THE ESSENTIAL NATURE OF LAW.

THE ESSENTIAL NATURE OF LAW

OR

The Ethical Basis of Jurisprudence

BY

WILLIAM S. PATTEE, L. L. D.

DEAN OF THE COLLEGE OF LAW

UNIVERSITY OF MINNESOTA

Fred B. Rothman & Co.

LITTLETON, COLORADO

1982

Library of Congress Cataloging in Publication Data

Pattee, William Sullivan, 1846-1911.
The essential nature of law, or, The ethical basis of jurisprudence.

Reprint. Originally published: Chicago : Callaghan, 1909.
Includes index.
1. Jurisprudence. 2. Ethics. I. Title.
K237.P37 1982 340'.11 82-12349
ISBN 0-8377-1011-1

THE
ESSENTIAL NATURE OF LAW

OR

The Ethical Basis of Jurisprudence

BY

WILLIAM S. PATTEE, L. L. D.

DEAN OF THE COLLEGE OF LAW

UNIVERSITY OF MINNESOTA

CHICAGO

CALLAGHAN & COMPANY

1909

To the Students
Who Have Been Under My Instruction
in the Graduate Department
of the
College of Law of the University of Minnesota
This Book is
Respectfully Dedicated.

"True law is right reason conformable to nature, universal, unchangeable, eternal, whose commands urge us to duty, and whose prohibitions restrain us from evil. Whether it enjoins or forbids, the good respect its injunctions, and the wicked treat them with indifference. This law cannot be contradicted by any other law, and is not liable either to derogation or abrogation. Neither the senate nor the people can give us any dispensation for not obeying this universal law of justice. It needs no other expositor and interpreter than our own conscience. It is not one thing at Rome and another at Athens; one thing today and another tomorrow; but in all times and nations this universal law must forever reign, eternal and imperishable. It is the sovereign master and emperor of all beings. God Himself is its author, its promulgator, its enforcer. And he who does not obey it flies from himself, and does violence to the very nature of man. And by so doing he will endure the severest penalties even if he avoid the other evils which are usually accounted punishment."—*Cicero, On the Commonwealth, Book III.* § *22.*

INTRODUCTION.

This volume grew out of an effort to emphasize and illustrate to the graduate students of the College of Law, in the University of Minnesota, the essential nature of law in its most general signification. After studying Jurisprudence for a period of three years, the student realizes that he has been considering but one of a numerous species of law. The Laws of God, the laws of physical nature, the laws of the human mind, and especially the moral law, have often been called to his attention in the legal works he has pursued during his course of undergraduate study. He has observed that the word "Law" is used in a great variety of senses, and that positive law is in some way related to natural and moral law; but just how and in what sense, he does not exactly comprehend. And the more he reads history, political science, economics and other subjects more or less closely related to Jurisprudence, the more confused and bewildered he becomes by the conspicuous use of the word Law and the various senses in which it is employed. And if, in the course of his reading, he makes excursions into philosophy, into the various branches of physical and mental science, into literature and religion, his perplexity and confusion are increased by the prominence the word assumes and the multitude of meanings it is used to convey. By some it is said that the worlds were "created by law," the universe is "run by law," the phenomena of the worlds "are caused by law." It is employed by others as synonymous with principle; it is employed as a substitute for the word "fact," and to it is often attributed a casual energy making it equivalent to the word "force."

The bewildering effect of this most conspicuous and

ambiguous term seemed to warrant an inquiry into the essential nature of law in its true and most general signification. And, moreover, the human mind craves a unified knowledge of whatever subject it studies. It desires to hold its knowledge of law, as its knowledge of every other body of facts, in the unity of a system. It craves the largest possible generalization. It desires to see the genus and species systematically arranged.

This inquiry seemed also desirable from the fact that, in making it, a large number of laws, as they have been formulated by the ablest thinkers in ancient and modern times, would naturally be grouped and presented to the student's attention in a body; and by that means he would be at least introduced to the various systems of metaphysical, scientific, psychological, ethical and sociological laws, a knowledge of which is necessary to every thoroughly equipped and liberally educated counsellor or jurist in these days of rapidly advancing knowledge. And moreover a general survey of the primary laws of reason and of their regulative function in the finite world of thought and of things; a similar survey of the laws or phenomenal order of mind and matter, and a special consideration of some of the most conspicuous laws operative in the world of individual and social life, furnishes the student a background upon which he can behold more clearly the facts and laws of any individual science to which he may devote himself as a specialist.

And this is particularly true of the student of Jurisprudence, because the science of human law is related in a peculiar way to all the branches of physical and mental science in that the courts of the civilized world judicially notice the laws of the various natural sciences as soon as they become a matter of general knowledge, and they give them effect where ever the interest of justice demands it.

It might at first appear that the student should master these various branches of learning as a part of his preparatory training for professional study. This, however, is hardly possible. It involves a wide range of reading requiring an amount of time not at the student's command, and a breadth of research for which he is not, as a rule sufficiently prepared. The wide range of subjects and the questionable number of electives now offered in the college and university curriculums, make it possible for students to graduate without having studied metaphysics, but few if any of the physical sciences, and little or nothing of philosophy, which subjects deal with laws that play a most important part in the moral and intellectual life of man. And even the subject of ethics, upon which jurisprudence is based, and which lays at the very heart of social life and good citizenship, has almost disappeared from the course of study in our institutions of higher education. While offered, but a very inconsiderable number of students ever elect it, and the result is that the persons coming to the study of Law have little knowledge of the science of ethics or of those other sciences whose laws are the most conspicuous and important in the discussions of this volume.

And besides the students coming from the college and the university to the study of Jurisprudence, large numbers from the high schools are attracted directly to it on account of the practical assistance it affords them in business life, and also from a desire to enter early upon their life work. This class of students is also unfamiliar with the natural sciences, with metaphysical, psychological and ethical truth, which are necessary to insure them an intelligent understanding of law in its widest sense.

In view of these facts it seemed necessary to offer those graduate students, who desire a broader view of law, a wider range of knowledge, and a more thorough comprehension of the ethical basis of Jurisprudence, a course of study embracing the fundamental truths of reason, the phenomenal order of the physical universe, the rational and ethical nature of man, and the true nature of law in its broadest signification as deduced from these studies.

But a stronger motive perhaps than any of these mentioned for making this inquiry into the essential nature of law, was found in the desire of many ambitious students to trace human laws to their origin. The scientist desires to know the origin of physical life, the origin of species, and the origin of mind itself. And this is not a modern passion. Before entering upon his discussion of the Civil Laws of Rome, Cicero said to Atticus, "Let us then once more examine before we come to the consideration of particular laws, what is the power and nature of law in general." He insists that both Justice and Law derive their origin from God Himself; that they are eternal and immutable. In his First Book, which abounds in the sublimest moral and religious sentiments, Cicero considers the origin and essence of law, its sources, its objects, and its operation. And in conclusion he says: "this then, as it appears to me, has been the decision of the wisest philosophers—that law was neither a thing contrived by the genius of man, nor established by any decree of the people, but a certain eternal principle, which governs the entire universe, wisely commanding what is right and prohibiting what is wrong. Therefore they call that aboriginal and supreme law the mind of God, enjoining or forbidding each separate thing in accordance with reason. On which account it is that this law, which the gods have bestowed on the human race is so justly applauded. For it is the reason and mind of a wise being equally able to urge us to good and to deter us from evil. * * * Therefore, the true and supreme law, whose commands and prohibitions are equally authoritative, is the right reason of the sovereign Jupiter."[1]

In other words, Cicero's position is, that the perfect reason of God is the supreme law. But to the average student, or to others unfamiliar with theistic philosophy this general statement seems transcendental and practically meaningless. We are prompted, therefore, to ask in what sense can *reason* be a *law*: in what sense can the perfect reason of God be the supreme law of the universe.

In answering these questions, we are obliged to consult theistic philosophy. There is a sense in which man's

[1] De Legibus, 431-2.

finite reason is said to be a law to his action. We are all subject to the regulative influence of certain self-evident and immutable truths, which are law to our action in the sense that they determine what we can and what we cannot do and what we can and what we cannot think. For example, we can change the form and position of matter but we cannot reduce it to non-existence. That "something cannot be reduced to nothing" is a law to physical power in that it determines what that power can and what it cannot effect. That truth says to power "you cannot." It is a law also to intellectual power in the sense that it determines what that power can and what it cannot conceive or imagine. The finite mind can conceive of something coming forth from something but not from nothing. It is a law of things also no less than of thought. Water may flow from a fountain in which there is water, but it cannot flow from a fountain in which there is no water. What is true of this common and familiar self-evident truth or law, is equally true of all the other primary or intuitive principles of reason: consequently we speak of the entire body or system of rational or intuitive principles, and all the necessary inferences that may be logically drawn from them, as law in its deepest and primary meaning. The term "primary law" then, as hereafter employed, embraces all the self-evident truths of reason with their necessary implications. It embraces the axiomatic truths of mathematics, all the self-evident principles of mechanics, and all others, such as those which demand that "every beginning or change of being must have a cause," that a "thing cannot both be and not be at the same time" and so on to the end of the list. In philosophy these principles are called the truths or principles of reason, because the mental faculty by which man recognizes and knows them is called his reason. These truths of reason then are law to man's actions: and when we say that "reason" is law to man's power, we mean to say that these "truths of reason" are law to his power. The term "reason" and the words "truths or principles of reason" are used synonymously.

It is in this sense then that reason is law. The individual "truths of reason" as above enumerated, and all others similar to them are law to physical and intellectual power in that they determine what that power can and what it cannot do.

But there is also a moral intuition—a truth of reason which lies at the very foundation of man's moral nature. Recognizing that he exists in a world of primary law, where every event must have a cause, where things cannot both be and not be at the same time, where the same space cannot be filled with both light and darkness at the same instant, where one body cannot be in two different places at one and the same time, where a statement cannot be both true and false, and where a certain act cannot be both right and at the same time wrong, where the same act cannot be at the same time both just and unjust, recognizing that he exists, I say, in such a world of law, man knows intuitively that he ought to conform his conduct to the demands of these laws, and not to waste his energies in the futile effort to attain his purposes in opposition to them, in other words, man knows that as a rational being he ought to act rationally. Here man comes out into the light of moral obligation. He knows intuitively that he ought to conform his choices and his conduct to the imperative demands of these fundamental principles. He knows them as law to his will. He recognizes himself now as living in a new world,—a world of moral obligation. Through his reason, man knows intuitively that he ought to conduct his life in harmony with these universal and immutable realities. He knows himself as a moral being, living with other moral beings in a moral system. That "a rational being ought to act rationally" is itself a truth of reason known intuitively. It is the basal principle in the moral constitution of rational beings. Without it a moral system and a moral life were impossible. Unless a person knew that he ought to obey law, he would be guiltless if he disobeyed it.

Such then are some of the fundamental realities recognized by finite reason, and known to reason as law to physical, intellectual, and voluntary Power. In this sense Cicero was correct in saying that reason, or the "truths of reason" are law.

Then arises the somewhat venturesome question as to whether these self-evident truths including the moral intuitions, are true to the perfect reason of God and hence are law to His will in the same sense that they are law to the action of man. Theistic philosophy does not hesitate to assert that this is so. It claims that all these self-evident truths are eternal in the Divine Reason, that they are law to the Divine Will, that they are, therefore, the supreme law of the Universe, that God created the Universe in harmony with them.

Cicero's statement, therefore, that the perfect reason of God is the supreme law, accords with this philosophic view. It means that the self-evident truths in the perfect reason of God are law regulative of all power in the Universe, physical, intellectual and voluntary. Those truths or laws, determining what physical power can and what it cannot effect, they determine what intellectual power can and what it cannot conceive, and they determine what voluntary power ought and what it ought not to choose.

Those truths may be thought of, therefore, as extending down from the Divine Mind, and as being operative within and throughout the realm of Physical Nature, and within and throughout the realm of finite mind.

So it seems to be the belief of the ancients and likewise of modern philosophers, that the perfect reason of God is the supreme law, and in seeking the origin of law, we find it in the *reason* and not in the *will* of God. These "truths or principles of reason" are eternal in the Eternal Reason. They are constituent elements in the Eternal Mind. They are eternal law to the Eternal Will. In harmony with them were all finite beings created, and obedient to their immutable demands the evolution of Nature and the history of man are determined.

And still another motive for making this inquiry was the desire to point out and emphasize the ethical basis of

Jurisprudence. That positive law has a moral basis is generally assumed; but in just what sense human law is founded upon Moral law is not so generally understood. To show this relationship it is first necessary to know in what the Moral law consists. What is the Moral law? How may it be stated?

We have endeavored to show that, as the law of gravitation is the all-comprehensive law of the physical world, so the "law of Social Service," or "the law of love" as it would be called in Christian ethics, is the all-comprehensive law in the Moral world. Auerback in the "Villa on the Rhine" translates the law "thou shalt love thy neighbor as thyself" into a slightly different form but substantially the same in essence "thou shalt *serve* thy neighbor as thyself." According to intuitional ethics man knows that he ought to seek the perfection of all his powers and susceptibilities so far as that is possible in this life. In this respect he is to serve himself. But such is the dependence and interpendence of human beings in society, that man finds his own highest well-being, or perfection and happiness, to depend very largely upon the highest well-being of his neighbors.

If one person owes another a debt he can attain his own highest good only by paying what is due to the other; if he has injured his neighbor, he can attain his own highest good only by compensating his neighbor for the damage he has suffered; if he finds his neighbor in destitution and distress he can secure his own highest welfare only by tendering such assistance to the unfortunate one as his means will warrant and the necessities of the case may require; and if his neighbor is seeking the truth to which he has a right, then the informer can attain his own highest good only by being truthful in his attempt to impart the desired information. In order to serve himself best, he must serve his neighbor also. In order to attain the highest degree of moral perfection and happiness, each one in society must perform his duties to others, and if each one performs all his duties to others then all of those others will have all of their rights, and no higher state of social existence can be conceived than that wherein all men have all their rights and all men perform all their duties.

Now according to Justinian, "Justice is the constant and perpetual wish to render everyone his due" (Justitia *est constans et perpetua voluntas jus sumus cuique tribuendi*).

Justice is of two kinds, subjective and objective. Subjective justice consists in the will's consent to the demands of the law. As Justinian has said it is the "constant wish" to render to everyone his due. If one wishes to pay his debt, or to compensate another for damage he has wrongfully inflicted upon him, if he wills to do so, though unable, he is nevertheless, a just man. His willingness to meet the demands of duty constitutes subjective justice. But on the other hand, if the debtor actually pays to the creditor the money due, and the creditor returns the note or other evidence of indebtedness if any, or if he who wrongfully inflicts an injury upon another, fully and actually compensates the injured one for the damage he sustained, and receives from him a full release and discharge of all claims for such damage, then objective justice has been fully met and obtained. Objective justice consists in the outward adjustment of the rights and duties of persons. The actual payment of the debt, the outward performance of the duty meets and satisfies the other's rights. After that, the former debtor has no further duty resting upon him with reference to that matter and the creditor has no longer any rights to be asserted. The rights and duties have both been fully canceled by their equitable adjustment. Justice in both its forms, as subjective and objective, is but one aspect of the moral law, "thou shalt serve (love) thy neighbor as thyself." In order to serve himself best, in order to attain his own highest good, man must be just, he must perform his duties to others, and in order to serve others most effectually, and help them attain their own highest good, he must regard and accord to them their rights. Man's own highest well-being and that of his neighbors can only be secured by mutual helpfulness, by the mutual discharge of their respective duties, and the mutual recognition of their respective rights. Such is the dependence of man upon man in society, such the solidarity of the human race, that the individual can attain his own highest good only by working for the highest good of other individuals, and this is all involved in the fundamental and all-comprehensive law of ethics, "thou shalt love (serve) thy neighbor as thyself." That rational beings, existing in a rational system, ought to obey reason, and recognize and regard their reciprocal rights and duties, and thus be just in spirit and just in conduct, is a "truth of reason" which man recognizes and knows intuitively. It is a fundamental truth of reason that men are under obligation to be just instead of unjust. Hence Justice has its origin in reason as the great Roman contended in his discussion upon the laws. "Let us begin then" he says "to establish the principle of justice on that supreme law (Right reason) which has existed from all ages before any legislative enactments were drawn up in writing or any political governments constituted * * * of all the questions which are ever the subject of discussion among learned men, there is none which it is more important to thoroughly understand than this, that man is born for justice, and that law and equity have not been established by opinion, but nature has given reason, she has given also right reason and therefore also law, which is nothing else than right reason enjoining what is good and forbidding what is evil.[1]

It is not contended that this all-comprehensive moral law of love is intuitively perceived in its completed formula as uttered by the Master "thou shalt love thy neighbor as thyself," but upon occasions in experience this truth that man ought to do his duty and regard the rights of others, came out into individual consciousness, and, at last, the truth in its generality was recognized and given expression.

As already said, justice, in both its forms, is involved

[1] Cicero De Legibus 407-411-413.

in this all-comprehensive law. Justice is but one aspect of love. Love is the choice of a person as an object of service. Benevolence and veracity are other aspects of the same principle, but we emphasize the fact that Justice is involved in and is an aspect of love because Justice, originating in the Eternal Reason, and intuitively known by the reason of Man, constitutes the Ethical basis of positive Law. It is not too much to say, that Justice, in its broadest meaning is the foundation of Jurisprudence, in the sense that Civil government and human law are chiefly instituted in order to establish and maintain objective Justice in the conflicting affairs of mankind.

To maintain justice is not, however, the sole object of civil government. As an individual is to seek his highest well-being, so an aggregation of individuals—a nation—is to seek its highest well-being. The well-being of the people is the supreme law. Public welfare must be regarded and such measures enacted, and such enterprises undertaken as will best secure its promotion.

And again, I have prepared these chapters particularly for the graduate students in our college of law, with the hope that they may inspire the young members of the Bar to extend their investigations beyond the narrow limits of positive law, and to familiarize themselves with the fundamental truths of philosophy, and science, and civil government. To say that these principles are of little or no practical consequence to the practicing lawyer, is to underestimate their value and importance. And be their practical value great or small, the culture that comes from their study, the satisfaction that a knowledge of them affords, the consciousness of strength which a familiarity with them awakens, the appreciation which one versed in them has for the labors of others devoted to their study, and the enlarged sympathies which an acquaintance with these truths quickens in the minds of men interested in their consideration, are sufficient reasons for bringing these principles, truths, and laws into one volume, where their essential nature may be readily recognized, and their relation to Jurisprudence clearly seen.

And finally, it is but justice to myself to say, that these chapters have been prepared during such fragments of time as could be procured from the busy periods of daily instruction in a growing college of law, and amid the exacting duties incident to its management and growth.

I publish them sincerely hoping that they may stimulate future students to a broader culture, and to wider and profounder thought, as I am frequently assured they have already so stimulated many former students who have pursued courses in the graduate departments of this College.

TABLE OF CONTENTS.

CHAPTER VIII.

The Ethical Basis of Jurisprudence.

CHAPTER IX.

Human Law.

CHAPTER X.

Divine Law.

THE ESSENTIAL NATURE OF LAW

Or The Ethical Basis of Jurisprudence

CHAPTER I.

Law.

Law is a term of extensive signification. It is generic, and among its various and numerous species, are embraced the fundamental laws of Reason, the general properties and orderly sequences of material things, the primary laws of finite mind, as the laws of thought and association, as well as those rules or laws of social conduct which human society endeavors to enforce, either through the established instrumentalities of public justice, or through the non-legalized agency of public opinion. In this general sense Law is primal. Before the worlds were, Law was. When all the shining inhabitants of space were yet in their primordial condition of nebulous vapor, the laws of chemical affinity and molecular motion were in full force and effect; and if we dare venture back in time to the origin of that nebulous mass itself, we must believe that the law of causation was operative in the workings of the Eternal Energy whence emanated that morning mist: and if that Eternal Energy is the personal God whom we worship, then the laws of Reason were regulative of His will, otherwise he could not have been a Moral Being.

Law is also universal. Nothing is beyond the reach of its influence. Matter and spirit are alike subject to its sway. From the swoop of a planet to the fall of a dew-drop, all is in conformity to Law. Even the choices of the human will made in the realm of personal freedom, are not thereby placed beyond its persuasive influence.

To law is due that order of the Universe, material and spiritual, which every finite mind, awakened to intelligence, adores, and seeks to discover and formulate. Law, as an object of investigation, is fascinating. It has ever been the quest of thoughtful men. It explains things. In its discovery the inquiring mind alone finds rest. To trace things to their beginnings is the natural tendency of every thoughtful mind. It was this craving that prompted Virgil to say: "Happy is the man who is able to discover the causes of things." The explorer does not rest until he has discovered the river's source: the scientist desires to know the origin of man, the genesis of life, the beginning of finite mind, and, if possible, the very beginning and nature of God. Prompted by this spirit, Caesar said he would gladly exchange the glory of all his victories, for a single glance at the sources of the Nile. So the mind craves to get behind the veil of outward manifestations, that it may see, not only their causes, but that it may also discover the laws that control their movements. The mind cannot rest amid the confusion of un-arranged facts. It can only rest in the genial light, and under the tranquilizing influence of Law. So man ever presses back through the infinite complexity of phenomena to the primal simplicity of controlling principle.

Influenced by this potent tendency, the ancient philosophic mind assumed the existence of some First Principle by which to explain the origin and orderly on-going of the universe. Thales taught that *water* was the one substance out of which all things were formed, but that in it there was an intelligence that directed all its operations as the soul in the body of man controls all his actions. Anaximenes differed from Thales in that he affirmed *air* to be the original substance; while Anaxagoras, recognizing the existence, without attempting to explain the origin of matter, conceived the necessity of an efficient cause, distinct from matter,which he found in an Infinite Mind that established order and controlled the on-going of the entire universe.

Recognizing the law of interdependence among the objects that make up the sum total of created things, Science came later to face the same question. In studying the individual man, Science found him to be related to humanity, and humanity to the rest of the animal creation, and the animal kingdom related to the earth, and the earth likewise, related to the solar system, and the solar system itself is but a part of the entire physical universe, and even the universe, in its totality, must be dependent upon some force or being for its existence and orderly development. But what is this First Cause, "Is it matter or spirit?" Agnosticism answers that it is an eternal energy, absolute and infinite, concerning which we know nothing more. Theism, on the other hand replies that it is a personal being, otherwise there is no explanation for the existence of finite persons now existing in, and forming a part of the universal whole,—the cause must be adequate to account for all that appears in the effect. Whether, therefore, we study Philosophy or Science, we are ever pressing back through the complex to the simple, or assuming the existence of the invisible, the invariable, and the eternal, in order to explain the tangible, the changeable, and the transitory. We are ever seeking for a *law* to explain the existence of order. And in passing out of the necessitated realm of impersonal things, into the region of personal freedom, we do not escape beyond the jurisdiction of law; for there is ever the law of moral obligation, operative upon the finite will. And in addition to these changeless laws of nature, into and under which humanity was born, we also find in human society all those constitutions, statutes, ordinances, and judicial decisions, comprising the self-imposed systems of jurisprudence.

Under the term jurisprudence is comprised all those rules of human conduct, enforced through the authorized or acknowledged instrumentalities of public justice. All such enforceable rules are, in common parlance, designated the laws of man while all other laws, of what kind or character soever, have been sometimes called the laws of Nature, and sometimes the laws of God. Importance attaches to the distinction between the laws for whose violation man has provided a sanction enforceable by human courts, and which are all embraced under the term jurisprudence, and all those other laws, under which man lives, embracing the first principles of Reason, the laws of the physical universe, and the psychic laws of finite personal beings. The first, for the purposes of this distinction, will be designated human law, or jurisprudence, and the others of every kind will be designated natural law. Constitutions, statutes, judicial decisions, decrees, and every other rule of human conduct, of whose violation human courts will take cognizance, fall under the first; while under the second are to be found the three classes of law embracing metaphysical truth, the laws of the physical universe, and the laws of psychic life, with the establishment and operation of which man has nothing whatever to do; hence, all of those laws may be properly designated natural, and for want of a better term, they will be so designated in this discussion.

Human law is conditioned by, and is founded upon, the natural, and one cannot thoroughly understand and fully comprehend the former, who does not also understand and comprehend, to some extent at least, the latter. The human is a natural outgrowth of the natural. Jurisprudence, which is temporary, rests upon a foundation of law which is eternal. The former is changeable, but the latter is changeless. Yet one essential characteristic of all law is common to both the foundation and the superstructure; therefore our investigation into the nature, the scope, and the necessity of human law, leads us to consider the fundamental principles of Reason, the laws of the physical world and of psychic life, as a necessary preparation to a thorough and comprehensive view of the changing and vanishing forms of jurisprudence.

What is Law?—At the very threshold of the investigation into its existence and nature, the inquirer is confronted with the question, "What is law?" and an answer must be given to this question before its influence, and its scope and function, in the universe, can be intelligently discussed. Before he can discover a law, the investigator must know what it is. The sportsman would hunt the gazelle to little effect, if he did not know one when he saw it.

That we live in a universe subject to unchanging law, has long been the assumption of the thoughtful. It has been customary for men in public discourse, whether political, legal, moral, or religious, to make frequent and impassioned reference to the eternal principles of right and wrong, to the changeless principles of eternal justice, to the unvarying principles of truth, to the immutable laws of the universe and to the supreme laws of God.

A universal order, conditioned upon law, was recognized long before man could formulate, define, or classify, the laws that secured that order; as the stars and their movements were recognized long before a correct system of astronomy was given to the world. Demosthenes says: "In short, we shall find nothing noble or useful which is not associated with law: indeed the whole universe, the heavenly bodies and the seasons, as they are called, if we may trust to what we see, appear to be governed by law and order."[1] And the poet, Sophocles, refers in sublime language to the higher law. Antigone had violated one of the king's decrees, by doing what she regarded as her duty under a law superior to his, and Creon says to her:

> "And didst thou dare to disobey the law?"

And Antigone replies:

> "Nowise from Zeus, methought, this edict came,
> Nor Justice, that abides among the gods
> In Hades, who ordained these laws for men.
> Nor did I deem *thine* edicts of such force
> That they, a mortal's bidding, should o'erride
> Unwritten laws, eternal in the heavens.
> Not of today or yesterday are these;
> But live from everlasting, and from whence
> They sprang none knoweth. I would not, for the breach
> Of these, through fear of any human pride,
> To Heaven atone."[2]

[1] Demosthenes. II Oration against Aristogiton. (Bohn, p. 87).

[2] Sophocles. Antigone. (Whitelaw, London, 1883).

With many of the ancients, law has been clothed with kingly and divine attributes, as in the Vedas, where it is declared: "Law is the King of Kings, far more powerful and rigid than they; nothing can be mightier than law, by whose aid, as by that of the mightiest monarch, even the weak may prevail over the strong."[3] And Pindar, the Greek poet, also uses language of a similar import: "Law is the king of all, mortals as well as immortals."[4] And Chrysippus has the same conception: "The common law, which is the right reason, moving through things, indentical with Zeus, the Supreme Administrator of the Universe."[5] And Cicero, who has been called the lens that collected all the rays of intellectual light in his day, speaks of law in much the same strain: "Let us then," he says, "once more examine, before we come to the consideration of particulars, what is the power and nature of law in general; lest, when we come to refer everything to it, we occasionally make mistakes, from the employment of incorrect language, and show ourselves ignorant of the force of those terms which we ought to employ in the definition of laws. * * * This, then, as it appears to me, has been the decision of the wisest philosophers,—that law was neither a thing contrived by the genius of man, nor established by any decree of the people, but a certain eternal principle which governs the entire Universe, wisely commanding what is right and prohibiting what is wrong. Therefore they called that aboriginal and supreme law the Mind of God, enjoining or forbidding each separate thing in accordance with reason."[6]

And again, he says: "Let us begin, then to establish the principles of justice on that supreme law, which has existed from all ages, before any legislative enactments were drawn up in writing or any political governments were constituted."[7] And in more modern times reference is frequently made to some "eternal principle," some "pre-existing law," but no definite conception of

[3] Sat. Br. 14.4.2.23., Br. Ar. Up. 1.4.14. (From Holland, Juris).

[4] Apud Plato, Gorgias. (Jowett, p. 73).

[5] Apud Diogenes Laertius, VII, 88.

[6] Cicero, De Leg. Bk. 2. IV.

[7] Cicero, De Leg. Bk. 1. VI.

its character is made known. Thus Burke, in the trial of Warren Hastings, indulges in several vague generalities. "We are all born," he says, "in subjection, all born equally, high and low, governors and governed, in subjection to one great, immutable, pre-existent law, prior to all our devices and prior to all our contrivances, paramount to all our ideas, and all our sensations, antecedent to our very existence, by which we are knit and connected in the eternal frame of the Universe, out of which we cannot stir. This great law does not arise from our conventions or compacts; on the contrary, it gives to our compacts all the force and sanction they can have; * * *"[8] So Tolstoi, in his book entitled "My Religion," paraphrasing the words of Christ, "think not I am come to destroy the law or the prophets," makes Christ say,—"I am not come to destroy the eternal law, of whose fulfillment your books of prophecy foretell. I am come to teach you the fulfillment of the eternal law, not the law that your Scribes and Pharisees call the divine law, but of that eternal law which is more immutable than the earth or the heavens."[9] Charles Sumner, in his renowned speech on the Barbarism of Slavery, said: "There is a better law above and a meaner law below that operate in the affairs of men;" and Lord Brougham says to the same effect: "There is a law above all human enactments of human codes—the same throughout the world—the same in all times; it is written by the finger of God upon the heart of man."[10]

Besides these confident references to the higher, immutable and eternal laws, so often made by both ancient and modern philosophers, orators, and poets, there are still more positive assumptions of universal and changeless law, adopted by the vigorous scientists of these later days, as they pursue their investigations, and construct their venturesome hypotheses regarding this world of matter and mind. Law is assumed, and Science is in

[8] Burke's Works, Speech on the Trial of Warren Hastings.

[9] Tolstoi, My Religion, p. 53.

[10] Heron, History of Juris. 24.

quest of it. Draper voices the sentiment of Science in the following lines: "It is of law that I am to speak in this book. In a world composed of vanishing forms, I am to indicate the imperishability and the majesty of the law, and to show how man proceeds in this social march in obedience to it. I am to lead my reader, perhaps, in a reluctant path, from the outward phantasmagorical illusions which surround us and so ostentatiously intrude themselves upon our attention, to something that lies in silence and strength behind. I am to draw his thoughts from the tangible to the invisible, from the limited to the universal, from the changeable to the invariable, from the transitory to the eternal, from the expedients and volitions so largely amusing the life of man to the predestined and resistless issuing from the fiat of God." And further he says: "The Government of the world is accomplished by immutable laws. * * * The laws of nature never vary, in their application they never hesitate nor are wanting. But in this ascending to primordial laws, and asserting their immutability, universality, and paramount control in the government of this world, there is nothing inconsistent with the free action of man."[11]

This brief view of expressed opinions as to the existence and universality of law would be incomplete without the oft-quoted words of Hooker. "Of law there can be no less acknowledged, than that her seat is the bosom of God, her voice the harmony of the world: all things in Heaven and Earth do her homage, the very least as feeling her care, and the greatest as not exempted from her power: both angels and men and creatures of what condition soever, though each in different sort and manner, yet all with uniform consent, admiring her as the mother of their peace and joy."[12]

These few citations of unqualified belief in the universal prevalence of regulative principles, superior to human enactments, taken, as they are, from the abund-

[11] Intellectual Development of Europe, Vol. 1, 20, 22.

[12] Eccl. Polity, Book I, Chap. 16, Sec. 8.

ance of similar references in the literature of philosophy, poetry, science, art and religion, testify to the fact that in all ages men in every field of investigation have seen in the movements and heard in the harmony of the spheres unequivocal evidences of the actual existence of certain regulative agencies supremely efficient and universally operative.

But to assume or assert the existence of law does not define or explain it. To believe that there is a law is one thing, to tell in what it consists is quite another. Everybody knows that there is water upon the earth, but that it is composed of two parts of hydrogen and one of oxygen in a fixed and changeless ratio is a further fact unknown to thousands who even spend their lives upon the sea. To know that things exist does not explain their nature: so the fact that law has been recognized from ancient days as a regulative factor in the universe, does not disclose its essential elements. Men, not knowing its real nature, have likened law to other things which they supposed they did know. They have likened it to a king, they have called it the mind of God, they have pronounced it a "certain eternal principle," but always and everywhere they have attributed to it a controlling if not an intelligent efficiency.

It is certainly desirable to know, if possible, the content of words so universally employed as the words "law" and "principle;" and especially as such universal consequences are ascribed to their influence in the world of mind and matter. What is this "better law" to which Sumner refers, and what is this "immutable pre-existent law" so important in the eyes of Burke? Can the "eternal laws of justice" to which the great English advocate says we are subject, be enumerated, defined and classified? Who enacted this "higher law"? Where can we find it? Has it been committed to writing? In short, if asked to state a single one of these eternal and immutable principles, what would the average layman or even lawyer reply? There is a general impression abroad that when the "higher law" is referred to, the ten commandments are meant. That cannot well be, for not a third of the human family ever heard of them, hence they would have no higher law. Some might reply that by the "higher law" is meant the "moral law." But the question then arises, what is the "moral law"? How is it stated? Where can it be found clearly worded so we may know just what it forbids or commands? The fact is that constant reference is being made to these higher and unchangeble laws, and this reference implies that men recognize a great body of law, distinct and separate, and above that which is taught in the school, and applied and enforced by the court. In fact, human law, such as our text-books and reports and statutes contain, is often condemned as being contrary to the laws of reason, contrary to the eternal principles of right and wrong, contrary to the first principles of justice, and therefore it is said that these human laws ought not to exist, or, at least, ought to be made to conform to the higher law. In this judgment and condemnation, these "eternal principles" are considered as the higher and more perfect, because the human law is pronounced unworthy of existence, being in conflict with them.

Now, if there is a code of laws higher, and better, and more obligatory, than those in our books, we want to know where that code may be found, where we can procure a copy, and, if not in book form, then where and in what form they are written. The reference which has been made from the earliest days to this superior system, and the fact that the human race has always believed in its existence, and referred to it as supreme, and tested to a certain extent its own humanly constructed enactments by it, are the strongest possible evidences that it has existence somewhere, and that the race turns instinctively to it for guidance. It is a worthy task to find this system of law, to define it, as far as possible, to examine its relations to mankind and to trace its remarkable influence in the text-books, the reports, the statutes, and in the orders and judgments and decrees of our courts. In this we are not undertaking something of no practical benefit. It is of the highest utility. In the Great Palace of Justice in Paris, behind and above the judges' chair is placed the crucifix, whose constant influence upon the judge is supposed to incite him to temper justice with mercy. So in every court room in the civilized world, there is present an invisible system of "higher law" influencing the judge, the jury, and the counsel, in the discharge of their respective duties. Though invisible, though we do not find it in a bound volume beside the statutes upon the judge's desk, or upon the counsels' table, yet its presence, like the invisible atmosphere, fills the room, and its influence, like that of the air, affects all persons incessantly, though perhaps unconsciously.

Its many senses.—The word law is used in so many senses that we are confused by it. We hear of the law of nations, the laws of nature, the laws of right and wrong, the laws of the mind, the law of the seasons, the laws of chemical affinity, the laws of general average, the laws of the heavenly bodies, the laws of trade, the law of supply and demand, the laws of thought, the laws of the feelings, the laws of the will, the laws of life, and the great law of human progress. And in these days of advancing science, we hear much respecting the law of evolution, the law of heredity, the law of reversion to original type, the law of the persistency of force, the law of the survival of the fittest, the law of the correlation of forces, and especially are we nowadays referred to the laws or "Principles of Sociology."

Over forty years ago Dr. McCosh said, that "Science, as it advances, has been widening the domain of law, and has detected its presence where the unlearned saw only caprice, and where the piously disposed mind was accustomed to contemplate the Divine Power, acting independently of all instrumental causes. It is now acknowledged that there are physical causes determining every 'fitful breeze, and every forming cloud, and every falling shower.' But while there is an universal recognition among the reflecting community of the existence of general laws, there is about as universal confusion of ideas as to the nature of these laws."[13] Often the word "law" is applied to the self-evident truths of reason, also to the general properties of matter; again to an "observed order of facts" in the realm of the finite mind, as when we speak of the laws of association; and besides being used in these different senses, it is often spoken of as an active agent. We hear it said that the universe was "created by law," that it is "controlled by law," that human progress and all financial disturbances are "regulated by law," as though "law" were an active agent, creating, regulating, and controlling things; and so imbued has our generation become with the idea that everything in the universe is subject to uniform regulation, that whenever we behold an unusual and unexplainable phenomenon, we at once ascribe it to some undiscovered law. Not infrequently we think of a person shortly before he calls upon us, and, commenting upon the inexplicable fact, we ascribe it to some probable law of telepathy not yet discovered.

Laws are again spoken of in a figurative sense, as when they are represented as running through the universe of both material and immaterial things. Henry Wood, in his work on "Economics," says: "Natural law is everywhere. Its lines, as they permeate the business world, may not be so easily traceable as in material science, but the evidence of their existence and rule is no less positive and unquestionable." So, Henry Drummond, in his work on "Natural Law in the Spiritual World," says: "The natural laws, then, are great lines running not only through the world, but as we now know, through the universe, reducing it like parallels of latitude to intelligible order."

That thinking people are rapidly becoming conscious that they live in a world of order, where all things material and immaterial, personal and impersonal, are subject to perfect and unchangeable principles, is undoubtedly a blessing; but to ascribe to law influences and powers and characteristics which it does not and cannot

13 The Divine Government,. Physical and Moral, 86, 87.

possess, and especially to apotheosize and exalt it to a control which it does not and cannot exert, is not only misleading, but it diverts the attention from the truth and thus retards our real progress. The many meanings attached to the word, the many powers ascribed to it, its identification with personal beings by some, and the assertion by others that it extends like "lines running through the universe;" the statement at one time that the universe is controlled by law, and the further statement at another time that the world "governs itself according to law," [14] all tend to confusion and perplexity. Vagueness, like a mist, enshrouds the whole subject; yet, from these numerous utterances of both ancient and modern authors respecting the existence and nature of law, we have unmistakable evidence of its importance as a factor in the world of thought, as well as in the world of being; and if we can sketch, through the mist of confusing utterances, but the faintest outline of law's essential features, it may possibly assist us to better understand the frail and fading imitations thereof, which humanity has made from age to age, for its own regulation, in its efforts to grow better and wiser.

[14] Buchner, "Force and Matter," 51.

CHAPTER II.

Natural Laws.

LAWS RELATIVE TO IMPERSONAL BEINGS AND THINGS.

In the preceding chapter we have seen that from the earliest historic times reference has frequently been made to law as a controlling agency. Its "immutability, universality and paramount control" are its generally recognized characteristics. The world is regulated by law says Demosthenes; the unwritten law divine cannot be abrogated for it is immutable, says Antigone; it governs the entire universe, says Cicero. That law in this generic sense is something fixed, changeless and universal seems to have been the idea of the race from the earliest days of reflective thought. Not only is this fact observed in these general references to law made by poets and orators but in the various languages of the world the word itself carries with it the same signification.

In the Greek, the Latin, the Arabic, and other ancient tongues the idea of fixedness, that which is decreed, laid down, and established, is the dominating thought, in the word "law." And in the modern languages also, the word conveys the same idea of permanency and changelessness. So, in our quest after natural law, we look for the fixed and abiding elements in the realms of mind and matter, and having found them we can then ascertain in what their essential nature consists.

As the definition of an object can only be accurately formulated at the close and not at the beginning of its analysis, so the definition of law can be properly framed only after our investigation as to what immutable realities there are in this world of mind and matter. Yet there are some advantages in having a general idea of the chief elements of law when we start out upon our inquiry as to its nature.

We shall find that law carries in it the two ideas of some fixed *reality* that resists or directs, and some *force* or *power* which is resisted or directed—some *reality* that regulates, and some *power* that is regulated. As in the chief languages "law" means that which is permanent, we must first search for the fixed and changeless realities in the universe, and then consider the forces or powers to which those realities set fixed and immovable limits. We shall find first that there are certain fundamental properties and realities in the material world which compose the true constitution of physical nature; and in the realm of finite personal beings we shall observe another group of fixed and changeless truths which compose the mental constitution of finite persons; and, considering the peculiar nature of these primary truths universally operative throughout the finite universe, we shall proceed to inquire whether they may not constitute the eternal laws so often referred to by writers in both ancient and modern times, and whether they may not in reality compose the supreme constitution in accordance with which the finite universe was constructed.

But in a discussion of law in general it is necessary to observe the distinction between law as a system of jurisprudence enforced by human authority and law as the totality of controlling principles operative throughout the universe of mind and matter. Jurisprudence, or positive law, such as the common law of a country, the constitutional and statutory provisions for the government of a people and the ordinances and rules of human conduct enacted by men for the purposes of social order and human progress, is the usual term employed by jurists to cover all those enactments or principles adopted and enforced by state authority. It is sometimes called human law in distinction from natural, and must be kept distinctly separate in thought from that system of fundamental principles which, independent of all human agency, reigns throughout the boundless realms of both the physical and spiritual universe.

Jurisprudence is the theme of the jurist. He discusses

its origin, its growth and its history. He analyzes and classifies its parts and reduces them to a scientific form and gives to the world the science of jurisprudence, or what is frequently but inaccurately called the "science of law." The "science of law," strictly speaking, includes within its classifications every known law in the universe be it human or otherwise. Jurisprudence is but one species under the genus "law"; and it is this distinction between jurisprudence as the body of principles enforced by judicial authority and that other system of controlling principles reigning throughout the world of mind and matter that is here emphasized. Prior to any human enactment there was a "reign of law." Even before the worlds assumed definite forms and selected their respective circuits in the heavens, and even while the primeval mist dwelt in the solitude of starless space, or even before the "eternal energy" gave the initial motion to that nebulous vapor, we are led to believe that there was the reigning law in the Moving Mind in accordance with which the primeval matter performed its motions, took on its forms and selected its sublime pathways.

While the laws of mind and matter have been classified under various terms, such as spiritual laws, mental laws, physical laws and material laws, the term "natural" will here be employed to cover all the laws of mind and matter, though that term has been used by different authors to cover more restricted portions of this field of inquiry. Laws that are self-enforcing are natural, and the term natural includes all the fundamental principles of mind and matter. The principles which are constitutive elements in the nature of any person or thing are natural and hence whenever those principles are regulative of power of any kind they are natural laws. The fundamental truth that "there can be no beginning or change of anything without a cause," is an original principle of reason, and may as properly be termed a natural law of mind as gravitation may be termed a natural law of matter. So in its most general signification the "Science of Law" may be considered under the two heads of Natural Law and Human Law.

Natural Law in its primary sense.—Directing our attention in this chapter to Natural Law, our first endeavor will be to consider the fundamental realities in the realm of material things. Our quest after law in its primary meaning is but a quest after the immutable realities that abide in the physical world. Pursuing the method of science, instead of that of speculative philosophy, we must begin our inquiry with the facts about us, and proceed from the things we know to the things we wish to know.

Looking upon the physical world about us, among the most obvious and changeless facts are the following so-called general properties of matter:

1. The extension of matter.
2. The indestructibility of matter.
3. The impenetrability of matter.
4. The divisibility of matter.
5. Inertia.

Extension.—All material objects have extension. Power cannot rob matter of this property. That material bodies must occupy space is axiomatic. Length, breadth and thickness are fundamental realities of all bodies from the atom to the planet. No power of thought can dissociate them from matter in the abstract and no physical force can do so in fact. Matter may be expanded, compressed, divided and changed from place to place, but it cannot by any kind or degree of power be deprived of its three dimensions. Force cannot create matter for whose existence space is unnecessary. Whatever else force may do respecting material things, it cannot deprive them of their space qualities. Extension then is a fundamental reality inseparable from matter and is a law in the primary sense of the term as that which determines what power can and cannot effect.

Indestructibility.—Matter cannot be destroyed. It is indestructible. It may be divided into countless parts, dissolved by acids, transformed from a solid into a liquid by heat and from a liquid into a vapor; it may be compressed and expanded, or changed into numberless forms, but never destroyed. That which is cannot be reduced to that which is not. "Something cannot be reduced to nothing" is a self-evident and eternal truth of reason. Indestructibility is a fundamental and necessary characteristic of matter. It is called a property of matter, and a law of matter.

This reality of indestructibleness, setting a limit as it does to power, is, in the true sense of the term, a law.

Impenetrability.—Not only is matter indestructible but it is impenetrable. One body occupies space to the absolute exclusion of all other bodies. Here again we find a self-evident truth operative in the realm of matter. To say that matter is impenetrable is to say that no two bodies can occupy the same space at the same time, which statement is axiomatic. Matter may be forced from place to place, it may be forced indefinitely upward or downward; planets may be whirled around one another with inconceivable velocity and atoms may be drawn together by chemical affinity with incalculable intensity, but neither atom nor planet can be compelled by any degree of power to occupy the same space at the same time with another atom or planet. This, too, is a fundamental reality respecting matter, and hence impenetrability being regulative of power is in the true sense of the term a law in the realm of material things. This is a universal and necessary truth and hence a universal law. Nowhere in space can power of any kind over-ride this dominant reality. It calmly resists all the conceivable assaults of power.

Divisibility.—In theory matter is infinitely divisible. The mind cannot conceive of a division of matter carried to such an extent that the parts may not be divided still further. Force can reach no limit in its dividing process, for infinite divisibility necessitates infinite time in which to make the division. Matter does, therefore, defy the action of power in its process toward an ultimate separation of matter into parts. If it is a fact, as theoretically assumed, that matter in its last analysis is composed of indivisible atoms, then the indivisibility of those atoms is a fixed and irrefragable reality pertaining to all the elements of matter, and hence it becomes a law to force in the primary and accurate sense of the word.

Inertia.—Matter is inert. It is not, like mind, self-active. At rest it cannot move, in motion it cannot stop by any power of its own. Every change must have a cause. If there is no efficient force within an atom or mass of matter, then there is no cause within it to produce a change of place. Being destitute of any inherent causal efficiency, the dead lump of matter cannot be conceived of as moving itself. As the mind cannot think of an effect without a cause, it cannot think of matter destitute of causal efficiency as moving itself. If there is no cause either without or within matter, its motion would be inconceivable. If there is a causal power without but none within matter, then its self-activity is inconceivable.

As to whether or not the inertia of matter is self-evident has been discussed by metaphysicians, as we shall hereafter observe, but that inertia is one of the general characteristics of matter as it is now known, is unquestionable. To move it when at rest, power is necessary, to stop it when in motion, power is also necessary. Power may overcome inertia, but it cannot make unnecessary a sufficient cause for its motions.

These general properties of matter, its length, breadth and thickness, its indestructibility, impenetrability and divisibility are fixed realities respecting matter and may be said to compose its fundamental constitution. These realities are the inexpugnable barriers over or through which power has no ability to break, but to whose regulative and directive characteristics all power is held in perfect subjection. These constitutional realities are regulators of power of all kinds,—of intellectual in that the mind cannot conceive of matter without these properties, and of physical in the sense that they determine what physical power can and what it cannot effect. The forces of nature must respect these essential laws of nature within whose inflexible framework they are permitted to exercise themselves. These realities are the things which we find to be fixed, immutable, invincible and as universal as matter. They are not active agencies but they are passive barriers. They are not intelligent self-active forces, but they are dumb realities setting limits to all the forces in the universe whether intelligent or unintelligent. They are simply realities regulative of power.

Primary Truth as Law.—In addition to these general properties of matter there are other fixed, immutable and imperative realities which operate throughout the entire physical universe. I refer to the primary principles of reason, generally called self-evident truth. They include the principles of mathematics and all the fundamental realities of reason and the necessary inferences to be drawn from them. Often spoken of as laws of thought, they are in fact permanent and changeless laws to physical force. Further consideration will be given these fundamental truths in subsequent pages, when their nature and importance will be discussed; but in order that their character as law in the material world may be recognized we mention the following, not as a complete enumeration of rational intuitions, but as examples of that important class of fundamental truths which constitute law in the physical system in its true and primary meaning. Among the many truths of reason and the necessary inferences that may be drawn from them which are regulative of physical forces and conspicuously obvious in the material world are the following:

(a) Every beginning or change must have a cause.

(b) The same complex of causes always produces the same effect.

(c) Something cannot come from nothing.

(d) With finite agents reception must precede production.

(e) Nothing can be and at the same time not be.

(f) If equals be added to equals the sums must be equal.

These truths are among the most common self-evident realities and at the same time they are true laws of nature regulative of all the physical forces in the world of matter. They tell force what it can and what it cannot do. No force of any kind can change or annul these realities. They are immutable, irreversible and universal. They are persisting realities in a material world of endless changes. They command material forces absolutely. It is always and everywhere true that "every event must have a cause." No kind nor degree of force can render a cause unnecessary to the production of an event. Force may be the cause of events, but it cannot make a cause unnecessary in a world of events. That is something which force cannot do. Stated in its positive form the law would be "Every change or new existence is and must be due to some cause." Wherever we observe a change in matter, either in composition, form, size, color, or otherwise, we know that such change must have had an adequate cause. We see the planets moving in their courses, the ocean surging, the vegetable kingdom undergoing constant changes from season to season and the animal world ever subject to countless beginnings and dissolutions, and behind all these mutations we know an adequate cause exists. That any event should occur without a cause is unthinkable.

The importance of this law, as illustrated in the material phenomena about us, warrants a somewhat lengthy quotation from Mivart:

"Every change in anything which already exists is, in fact, a new mode of being; and therefore equally demands a cause for its existence. It must, then, be due either to something distinct from it, or to some antecedent mode of being of that which now exists in its new mode.

"Thus, when we awake from sleep, our awakening must be due either to something external which has awakened us, or to some change which has taken place in our own organism. In the latter case, that change or new mode in our being, which we call 'wakening from sleep,' had for its cause an antecedent state of our body—increased vigor of the circulation or what-not.

"Moreover, all the various objects we see or feel must, each of them, we know, be a result of the action of some cause or causes external to it. This is, of course, most manifestly evident with respect to every artistic product, and everything which has been made by man. But a little reflection will show that the same is the case with all the products of nature. No stone we tread upon, no patch of sand or mud, can have come to be what it is, save by the action of antecedent causes. The shape of every mountain is, at least, largely due to the action of water, and so on. And this law of causation applies to the most minute and simplest, as well as to the largest and most complex, of bodies. Even pieces of matter, which, so far as we yet know, consist of but one chemical element—such as a fragment of gold or carbon—owe the shape, place and the relations in which we find them, to conditioning causes. And carbon in its brilliant condition as a diamond (a state we term crystalline) is equally an effect of causes; and, as yet, all the causes which have produced all the diverse and most definite forms of crystallisation, which are characteristic of different minerals, are for us mysterious.

"Any and every such object demands a cause for its actually being in the place it is, at the time it is there, for its size, its shape, etc., and for its relations to surrounding things, as well as for any special qualities of its own internal conditions. These special conditions would demand a cause, even if such a body existed alone and by itself in an otherwise empty universe—if we may permit ourselves to frame for a moment so absurd an hypothesis."[1]

This self-evident principle is a law to physical force in that it determines what that force can and what it cannot do. Physical forces can cause changes, produce effect, but it is not possible for force by any conceivable exertion to render a cause unnecessary for any particular change in matter. In this sense this truth is a law to physical power.

Complex of Causes.—The truth that "the same complex of causes will always produce the same effect," needs only to be incidentally referred to. This is a primary truth, and no kind or amount of power can change its nature or influence as a regulative reality in the finite universe. In rowing a boat across a running stream, the

[1] Mivart, Groundwork of Science, 258.

force of the current and the force exerted by the rower will combine to effect a certain result, which, under like conditions, will always be the same.

Another universal law is found in the truth that "something cannot come from nothing." This is true in the realm of matter and mind alike. Water cannot flow from an empty fountain, a living tree cannot come from a lifeless seed, and the feelings of love cannot exist in the heart where there is nothing but hate. In all the affairs of life this truth finds application. He who has no title to property cannot convey one to another, and he who has no money cannot give money to the poor.

The Law of Reception and Production is Self-evident.—No finite being can give out that which it does not have, and no finite being can have that which it has not first received. In mechanics this law finds constant and universal application. A machine can produce results only in proportion to the power it has received. The locomotive can draw a train across the continent upon condition that it has first received the necessary power. The same law operates throughout the vegetable world. The tree can put forth its foliage and its fruit only as it first receives from the earth, the atmosphere and the sunlight the necessary elements for their production and development. All the cosmic forces are focused upon the plant imparting to it their energy, in order that the plant may issue its flower and perfume. And even man himself can accomplish nothing save as he receives his existence and his powers from parents associates, food, air and countless agencies that play upon him from without.

Law of Contradiction.—Nothing can be and at the same time not be. This so-called law of logic finds endless illustrations in the realm of matter. It is a law of things, no less than a law of thought. A piece of paper cannot be white and at the same time black. A door cannot be open and shut at the same instant. A person cannot be present with me and at the same time absent. Water may be either hot or cold at any moment but it cannot be both hot and cold at the same moment. A star may be within the range of human vision or it may be beyond it, but it is impossible that it should be both in sight and out of sight of the same observer at the same instant of time. A body may be either square or cubical, but it is not possible that it should be both. So the illustrations of this fundamental truth in the world of matter might be carried to an indefinite extent. This truth determines the possibilities of physical force. It may fashion a block of marble into the form of a Venus, or into the form of a Hercules, but it cannot by any conceivable degree of energizing give it both forms at the same time. The truth or reality itself is a law to power determining what it can and what it cannot do.

Concerning this principle as a law of objective phenomena it has been well said:

"But, once more, it is no mere law of our own minds, no affair of mere logic, since, if we are to accept as absolutely true what our reason declares to be self-evident, it is a law which applies to all things from physical phenomena to mental states. Such we have seen to be the case with respect to the various instances we have put forward as examples. When we say that the number of balls in a bag cannot at the same time be both "odd" and "even", we are certain that this is not a truth due to our organization, but to the real necessary objective conditions of existence of the balls themselves. Our reason declares that the law of contradiction is no 'form of thought' imposed on our intellect, but is a certain and inevitable law of objective existence independent of our intellect.

"To doubt this would be to destroy all certainty, since it is a fundamental truth on which all reasoning depends.

"If we could not be sure that the fact that 'all men are mortal' did not necessarily imply that none could live forever we could never infer the mortality of anyone as a consequence of his humanity. Thus for anyone to attempt such a task as that of 'proving' the law of contradiction would be in the highest degree absurd, since he would be compelled already to assume its certainty at the very outset of his demonstration—at the very first assertion he made.

"Our perception, therefore, of the necessary validity of the law of contradiction, teaches us both an absolute verity with respect to objective existences—with respect to the matter of all science—as well as the existence of our own mental perception thereof."[2]

That "things which are equal to the same thing are equal to each other" is known and daily acted upon as a valid and incontrovertible principle, not merely as a form of thought, but as a universal truth respecting bodies and masses in the world of things. It is a law to physical power in that it sets limits to the possibilities of power. Power cannot make things that are equal to the same thing unequal to each other.

Referring to this principle as a law of things as well as of thought, Mivart also says:

"As with the law of contradiction, so with this axiom—it is practically known and constantly acted on in every-day life without advertence to its axiomatic character, and even without any knowledge of it as a recognized truth at all. The familiar application of a yard measure to different objects is an amply sufficient demonstration that such is the case. But the principle applies not only to the equality of material things but to every kind of equality—equality of motion, illumination, and feeling—and it is evidently a principle of objective validity, and is a law of things no less than of thought."[3]

So it might easily be shown that all the self-evident or primary truths of intuition and the necessary inferences drawn from them are laws in the physical world, except those moral intuitions which have to do exclusively with the power of free-will. But enough has already been said to illustrate how these first principles are fixed realities regulative of physical force.

Persistency of Force.—It is interesting to observe that the fundamental law of the persistence of force rests, as a doctrine of science, entirely upon the self-evident truths of reason. The whole structure of physical science rests upon this simple principle. If this principle is unsound,

[2] Mivart, Groundwork of Science, 246.
[3] Mivart, Groundwork of Science, 247.

the science of material things is without foundation and falls worthless to the ground. This is the basal principle of Physics, and it has an immovable foundation because it rests entirely upon the changeless laws of reason. That the amount of force existing at any moment in the universe never varies but must forever remain the same is a necessary inference from the axiomatic truths, that something cannot become nothing—as would be the case if a quantity of force should cease to be—and that "nothing cannot become something,"—as would be the case if a quantity of force should appear when there was no such force before. Force cannot create other force from nothing, so the assertion that the sum total of force existing at any time is always the same, is a fundamental reality respecting power itself. This reality also is a law to power, for it is as impossible for power to create other power from nothing as it is for it to create more matter from nothing. Concerning this point Prof. Fiske says: "How do we know that force is persistent? If force is not persistent, if a single unit of force can ever be added or subtracted from the sum total at any moment existing, our entire physical science is, as we have seen a mere delusion. * * * What proof have we that no force is ever created or destroyed? Logically speaking we have no proof. An axiom which lies below all frameable propositions cannot be deductively demonstrated. * * * Nor can an axiom be demonstrated inductively, without reasoning in a circle. We cannot adduce the observed equality of action and reaction in proof of the persistence of force, because this persistence is taken for granted in every observation by which the equality of action and reaction is determined. Obviously it is impossible to prove the truth of an axiom by any demonstration in every step of which the truth of the axiom must be assumed. * * * We are compelled to believe in the persistence of force, because it is impossible to conceive a variation in the unit by which force is measured. It is impossible to conceive something becoming nothing, or nothing becoming something, without establishing in thought an equation between something and nothing, and this cannot be done. * * * Thus, the proof of our axiom is not logical but psychological, and as was formerly shown this is the strongest kind of proof."[4]

It may be that the time will come when every antecedent and consequent, when all the orderly and uniform sequences with which physical nature abounds, may be traced each to its underlying principle of reason, in accordance with which it operates, and because of which it cannot be otherwise than it is. Already many of the phenomena of nature which appear as mere uniform sequences, have been found to rest on some rational first principles and to owe their uniformity to the immutability and universality of the underlying law. Upon this point Doctor Harris observes:

"Some laws of nature, which are usually regarded as merely uniform sequences, do in reality rest on rational principles from which they derive all their significance as laws. The law of gravitation is commonly spoken of as expressing merely an observed uniform sequence, but in truth this law is not known by experience, but is deduced from an *a priori* mathematical principle. The same is true of the law of dispersion of light. Also, when science carries an observed sequence beyond the observed facts, the induction rests entirely on self-evident intuition of reason. Also, the laws of mechanics rest partly on the law of causation and partly on mathematical principles both of which are first principles of reason."[5]

Indeed we are already taught that "the uniformity of nature is a necessary result of the law of causation, which necessary and self-evident truth gives the efficient and necessary support to that expectation which good sense and human testimony combine to produce in us."[6]

That these self-evident, universal and immutable principles, disclosed through man's rational intuition, have an objective reality and are fundamental truths regulative of the material forces of the universe and hence laws

[4] Fiske, Outline of Cosmic Phil., I. vol., 284-5.
[5] Harris, Phil. Basis of Theism, 186.
[6] Mivart, Groundwork of Science, 262.

in the primary meaning of the term as that which regulates power, seems to be incontrovertible, unless we deny unqualifiedly the trustworthiness of the human intellect.

Natural Law in a Secondary Sense.

Generalized Facts as Law.—But in this physical universe there are many so-called laws which are law only in a secondary sense. We hear the word "law" constantly upon the lips of men devoted to the physical sciences, when they have in mind nothing but the generalized facts or an orderly sequence of phenomena or events. They speak of the laws of motion, the laws of light, the laws of heat, the laws of sound, the laws of electricity, the law of the seasons, the law of evolution, and the law of gravitation. Let us state some of these laws as they have been formulated by science, and examine them with a special view of ascertaining whether they are laws in the true sense of the term, or whether they are laws only in the secondary sense; meaning the general facts and orderly sequences in the realm of nature. Among the multitude of natural laws now generally understood are the following:

Gravitation.—"Every particle of matter in the universe attracts every other particle with a force directly proportioned to the mass of the attracting particles, and inversely to the square of the distance between them."[7]

Newton's Laws of Motion:

1. "Every body continues in its state of rest, or of uniform motion in a straight line, except in so far as it is compelled by force to change that status."

2. "Change of (quantity of) motion is proportional to force, and takes place in the straight line in which the force acts."

3. "To every action there is always an equal and contrary reaction; or, the mutual actions of any two bodies are always equal and oppositely directed."[8]

[7] International Encyclopedia, Vol. 7. page 28.
[8] Ency. Brit. Vol. 15, Page 676.

Kepler's Three Laws:

1. "Every planet moves in an elliptical orbit, in one focus of which is the sun."

2. "The line drawn from the sun to a planet, or the radius vector of the planet, sweeps over equal areas in equal times."

3. "The squares of the numbers representing the periodic times of the planets vary as the cubes of the numbers representing their mean distances." [9]

Liquids.—Besides these laws pertaining to solid masses, we have the same term applied to certain facts respecting liquids, as "Where pressure is exerted on any part of the surface of a liquid that pressure is transmitted undiminished to all parts of the mass and in all directions." [10]

Gases.—And in the case of gases we have the law of Avogadro: "Equal volumes of all gases under the same conditions of temperature and pressure, contain the same number of molecules." [10]

Atoms.—And when we pursue our investigation down into the very atoms of which matter is supposed to be constructed, we find the law of definite proportions,—"Chemical combinations always take place between definite masses of substances." [11] And to this may be added the law of multiple proportions,—"If two elements form several compounds with each other, the masses of one that combine with fixed masses of the other bear a simple ratio to one another." [12]

Heat:

1. "Every body has a definite melting point assignable on the thermometric scale, if the pressure to which it is subjected be the same."

2. "When a body is melting it retains that fixed temperature, however much heat may be applied, until the last particle is melted." [13]

Light.—To these may be added the laws of light:

[9] Ency. Brit. Vol. 2, p. 779. (9th Ed.)

[10] Inter. Ency. Vol. 7, p. 746.

[11] Remsen, Introduction to Chemistry, 194.

[12] Id. p. 74.

[13] Inter. Ency. Vol. 7, 396.

1. "In a medium of uniform density light goes in straight lines with a uniform velocity."

2. "The intensity of light varies inversely as the square of the distance from its source."

The laws respecting refraction of light are stated as follows:

1. "In passing into a denser medium light is bent toward a perpendicular to the surface at the point of incident."

2. "In passing into a rarer medium, light is bent from the perpendicular."

Electricity.—In electricity we have Ohm's law that: "In electricity the quantity of current which will pass through a conductor is proportional to the pressure and inversely proportional to the resistance."[14]

Sound.—The laws regarding sound have been stated as follows:

1. "The velocity of sound varies inversely as the square root of the density of the substance."

2. "The velocity of sound varies directly as the square root of the elasticity of the substance."

Then again we have the law of reflection of light and sound which is that: "The angle of incident is equal to the angle of reflection."

We may take these few selected specimens of the laws of nature as illustrations of that vast Natural Code to discover and formulate which is the arduous task of science. But when we carefully examine these so-called laws we shall find them to consist of generalized facts respecting the behavior of matter, rather than truths or general properties of matter regulative of power. For example, when it is said that, "every particle of matter in the universe attracts every other particle with a force directly proportional to the mass of the attracting particle," the statement is one of uniform fact. Masses of matter always attract one another in that way. If we conceive of matter as a substance by itself, and force as a power outside of matter, but exerted upon it, then the

[14] Inter. Ency. Vol. 5, 330.

statement is simply one asserting how force behaves toward matter. It uniformly compels all masses to tend toward each other in a uniform manner. And if we conceive matter as a substance possessed of attracting forces within itself, then the statement is simply an assertion as to how such matter uniformly behaves. To say that any body unsuspended in the air will tend to fall toward the center of the earth sixteen feet the first second is simply to make a general statement as to how all bodies uniformly act; and it is this uniformity of action which is by science called a *law*.

To say that every body at rest continues at rest, or, if in motion, continues in motion in a straight line, except in so far as it is compelled by force to change that state; to say that the change of motion is proportional to the force, and that to every action there is always an equal and contrary reaction is to make simple statements of fact respecting the behavior of matter or the conduct of force. To say that all planets move in an elliptical orbit, with the sun in one of its foci, is to make a statement of fact respecting the relation of planets to the sun. And if this is true as to the orbit of Mars and Venus and Jupiter and so on through the entire solar system, then this is a uniform arrangement in that particular, and science calls that uniform, orderly arrangement a *law*. If the radius vector of a planet sweeps over equal areas in equal times, and this is true of all planets, this is but a generalized fact,—the uniform manner planets have of behaving themselves. If the pressure exerted upon one part of the surface of a liquid is transmitted undiminished to all other parts of the mass in all directions, and this is true of all cases of pressure upon all kinds of liquids, then this is but a statement of fact which is found to be uniformly and universally true. If equal volumes of all gases, under the same conditions of temperature and pressure, contain the same number of molecules, this is a uniform fact throughout the realm of gases, and science calls it a *law*. If two elements forming several compounds with each other always combine in a fixed ratio chemically, this is simply stating how atoms behave themselves and is therefore a mere generalization which the chemist calls a *law*. If when a body is melting, it retains a fixed temperature however much heat may be applied until the last particle is melted, this is but a statement as to how melting bodies retain their temperature, but science calls it a *law*. To say that light goes in straight lines with uniform velocity is but a statement of fact respecting light. And if the velocity of sound varies inversely as the square root of the density of the substance, this too is but a bare statement of fact.

And so we might go on through the entire realm of nature, and wherever we find matter or force operating in a uniform manner we shall find science pronouncing this uniformity a law of nature. It is true, as Mr. Fiske says in his Cosmic Philosophy, page 393: "A law of nature, as formulated in a scientific treatise, is a statement of fact and nothing more." And, as Mr. Drummond says: "The laws of nature are simply statements of the orderly condition of things in nature;" and further he observes, "The natural laws originate nothing, sustain nothing; they are simply responsible for uniformity in sustaining what has been originated and what is being sustained."[15]

In this age of investigation, when so much is attributed to law, it is worth our while to examine others of these general facts which are so often referred to as laws of nature, and by analyzing, ascertain their real nature. Among them we may profitably consider the following:

The Law of Conditioning and the Conditioned:—In his illustration of this law, of which he makes much account, President Hopkins says: "Let us see how this is with reference to the great forces by which the Universe is controlled * * * In the beginning the earth was without form and void—mere differential, nebulous, chaotic, surging matter in space; what would be the force which must act in order to bring this matter into such a condition that it might serve the purpose of a world? * * * Evidently it would be the force of gravitation; that is to

[15] Natural Law in the Spiritual World, p. 5.

say, it would be that force by which all matter tends towards all matter by a certain definite law. It would be necessary that such a force or mode of force should exist and apply itself to every particle of matter in order to its aggregation in such a way that it could become subject to the action of another force or mode of force. Being thus the condition for the action of any other force we may set Gravitation down as the lowest and most universal of all the forces or forms of force. * * * By gravitation matter is brought together, but simply as loose particles. That it may be serviceable as matter now is, there must be a force which will unite the particles into separate bodies. What is this? It is the attraction of cohesion. This exists between the particles of all bodies whether solid or fluid that can be defined or limited as separate bodies. This would give us a world made up of the different kinds of matter indiscriminately mixed, or with kinds separated as in crystallization.

"What force then is there by which such indiscriminate mixture may be avoided, and the varieties and combinations of matter as we now have them be given us? It is Chemical Affinity, which is the next higher power as conditioned upon gravitation and cohesion. Under this, also, as under gravitation, we have uniformities so perfect that they may be represented by mathematical formula. These laws being given, and working upon suitable materials we have the condition on which the cause of vegetable life, whatever that may be, can work. Without them vegetable life could not be.

"Again, having vegetable life given, mediating as it does between inorganic nature and animal life, by converting inorganic matter into food, by absorbing superfluous carbon, and by giving out oxygen to supply the waste made by animals, we have the conditions, and the only conditions, on which animal life could be produced and permanently maintained. This then gives us our next higher force—Animal Life.

"But one higher force remains, that is, Rational or Spiritual Life. That an animal life is a necessary condition of this in all beings, is not claimed or supposed.

But in man it is. Man exists in his present state only as the laws and forces already mentioned are given as a part of himself, and to be subjected under the force of a Rational and Free Will. This gives us Man * * * Looking at the relations of the forces and powers, we see that man has a right to the highest place on two grounds. First, all other things are a condition for him. He is conditioned upon them. They precede him, not arbitrarily, as a herald precedes a king, but in the way of preparation, as soil precedes vegetation, and as vegetable precedes animal life. So far as the creation was a process of upbuilding, that which came last was of course highest. But again, man is also highest because he subordinates all things to his own ends and uses them as they do not use him. * * * So we can trace the law still further by observing that the physical constitution of man including the brain is a condition precedent to the human intellect. The intellect is a condition in order that there may be feeling or sensibility, and sensibility in turn is a necessary condition in order that there may be motive for the exercise of a free will, and a free will is essential in order that there may be moral responsibility.''[16]

Thus this law of the ''Conditioning and the Conditioned'' is seen to extend throughout the universe of created things. And even back of material things the universe itself must depend for its existence and continuance upon the unconditioned but all-conditioning Being whence all things proceed.

This truth expresses a universal *fact*. The earth must exist before the roots and trunk of the tree can have existence, the trunk must precede and condition the branches, the branches condition the twigs, the twigs condition the leaves and the buds, and the buds precede and condition the fruit, and so on throughout the finite universe we find the law of the Conditioning and the Conditioned necessarily operative.

Some philosophers make no distinction between a con-

[16] Outline study of Man. 18-22.

dition and a cause, but the foundation of a house cannot be regarded as the cause of the superstructure, though it is a necessary condition for the erection of the edifice. There is in the idea of a cause some force, some causal efficiency that works changes which is lacking in the mere idea of one thing being a condition for another, as water is a condition for a floating steamer.

The existence of force is a condition precedent to all effects or change in the sense that the force must precede the change; but it is more than simply a precedent condition; it is a causal agent, an efficient power producing effects. But apart from the element of power, the law of Conditioning and Conditioned reigns throughout all nature. The mineral kingdom conditions the vegetable, the vegetable conditions the animal, the animal organism conditions intelligence, and intelligence conditions moral consciousness, and moral consciousness in turn conditions man's religious or spiritual nature.

These conditions are necessary. The conditioning must precede the conditioned: the foundation must precede the superstructure: the mineral must precede the vegetable: the vegetable must precede the animal: the animal must precede intelligence. There cannot be an intelligent being until there is a being to be intelligent: there canot be an organism vegetable or animal, without material from which such organism can be constructed. This is self-evident, and hence the law of the conditioning and the conditioned rests upon law in the primary sense of the term.

The Law of the Survival of the Fittest:—Mr. Darwin in the "Origin of Species" explains in what sense he employs the term "struggle for existence." He says: "I use the term in a large and metaphorical sense, including dependence of one being upon another, including (what is more important) not only the life of the individual, but success in leaving progeny. Two canine animals, in the time of dearth, may be truly said to struggle with each other which shall get food and live. But a plant on the edge of a desert is said to struggle for life against the drought, though more properly it should be said to be dependent on the moisture. A plant which annually produces a thousand seeds, of which one on an average comes to maturity, may be more truly said to struggle with the plants of the same and other kinds which already clothe the ground. The mistletoe is dependent on the apple and a few other trees, but can only in a far-fetched sense be said to struggle with these trees, for if too many of these parasites grow on the same tree, it languishes and dies. But several seedling mistletoes growing close together on the same branch may more truly be said to struggle with each other. As the mistletoe is disseminated by birds, its existence depends on them; and it may metaphorically be said to struggle with other fruit-bearing plants, in tempting the birds to devour and thus disseminate its seeds. In these several senses which pass into each other, I use for convenience' sake the general term of struggle for existence."[17]

In both vegetable and animal life, there are found certain individual differences and variations, which prove to be an advantage or hindrance to the individual in its struggle, and Mr. Darwin proceeds to say, "Can it then be thought improbable, seeing that variations useful to man have undoubtedly occurred that other variations useful in some way to each being in the great and complex battle of life, should occur in the course of many successive generations? If such do occur, can we doubt (remembering that many more individuals are born than can possibly survive) that individuals having any possible advantage, however slight, over others, would have the best chance of surviving and procreating their kind? On the other hand, we may feel sure that any variation in the least degree injurious would be rigidly destroyed. This preservation of favorable individual difference and variations and the destruction of those which are injurious I have called Natural Selection, or the Survival of the Fittest."[18]

In this struggle for existence, other things being equal, the individual possessing the greatest power, or power

[17] Origin of Species, p. 56. [18] Origin of Species, p. 70.

working at greater advantage by reason of some favorable difference or variation of structure or otherwise, must prevail over the individual with less power or with less favorable variations; and the stronger is thus said to be selected by Nature to survive,—selected by reason of its superior natural powers or its natural and advantageous variations or differences. Or, in other words, the stronger survives, and the weaker succumbs. So this law of the Survival of the Fittest is simply a statement of the fact that whenever a greater power, or a power working at greater advantage, comes into opposition or competition with a lesser power, or a power working at lesser advantage, the greater must prevail.

"The law of the survival of the fittest declares merely what must result when a stronger force encounters a weaker." Is it not self-evident that a greater power opposing one that is less must prevail? Is this not a necessity under the law of causation? Equal powers, when opposed, must hold each other in check. Two locomotives upon opposite ends of a train of cares, pulling with equal power in opposite directions, would produce no motion of the train, but add to the power of one locomotive fifty horse power more and this extra power becomes the cause by which motion is effected in the direction whither the increased power is exerted. The motion is affected by the increased power; hence the power and motion stand to one another in the relation of cause and effect. Consequently the "law of the Survival of the Fittest," in so far as it signifies that the stronger individual plant or animal, other things being equal, will prevail over the weaker is but an application of the more general law of causation. Of this law it has been said, "The application of this becomes less easy as the arrangements of nature become more complicated, and especially in organic and conscious life. But in all complications the law of causation remains true, and the greater power or the power working at greater advantage must always prevail over the less when they come into opposition. In organic life this is the law of the survival of the fittest." [19]

[19] Harris. Self-Revelation of God, 534.

As Mr. Darwin uses the terms "Natural Selection" and "The Survival of the Fittest" interchangeably, so the so-called "law of Natural Selection" and the "law of the Survival of the Fittest" are identical. Nature selects the fittest as the one to survive in the struggle for existence.

But, on the other hand, in so far as the term law has reference to the existence simply of "individual difference and variations" it is simply the statement of a generalized fact, and is a law only in the secondary sense of the term.

The Law of Compensation.—This law has a varied and extensive application. In discussing it at great length Emerson has said, "In the animal kingdom the physiologist has observed that no creatures are favorites, but a certain compensation balances every gift and every defect. A surplusage given to one part is paid out of a reduction from another part of the same creature. If the head and neck are enlarged the trunk and extremities are cut short—also in mechanics 'what we gain in power is lost in time'—The cold climate invigorates, the barren soil does not breed fevers, crocodiles, tigers, or scorpions. Every sweet has its sour, every evil its good. For every grain of wit there is a grain of folly. The President has paid dear for the White House. It has commonly cost him all his peace and the best of his manly attributes." [20]

And speaking of the same law Mr. Darwin has said, "The elder Geoffray and Goethe propounded, at about the same time, their law of compensation or balancement of growth, or as Goethe expressed it, "in order to spend on one side nature is forced to economize on the other side." I think this holds true to a certain extent with our domestic productions: if nourishment flows to one part or organ in excess it rarely flows, at least in excess, to another part; thus it is difficult to get a cow to give much milk and to fatten readily. The same varieties of the cabbage do not yield abundant and nutritious foliage and a copious supply of oil-bearing seeds. When the seeds in our fruit become atrophies, the fruit itself gains

[20] Essay, Compensation.

largely in size and quality. In our poultry a large tuft of feathers on the head is generally accompanied by a diminished comb, and a large beard by diminished wattles. With species in a state of nature it can hardly be maintained that the law is of universal application, but many good observers, more especially botanists, believe in its truth.''[21]

To whatever extent Goethe's statement is true that "in order to spend on one side nature is forced to economize on the other'' it is not a necessity in the sense that we cannot conceive the process to be otherwise. That it is a general truth is the most we can say of it, and hence a law in the secondary sense.

The Law of Use and Disuse:—This law is one of universal application. The use of the power we have increases it. The use of the muscles of the body increases their capacity, the proper use of memory makes it more retentive and ready, the exercise of the imagination increases its strength and vividness. Of this law Professor Fiske has said, "The principle in accordance with which the gloved hand of the dandy becomes white and soft while the hand of the laboring man grows brown and tough is the main principle at work in the improvement of humanity. Our intellectual faculties, our passions, our prejudices, our tastes and habits become strengthened by use and weakened by disuse, just as the blacksmith's arm grows strong and the horse turned out to pasture becomes unfit for work. This law of use and disuse has been of immense importance throughout the whole evolution of organic life. With man it has come to be paramount.''[22]

This too is the statement of a general fact. It is not inconceivable that use should weaken and rest should strengthen both mind and body.

Mr. Darwin gives interesting illustrations of the same law. "It is well known that several animals, belonging to the most different classes, which inhabit the caves of Carniola and Kentucky are blind. In some of the crabs the foot-stock for the eyes remains though the eye is

21 Origin of Species, p. 131. 22 Destiny of Man, 98.

gone. The stand for the telescope is there, though the telescope with its glasses has been lost. As it is difficult to imagine that eyes, though useless, could be in any way injurious to animals living in darkness their loss may be attributed to disuse. In one of the blind animals, namely the cave-rat (Nestoma), two of which were captured by Professor Silliman at above half a mile distance from the mouth of the cave, and therefore not in the profoundest depths, the eyes were lustrous and of large size, and these animals, as I am informed by Professor Silliman, after having been exposed for about a month to a gradual light, acquired a dim perception of objects.''[23]

This is nature's method of operation, and the uniform method is spoken of by scientists and by the public generally as a law.

The Law of Inertia:—This law is a generalized fact, rather than a self-evident truth or principle. The law as stated is not ''an a priori necessity,'' though many attempts have been made to show that it is. We shall not submit this law to a metaphysical examination for the purpose of ascertaining whether it should be classified as law in the primary or the secondary sense, for it is not a matter of prime importance whether the classification of the laws we are enumerating should be metaphysically correct. Inertia of matter is a fact, and being of general application it is a law, as are other generalized facts. Concerning this law, however, Professor Bowne has said, ''The first and basal law of motion is that of inertia, according to which a body cannot start or stop itself. If at rest it remains at rest, and if in motion it remains in uniform motion in a straight line unless interfered with from without. Many attempts have been made to show this law to be a necessity of thought, but without success. If the non-sponteneity of the elements be allowed, the law is of course an identical judgment, for the law is simply a denial of sponteneity with regard to space-relations. A change of condition is always an effect and pre-supposes some cause; and if an element

[23] Darwin, Origin of Species, p. 123-4.

has not influence over its own states of course all changes come from without. But when the point is to know whether the law is an a priori necessity, we must inquire whether there is any ground for saying that the elements must be of this sort. That they are such may be allowed; but that they must be such is not made to appear. The apparent self-evidence in the case is largely due to the abstraction of a material point with which mechanics is wont to begin. This point is conceived as the inert and rigid subject of possible motion, and in itself is so emptied of all quality as to contain no ground of activity of any sort. The deduction of the law from this conception is easy enough; but this conception is a pure figment of the imagination. As applied to a real element, even the first part of the law, which asserts that a body at rest will remain at rest unless moved by something outside of it, is not self-evident. It is not self-evident that an element, if it could exist alone in space, could not, whatever its nature, begin motion; for motion, as we have seen, is but the spacial expression of an internal state, and if that state were given motion would result. It is not self-evident that the inner changes of such a thing could never result in that state which expresses itself in motion."[24]

After further argument Professor Bowne concludes that "it is not self-evident that motion must take place along the line which joins the bodies, for all we can say it might be in any other line whatever. * * *

He then concludes his comments with the following reflection: "We must reduce the whole apparent world in space and time to phenomenal existence, the study of the phenomenal laws, leaving the metaphysical question to philosophy. As a matter of fact phenomena have laws. They come together, vary together, succeed one another according to rules. These laws are largely spacial and temporal and admit of geometrical and numerical expression. Every such expression is valuable if it helps us to a knowledge of the order of phenomena, and especially if it gives us any practical control of them.

24 Bowne, Metaphysics, 227.

These laws have to be learned from experience. Neither the laws of motion nor the so-called laws of force admit of a priori deduction, and all alike are valuable only for the practical control of phenomena to which they may help us.''[25]

Conformity to Type.—Huxley says that ''It is the first great law of reproduction, that the offspring tends to resemble its parent or parents more closely than anything else.''

Attention is called by the Botanist to the wide difference between the lichen, the oak and the palm tree. In structure, in form, in the variety of fruit and flower they are distinct, and as unlike as organic life can well be. But the germs of these three organisms are so similar that it is difficult and even impossible to discover by aid of the most powerful microscope any difference in their structure. While these germs are alike so far as discoverable even by the Chemist, yet they develop into structures bearing the slightest possible resemblance to one another. Each germ contains a type in itself.

Darwin states this law under the name of ''Unity of Type,'' and says that by it ''is meant that fundamental agreement in structure which we see in organic beings of the same class and which is quite independent of their habits of life.''

According to this law the hemlock produces the hemlock, the birch the birch, the bird according to its type produces the bird, the lion produces a lion and so on throughout the realm of organic life.

This law is a general fact and we call this uniform tendency for like to produce like, the Law of ''Unity of Type'' or ''Conformity to Type.''[26]

Every living thing that comes into the world is compelled to stamp upon its offspring the image of itself.

The Law of Reversion to Type.—If animals or plants, which have once been improved by care or cultivation, are neglected or allowed to care for themselves, they will deteriorate and return to the type of their progenitors.[27]

25 Bowne, Metaphysics, 242.
26 Origin of Species, page 186.
27 Nat. Law in Spiritual World, page 97.

This is a law often referred to by naturalists, and it is illustrated by Mr. Drummond as follows:

"If a garden is planted with strawberries and roses and for a number of years left alone, * * * it will run to waste. But this does not mean that the plants will really waste away, but that they will change into something else, and, as it universally appears, into something worse; in the one case, namely, into the small, wild strawberries of the woods, and in the other into the primitive rose of the hedges. * * * And if we neglect a bird, by the same imperious law it will be gradually changed into an uglier bird. And the law of reversion to type runs through all creation.

If a man neglect himself for a few years he will change into a worse man and a lower man: if it is his body that he neglects, he will deteriorate into a wild and bestial savage,—like the de-humanized men who are discovered sometimes upon desert islands. If it is his mind, it will degenerate into imbecility and madness. If he neglect his conscience it will run off into lawlessness and vice."

Mr. Darwin throws some doubt upon the universality of this law that our "domestic varieties, when running wild, gradually but invariably revert in character to their aboriginal stock."

So far as it is a law, however, it states no more than a general fact and is a law only in that sense.

The Law of Battle.—By the law of battle is meant the struggle that goes on between the individuals of one sex in the lower orders of animal life, generally the males, for the possession of the other sex. The males contend for the favor of the females in the lower orders of animal life as well as in the higher. The fact that such a battle is resorted to, and is quite general, has been designated the law of battle. The males fight for the possession of the females. Mr. Darwin says, "How low in the scale of nature the law of battle descends I know not. Male alligators have been described as fighting, bellowing, and whirling around, like Indians in a war-dance, for the possession of the females; male salmons have been observed fighting all day long; male stag beetles sometimes bear wounds from the huge mandibles of other beetles; the males of certain lymenopterous insects have been frequently seen by that inevitable observer M. Fabre fighting for a particular female, who sits by, an apparently unconcerned beholder of the struggle, and then retires with the conqueror." This general fact that the lower orders of animal life are pugnacious and that the males contend for the possession of the females has been designated the law of battle.

The Law of Evolution.—"Evolution is an integration of matter and concomitant dissipation of motions; during which the matter passes from an indefinite, incoherent homogeneity to a definite coherent heterogeneity, and during which the retained motion undergoes a parallel transformation."[28] This, as it will be observed, is the mere statement of a fact, a phenomenal process as Mr. Spencer understood it; and as it is the general process which Nature follows in all her productions, it may be termed the world process—a general fact. It does not state a necessary truth; it simply points out "the steps by which any living being has acquired the morphological and the physiological character which distinguish it."[29]

It states the world process, the order pursued by nature as a mere matter of fact. It has nothing to say about causation. It does not tell us how vegetable or animal life came upon the earth, but it simply recounts the fact that "the simplest and lowest forms of existence preceded the higher and more complex forms. Nothing begins ready made. The present grew out of the past, the complex out of the simple, the high out of the low, the heterogeneous out of the homogeneous. In the inorganic world, if one should trace its history backward, we should find simpler and simpler physical conditions, until we came to some simple state of dispersed matter, say a nebulous cloud. In the organic world, if we should trace living forms backward along genealogical lines, we should find those lines converging towards a common point of radiation. The forms of life would grow simpler, until in some very simple forms we should find the common

[28] First Principle, 407. [29] Huxley, Ency. Brit. 9ed.

starting point from which the complex forms of today have been developed. The same order is to be observed in the development of mind, society, civilization and institutions in general.

"Evolution in this sense is simply a description of an order of development, a statement of what, granting the theory, an observer might have seen if he had been able to inspect the cosmic movement from its simplest stages until now. It is a statement of method and is silent about causation; and the method itself is compatible with any kind of causation. One might hold to this phenomenal order and be an agnostic, or a positivist or an idealist, or a theologian, as to the causation.

"This conception of the phenomenal history of the world as showing such a continuous progress from the simple to the complex, from the low to the high, we may call the doctrine of evolution in its scientific sense. It lies within the field of science, and is open to scientific proof or disproof. Whenever the doctrine transcends this field of phenomenal description, and claims to give a theory of the productive causes, it then becomes metaphysics, and must be handed over to the philosophical criticism for adjudication.

"Evolution then, in the scientific sense is neither a controlling law nor a producing cause, but simply a description of a phenomenal order."

While this law is generally accepted as the general order of nature in the organic world, yet "how the ascent even of species has been brought about" is a matter of dispute.

But whether this cosmic formula be accurately stated or not, and whether it be true or false, the general order of nature as we observe it is a matter of fact rather than a self-evident truth of reason, and in our classification of laws it must be regarded as a law in the secondary rather than in the primary sense of the term.

Law of Continuity.—It is claimed that Leibnitz first formulated this law and confined it to motions, but it is now stated in various forms and finds numerous applications. "Motion is continuous." "Natural causality is continuous." "The order of phenomenal law is continuous," and the more comprehensive statement of the law may be that "Nature is continuous."

This law has been the subject of much comment by scientists and of much analysis and criticism by metaphysicians. In a superficial sense this law is a mere statement of an apparent fact and belongs to the class of secondary laws.

Professor Bowne indulges in the following comments upon this law: "What is it then, in the case of Nature, that is continuous? Is it natural things in their existence, or natural causality, or nature as phenomenon? The suspicion begins to dawn upon us that nature is not continuous in any of these senses, and that the continuity is to be found in the continuous validity of the system of law and in the continuity of thought of which nature is the flowing expression.

That nature is continuous in its existence is a metaphysical proposition. It might mean that nature itself is a continuous substantial somewhat, or that the material elements are continuous in their existence, and suffer no increase or diminution of their number. Both propositions are already condemned. The necessary dependence of the finite on the fundamental reality reduces it to contingent existence, and leaves us entirely unable to say how, or when, or in what order, they shall cease to be. A metaphysical doctrine with so many riders as this can never be put forward as a first principle. In addition, metaphysics reduces all impersonal existence to a flowing form of the activity of the fundamental reality. The only metaphysical continuity in the case is the continuity of the infinite being in which nature has its root.

But natural causality is continuous. To question this would be fatal to all science. But here again we have confusion. Some causality must be continuous, without doubt; the cessation of all causality would be the vanishing of nature. If natural causality means the causality which supports nature, it is continuous, not indeed as a necessity, but as a matter of fact. How long it shall remain continuous however, is unknown to all but the uncritical dogmatist, and he simply mistakes the monotony of his thinking for a law of existence. If by natural causality we mean the causality of nature, considered as an impersonal agent or system of agents, we have to say that there is no such thing.

Again, what the uncritical speculator really needs here is not a metaphysical doctrine about natural causality, but rather an inductive postulate of the continuity of natural law. As long as the order of law holds we may hope to construe experience. If this order should fail us, all hope of dealing with experience would vanish. But no metaphysical principle whatever can assure us of this continuity. There is nothing in the conception of impersonal causality to assure us that it is shut up to a uniform manifestation. The continuity of law, therefore, is a pure postulate which must either be referred to an abiding purpose in the cosmic intelligence, or else be accepted out of hand as an opaque fact.

The continuity of nature as phenomenon means the same thing, the continuity of phenomenal laws. In the strictest sense a moving world has no continuity in itself, but only for the observing or producing mind. Apart from this mind, nature, supposing it to exist at all, would be a mirage of vanishing phantoms, each and all perishing in the attempt to be born. But granting the observer and the phenomenal world, the only continuity possible would be the continuous succession of phenomena according to the same laws. The new phenomena as events would be other than the old, however similar that might be, as a new day is another day notwithstanding its logical equivalence to old days. But all the phenomena, new and old alike, would be comprehended in the same scheme of law and relation; and this fact constitutes the unity and continuity of the system. From the phenomenal standpoint nature has no other continuity. The only inductive continuity we can find or allow is one of phenomenal law. And this law produces nothing and really prescribes nothing. It merely states a uniformity of the phenomenal order."[30]

30 Bowne, Metaphysics, 264.

Orderly Sequences as Law.—There are in addition to these generalized facts certain orderly and uniform sequences to which the term "law" is also applied. The earth, rotating upon its axis, is attended by alternate and orderly sequences of light and darkness; in its revolutions around the Sun it is also attended by the orderly succession of the seasons as a natural and necessary sequence. So in the vegetable realm a seed dropped into the soil swells and bursts forth into the blade, then unfolds into the trunk of a tree developing its branches and twigs upon which later appear the leaves, the buds, the flower and finally the fruit which, passing gradually through its various stages, comes at length to its final maturity. In the animal world the same rule of invariable and orderly sequence applies. An egg subjected to the proper degree of heat passes through its various stages of development until bursting the shell the young chick appears, only to proceed along another gradual course of progression and so on through its natural period of life to maturity and to final dissolution. The heart of an animal throbs and as a result the blood courses throughout the system, carrying the proper materials for upbuilding the tissues, and the process of reconstruction goes on year after year through the allotted stages of animal life; and so throughout the entire physical universe unvarying antecedence and consequence prevail, and to this orderly ongoing of nature is also applied the term law. The infant mind of man, appearing at first little more than instinct, gradually unfolds until slight indications of intelligence are followed by the intellectual processes of reflection, then follow analysis, synthesis, moral perceptions, conscience and voluntary determinations of the will. All of these progressive unfoldings of the seed, the egg and the mind are the natural and orderly sequences of forces apparently inherent in nature, regulated by the principles of reason amid the conditions of physical and mental existences. These uniform and invariable sequences are themselves called laws. They are the necessary results of law in its deeper and primary meaning, but as scientific usage has conferred upon them the term "law" it is necessary to distinguish them from those controlling principles which constitute law in its primary sense.

Referring to both the generalized facts and the orderly sequences of nature Henry George says:

"Thus, then, when we find in Nature certain invariable sequences, whose cause of being transcends the power of the will testified to by our own consciousness—such, for instance, as that stones and apples always fall towards the earth; that the square of a hypothenuse is always equal to the sum of the squares of its base and perpendicular; that gases always coalesce in certain definite proportions; that one pole of the magnet always attracts what the other always repels; that the egg of one bird subjected to a certain degree of warmth for a certain time brings forth a chick that later will clothe itself with plumage of a certain kind and color, and the egg of another bird under the same conditions brings forth a chick of a different kind; that at a certain stage of infancy teeth appear, and later decay and drop out; and so on through the list of invariable sequences that these will suggest—we say, for it is really all that we can say, that these sequences are invariable because they belong to the order or system of Nature; or, in short, that they are 'laws of nature.' "[31]

To the same effect but with greater discrimination Doctor Harris observes: "The uniform factual sequences observed in nature are also called laws of nature, but these are so called only in a secondary sense. In truth they are only factual manifestations or revelations of law in its true significance which is always the appliance of law or reason." And further he says: "But the so-called laws of nature are mere observed factual sequences. The name 'laws' can be applied to them only in a secondary application. * * * The principles of reason regulating physical force are the laws of nature in their true and deepest meaning. The terms have become to be called laws because they are seen to reveal in nature this

[31] Henry George Science of Political Economy, 55.

intelligent and rational regulation by the power above nature."

Theories and Hypotheses as Law.—Theories and hypotheses regarding the origin, development and on-going of physical nature have frequently been dignified by the name of "law" before they have been sufficiently verified to be generally accepted as facts.

The nebular hypothesis, as the correct explanation of the origin of the whole physical universe, the theory of universal gravitation, the atomic theory, the theory of spontaneous generation, the materialistic theory of the transformation of motor force into thought and emotion, and the theory of evolution, and others, are sometimes designated as "laws of nature."

Strictly speaking, a theory or hypothesis, as used in this connection, is simply an intelligible conception as to how phenomena are brought about. This conception is assumed because it tends to explain the origin of things and how and why one event follows another. When any such theory is so verified as to be practically demonstrated as true, as in the case of gravitation, as formulated and expressed by Newton, and as in the case of Kepler's laws which he held as theories long before he proved them to be true, the term "law" in its secondary meaning is properly applied to it. The theory has ripened in such case under the light of successful investigation, into a natural law as an established fact.

But a theory that has been proved to be a true conception as to how things are related and how they operate, is quite different from one that has few if any facts to support it. We can speak of the law of scientific evolution with much more propriety than we can of the law of materialistic evolution, because the latter assumes spontaneous generation to be an established fact, when there is no adequate, if indeed, any proof of it whatever.

In this connection we find the same carelessness respecting the use of the term "law" as prevails generally in the use of that word. It is applied to the supposed order quite as freely as it is to the known order of events. Thus we speak of the law of telepathy, when no such law has ever been formulated. The fact that one person sometimes thinks of another just before seeing him, and other similar facts lead to the supposition that one mind acts upon another at a distance without the use of words or the other ordinary signs of expression. But that one mind does in fact act upon another, under such circumstances, is a pure assumption. It is an easy method of quieting the inquiring mind to refer the unknown relation of events and their causes to the influence of some law. The mind naturally seeks the causes of things and not infrequently, as we have before observed, we find "law" referred to as a causal agency. Confusion of thought is inevitable when we confound law which directs with the causal agencies which are directed.

Force as Law.—Force itself is sometimes referred to as a law, but without justification if law is that which regulates force. The Force of Gravitation is one thing; the manner of its action is another. We know it as a "force of attraction operating between all the particles of matter in the exact measure which was ascertained by Newton—that is—directly as the mass, and inversely as the square of the distance."[32]

The force of attraction is the causal agency, but the manner in which it acts upon matter, namely, "directly as the mass and inversely as the square of the distance" is the law of its action. The force and method of its action are not identical. The method is called a law, but it can be such only in the secondary sense of the term.

Electricity or lightning is said to follow the line of the least resistance, but the electric force is one thing and the manner of its behavior is quite another. The force is a causal agent, but the fact that "it acts uniformly in the line of least resistance" is called the law of its action—but law in the secondary sense.

Organic Life.—The preceding illustrations of law in the secondary sense of the term have been drawn from the inorganic and organic realms indiscriminately. No attempt has been made to separate and group certain laws

[32] Argyle Reign of Law, page 72.

as those prevailing exclusively in the organic or inorganic kingdoms respectively.

The phenomenal order discovered to exist in any one of these realms embraces all the so-called laws of that particular realm. The laws of planetary motion and others enumerated in our astronomy belong to the inorganic world; the law that all vegetable life springs from a seed, and others named and discussed in our botany, prevail in the vegetable sphere; while the law that all animate life comes from an egg, and the numerous other laws pertaining to the senses, digestion, circulation, respiration and secretion announced in our zoology operate throughout the animal kingdom.

Then there are certain of these laws like gravitation, chemical attraction and combination which prevail in both the inorganic and organic realms; and still others like the law of growth and decay, and the geographical distribution of life on the globe, which are confined in their operation to the organic world, but are present in both the inanimate and animate spheres. And still others like the laws of vision, locomotion, nervous excitability, and intelligence, exist only in the animal world. To understand all the laws in the organic realm would be to know its entire phenomenal order in all its details. Science here has but just entered upon its work.

Law of Biogenesis.—The law of biogenesis is a fundamental principle in the organic sphere. It illustrates how a fundamental truth of reason operates as a law in the realm of phenomena. Harvey's statement of the general fact that all life comes from life, "*Omne vivum ex vivo,*" expresses the basic principle in the phenomenal order of the organic world. Everywhere we behold life springing from life. "Life is the gift of life." The growing corn sprang from the living seed, the living tree and shrub and bush and grasses all spring from a vitalized source. The fishes and birds and beasts and insects all have their origin in some egg containing the principle of life. Though attempts have often been made to experimentally establish the alleged fact of spontaneous generation, yet the prospects are not good for demonstrating that life can be extracted or generated from materials in which there is no life. Water cannot flow from an empty fountain. Something cannot come from nothing. This fundamental truth holds throughout the realm of nature.

Animal Intelligence.—Crossing the line which separates the inanimate from the animate realm, we encounter at once a new factor in the organic world. Intelligence varying in degree from the lowest order of simple perception to the highest order of the animal mind appears and presents a most difficult field for investigation. Of the impersonal or animal intelligence comparatively little is known. The psychic nature of the animal world has arrested the attention of thoughtful and industrious men; but the phenomenal order of an invisible existence, where introspection is impossible, eludes the investigator. That intelligence exists in the brute being, that the process of memory and reasoning go on in some fashion, and that the elements of fear and joy and sorrow and affection exist in the mind of many grades of animal life is unquestionable; but the discovery and the formulation of the laws prevailing in the impersonal mind of the animal kingdom must of necessity be extremely slow.

The most conspicuous element of animal life is the instinctive element, and as that plays such an important part in regulating animal conduct we will refer to that alone in this connection.

Instinct as Law.—Besides the truth of reason, the generalized facts and orderly sequences of physical nature there are the instincts of animal life, which are fixed and regulative agencies in the realm of animate existence. Instinct is a constitutional element in animal life, and its office is to guide the forces of animate being. It is found throughout the whole scale of animal creation, from the lower orders of life to man himself. It is a regulative propensity. It is distinct from the power which it guides. The physical force exerted by the bird which migrates from one clime to another is not identical with the native propensity which directs that force. Instinct has been defined as "a special internal tendency to perform blindly a series of definite and useful actions." [33]

Whether it is in the nature of a feeling as some contend, or whether it is in the nature of intelligence as others believe, it is in either case directive and regulative. Even if it is a psychical force, it is nevertheless changelessly and blindly regulative of physical power and hence it is a law to such power. Its range of influence in the animal world is co-extensive with animal life, and forms a most interesting chapter in its history. I quote from Mr. Mivart the following examples of this regulative tendency in animal life.

"But instinct, as it exists in man, is very feebly and obscurely developed, compared with the manifestations of that faculty which may be met with in various orders of the lower animals, and especially among insects. Chickens will, very soon after they are hatched, peck at small objects, grains and insects, and but little later will at once perform, when they come in contact with water, the movements for making it flow over their backs and fall off. Some birds will feign lameness, or some other injury, to draw off attention from their eggs or young. Birds of the first year, when the time of migration arrives, are often the earliest to depart, and duly accomplish their journey, though they can have no knowledge of the route they have to pursue, or the region it is the object of their journey to attain. Snakes taken out of their mother's body just before their natural birth will even then threaten to strike, and, if rattle-snakes, to rattle, or at least rapidly vibrate the end of the tail. Ichneumon flies will lay their eggs within the bodies of caterpillars, that they may find abundant suitable food when they are hatched, but we cannot believe that they foresee the purpose and practical utility of their action.

"A kind of wasp, called 'sphex,' provides for the nutrition of her unhatched young in an analogous but yet more remarkable manner. She will hunt about until she finds a suitable caterpillar, grasshopper, or spider, which she adroitly stings on the spot which induces, or on the

[33] Mivart, Groundwork of Science, 133.

several spots which induce, complete paralysis, so as to deprive it of all power of motion, but not to kill it, as to kill it would defeat her purpose. This done, she stores away the helpless victim along with her eggs, in order that when her eggs are hatched the grubs which issue from them may find living animal food ready for them and in a suitable state of helplessness; for were they not in such a state, the grubs would be utterly unable to catch, retain and prey upon them. The species of sphex which preys upon the grasshopper first stings it and then throws it upon its back, so as to get at the delicate membrane which unites the pieces of its hard armour at their joints. This it bites through to reach a specially enlarged portion of nervous tissue there concealed by mutilating which it attains its practical but surely unforeseen end.

"But if the adult insect cannot reasonably be supposed to understand the future conditions of its unborn young which it will never see, still less can the poor grub be expected to understand what will be the future conditions of its own life when it is a grub no longer,—conditions so utterly different from those of which it has had any experience. Yet many species of caterpillar form cocoons in modes and places most suitable for their protection and for their own easy emergence when they have changed into the adult form. The caterpillars of a moth found in Africa will unite their efforts to form, as it were, a great common cocoon, within which external envelope each caterpillar makes its own special cocoon, but which are so skillfully arranged as to leave passages between them to facilitate their departure when, as moths, the time has come for them to fly away.

"The caterpillar of the emperor moth is described as spinning for itself a double cocoon, but leaving an opening fortified with elastic bristles pointing outwards, and so directed that while they readily yield to pressure from within, they firmly resist pressure from without. Thus the caterpillar is at the same time both protected from intrusion from the outside, and enabled easily to obtain its own exit when fully developed.

"As an example of the blindness which characterizes

these instinctive actions, we may refer to a kind of wasp which does not enclose living food with her eggs, but from time to time feeds the grubs which thence emerge with fresh food, visiting her nest for that purpose at suitable intervals. She covers her nest so carefully with sand that it is completely hidden, and this covering is replaced with equal care after each of her visits. While it remains thus hidden she, it is said, can always find it; but if an entrance is made ready for her, this, instead of helping her to get to her young, seems to puzzle her completely, and even to prevent her from recognizing her own offspring.

"But as everyone knows, moths and butterflies habitually lay their eggs on the leaves of such plants as will form suitable food for the grubs when hatched, although the parents themselves neither feed on such leaves nor make any other use of them than that of serving as a receptacle for their eggs. It may be that the parents are insects which, in the adult condition, do not feed at all, and it is incredible that they foresee the use to their unhatched young of leaves useless to themselves, and the past utility of which to the grubs they once were they cannot be supposed to remember. Still more incredible is it, however, that a grub should foresee the shape of the body it is destined later to acquire, especially when this shape is widely different in the two sexes. Yet the grub of the female stag-beetle, when she digs the hole wherein she will undergo her metamorphosis, digs it no bigger than her own body; whereas the grub of the male stag-beetle makes a hole twice as large as his own body, in order to leave room for the enormous jaws (the so-called 'horns') which he will have to grow.

"One more example of that function of the nervous system which results in instinct must here suffice. There is a kind of beetle called 'sitaris,' which is parasitic on certain bees, while its relation to those insects is very different during the different stages of existence which make up its life history. It is hatched from eggs which the mother sitaris lays in passages in the bees' nest. Instead of being in the form of a grub (as is the case with beetles generally), it comes forth from the egg as an active six-legged little insect with eyes and two 'feelers,' or antennae. In the spring, as the male bees (drones) pass out for their nuptial flight with the queen, the sitaris attaches itself to one of them, and as soon as the opportunity offers, passes from it to the body of the queen bee. When afterwards, the queen bee lays her egg in the hive, the sitaris springs upon it, and is unsuspectingly enclosed in a cell with the honey destined to nourish the bee-grub when the queen's egg is hatched. Thus left alone with the egg, the sitaris devours it, and then undergoes a transformation in the empty egg-shell. having been active in the earliest stage of its life it assumes the helpless form of a fleshy grub, which floats on the honey and gradually consumes it. Afterwards it transforms itself once more, and regaining its six legs, emerges as a peaceful beetle, and so with its egg begins again the cycle of this species' strange life-history."[34]

For our purpose it is unnecessary to go further into this subject than to call attention to the guiding and regulating nature of instinct. It is a law to the power it regulates only in the secondary sense of that term. It is not one of the immutable, universal and self-evident truths which constitute law in its primary meaning, but falls into that class of laws where are classified the orderly sequences and uniformities of nature. Instinct is uniform in its regulative tendencies, and orderly in its results, and, as a constitutional characteristic of animal life, it is a law in the secondary sense of the term. It is a reality regulative of power.

The Material World Itself a Law.—But there is a sense in which all these generalized facts and orderly sequences of nature are laws to man in the true and real significance of the term. Man is a force in nature. He is a finite personal power, placed in a world of fixed and uniform physical phenomena. To man the so-called law of gravitation is a fixed and unalterable fact regulative of his power. Relative to man, the laws of rotary motion, the laws of chemical combination, the laws of

[34] Mivart, Groundwork of Science, pp. 127-131.

heat, light and sound are facts fixed, laid down, and unalterably established, as much so as the laws of reason themselves. Man, by all his native force, and by all the forces he can command, can no more change the course of the stars than he can make two bodies occupy the same space at the same time; he can no more interrupt the course of the seasons than he can enclose a portion of space with a straight line; he can no more make oxygen and hydrogen unite chemically in other than their established proportions than he can make two and two equal five; he can no more make solid bodies tend to fly away from the center of the earth than he can hasten or retard the flight of time; he can no more prevent light from dispelling darkness than he can make a circle whose diameter is greater than its circumference; he cannot prevent the rotation of the earth, nor the reflection of the moon, nor the ebb and flow of the tides, nor the growing of the flowers, nor the movements of the atmosphere, nor the chemical effects of sunlight about him, any more than he can change the constitution of the multiplication table, or make the whole of anything less than the sum of its constituent parts.

All these so-called laws of nature, all these uniformities in the physical world, are fixed, and unchangeable by human power, and are therefore regulative of human power in that they determine what man can and what he cannot do. Whatever he accomplishes must be accomplished in harmony with, and not in violation of these uniform tendencies and sequences of nature. If man would float an ocean steamer he must conform his work of its construction to the uniform demands of liquids and mechanics. If he would scale the heavens in a balloon he must harmonize its construction with the laws of the atmosphere,—in defiance of them he must fail, in compliance with them he may succeed. They regulate his power, in that they determine what he can and what he cannot do.

Enough of these so-called laws of Nature have now been examined to illustrate their character. Aside from the primary truths of intuition, and the necessary inferences therefrom, which are regulative of all the finite energies of the physical universe and, as we have seen, are laws in the primary and true sense of the term, there are the generalized facts and orderly sequences of impersonal nature and the manner in which certain forces act, to all of which the term, "Natural Law" has been applied.

We have observed in our examination that these facts are not forces. Orderly phenomena are the effects produced by forces. Natural laws in the realm here referred to, are simply the modes in which energy uniformly manifests itself. They have no real existence apart from the energy whose uniform methods of action they are, any more than motion has an existence independent of the body that moves. It is easy for the human mind to hypostasize these modes of action, and thus give to them an apparent existence as actual entities. We think of these laws as real things, as a frame-work of changeless realities. They are sometimes conceived as things distinct and separate from Matter and Force, as we think of the earth's orbit around the sun as a real elliptical path. Were the earth removed from the Solar System, no orbit or path would remain. The orbit is simply the imaginary figure described by the earth's motion. So when we say it is a law of nature that planets revolve around the sun in elliptical orbits, the law referred to is nothing more than the uniform manner in which the planets revolve around the sun. The "law" is not the planet nor its orbit, but it is the name given to the general fact that each one of the planets, and hence all of them in general describe an ellipse in their respective revolutions around the sun. In this sense the law is simply a generalized fact.

From this, the inaccuracy of attributing to "Natural Law" causal efficiency is clearly seen. Force produces results. The orderly phenomena of Nature are effects, not causes. We give the name law to the whole phenomenal order of impersonal nature; and to each specific phenomenal process we give a specific name, as, to the uniform phenomena of attraction between masses of matter we give the name, "Law of Gravitation," to the uniform attraction between atoms of matter, we give the name, "The Law of Chemical Affinity," and so on throughout the known realm of the physical universe.

When we speak of the "Laws of Nature," producing this or that effect, as when we say that the universe was created by law, we are attributing to law a certain efficiency which it does not possess, and we are likely to be lead thereby to false conclusions in our reasoning about Nature.

"The laws of nature which declare mere uniform factual sequences are laws only in the secondary sense. In the lapse of time these sequences may change and give place to new arrangements. On the contrary, it is the principles and laws of reason which extend over nature and its ideals and ends which are progressively realized in the ceaseless course of nature. It is these principles and laws which persist in all physical sequences, survive all their changes, reappear and persist in every new arrangement. Such, for example, persisting unchanged through all changes, are the laws of causation, the law of uniformity, and continuity, that the same complex of causes must everywhere and always produce the same effect, the law of the correlation and conservation of motor force, the principles of mathematics, the laws of falling bodies, or gravitation, of the dispersion of force, and all laws of mechanics founded on mathematical principles—these are the true laws of nature."[35]

[35] Harris, Self-Revelation of God, 506.

CHAPTER III.

Laws Relative to Personal Beings.

INDIVIDUALS.

Having examined the general properties of matter and certain universal and necessary truths which together constitute the laws of physical nature in the primary meaning of the term, and having also examined certain generalized facts and orderly sequences which are laws only in a secondary sense, we now come to look for those realities in the realm of the human mind which, regulative of mental forces, constitute laws in the mental realm.

Mind differs from matter in many respects, but the one chief distinction which concerns our inquiry is, that while matter is inert, mind is self-active and self-directive. It has the power to know, the power to recall its own past experiences, the power to construct ideals through the imagination, the power to choose the ends toward which it will exert its energies and to choose the means it will employ for the attainment of those ends. The mind of man is an energizing entity. It is a causative power. Man is a sub-center of causal force in a universe of physical and mental laws. We have seen in what the laws of matter consist; and now, pursuing the same method of investigation, we are to inquire in what the laws of mind consist. What are the realities in the realm of mind regulative of mental energy?

For reasons more clearly to appear later in the discussion of moral law, it is necessary to notice the fact that while various faculties and powers—as intellect, memory and imagination among others —are ascribed to the human mind, the mind is nevertheless a single or indivisible entity. It is not composed of several faculties constituting a compound, as water is composed of oxygen and hydrogen, but the soul is a single, rational, emotional, self-conscious and self-directive force, called a person. When this mental force exerts itself in the act of knowing it is called Intellect, when it is considered as susceptible of motives and emotions it is known as Sensibility, and when it puts itself forth in self-determination or choice it is regarded as Will; but it is always an indivisible energy, employed though it may be in various kinds of activity. When recalling its past experiences the mind is known as Memory, when constructing some ideal as the plan of a mansion or cathedral, it is regarded as Imagination, when cognizing self-evident truth it is known as Reason, and when cognizing moral truth it is known as Conscience; but these terms are employed as a matter of convenience to denote that the mind is capable of various activities or states. This general division of the mind's power into Intellect, Sensibility and Will is now quite generally adopted by psychologists, respectively denoting the mind's power to know, capacity to feel, and power to choose.

Intellect.—The mind acquires all its knowledge through Intuition, Representation and Reflection. Through Presentative Intuition the mind acquires a knowledge of facts,—a knowledge of the phenomena of both the external world and of the internal world of mind itself; as when through sense-perception a person gains immediate knowledge of the objects and beings about him constituting his environment; and as when through self-consciousness or introspection he acquires immediate knowledge of the mind in its various states and operations. Through sense-perception the mind acquires a knowledge of external phenomena, and through self-consciousness it acquires a knowledge of internal phenomena, and thus through both processes it acquires immediate knowledge —not mediate knowledge—of the facts in both the worlds of matter and mind. These physical and mental phenomena or facts, thus acquired and known immediately by the mind, supply the raw materials upon which the mind further operates in its various processes of thought.

Through Rational Intuition the mind gains immediate knowledge, not of facts, but of self-evident, necessary and universal principles,—those principles which, as we have observed in the foregoing pages, are regulative of all the forces in the physical universe. Upon some occasion in experience, as the falling to the ground of a body unsuspended in the air, the truth of the principle that "every event must have a cause" is brought out into the conscious recognition of the perceiving mind. So one after another these self-evident principles, now known and admitted to be true, have come out into the consciousness of mankind. That "something cannot spring from nothing," that "something cannot be reduced to nothing," that "a thing cannot both exist and not exist at the same time," that "any action conforming to a universal law is right, and any action not conforming thereto is wrong," and many other similar principles are known through Rational Intuition, and are regulative principles in every process of mental activity. The origin and nature of these principles will be considered more in detail in the following pages.

Through the process of Representation, a phenomenon, once before the mind through sense-perception or self-consciousness, is called up from the past and again presented to the mind in a mental image. This mental image is known by the mind immediately as a re-presentation of the reality which was before it on a former occasion. It is not sufficient that the mind have the power of acquiring, it must have the power of retaining and representing its knowledge as well; otherwise the mind's present knowledge would be its entire knowledge, and progress would be impossible. The mind's power of retaining knowledge which has passed out of consciousness, and of re-presenting and immediately knowing it again, is generally designated by the term memory. "Memory is the power of representing the past and of knowing it again through the representation."[1] Hamilton and others, however, apply the term memory to the mind's power of retaining knowledge, and its power of reproducing knowledge in consciousness they call the Repro-

[1] Harris, Philosophic Basis of Theism, 47.

ductive Faculty.[2] The knowledge gained in memory is that of a reality once known by the mind, but now known again through a representation.

In Reflection the mind gains still further knowledge through its processes of thought. Having already before it the materials or facts supplied by Presentative Intuition, the mind, analyzes, compares, notices the similarities, differences, attributes, properties and relations of these raw materials; and through the processes of inference, reasoning, generalization and classification, and all in obedience to the regulative principles known through Rational Intuition, the mind acquires a more exhaustive, elaborate and unified knowledge of the materials under its consideration. Through the three processes of, first, apprehending or inspecting the objects before it; and, secondly of observing their similarities and differences; and, thirdly, of arranging the objects according to some common relation or characteristic and thus comprehending them in the unity of a class, the mind progresses from individual things to classes, from classes to still greater groups and from the greater groups to the sublime unity of the Cosmos.

Sensibility.—By Sensibility is meant man's capacity to feel, and experience emotion. Under this head fall his appetites, such as hunger and thirst; his natural and benevolent affections, such as love of country, parental and filial love and pity for those in distress; and also those others generally known as malevolent affections, such as revenge, fear, anger, hate and envy; and also the desires such as those for property, for knowledge, for power, for esteem, and in addition to these the instincts. And besides these man is distinguished from the impersonal world by certain rational emotions, such as the esthetic, or the emotion of beauty; ethical, as self-approval and the joy and peace that follow righteous action, or remorse and self-loathing that follow unrighteous conduct; scientific, as the joy experienced by one who has discovered a new truth; and religious, as that of adoration and praise.

[2] Hamilton's Metaphysics, 274.

These natural and rational sensibilities furnish the motives that influence man to action. They are not forces that compel and thus necessitate the action of man's will, but rather feelings that incite it to free and voluntary self-determination. The appetites and desires which incite one to procure something for self, and the affections which incite one to impart benefits to others, precede in time the action of the will; and the emotions awakened by such action necessarily follow. A desire for knowledge may incite a Newton to investigation, through choice and volition the investigation is made and the exact law of attraction established, and then follows the emotion of joy and triumph. The motive incites, the will chooses and the satisfaction or emotion succeeds.

The Will.—The will is the mind's power of self-determination. It is not a particular part of the mind acting in a particular manner, but it is the entire self-active indivisible mind as a conscious unit exerting itself in the act of self-determination. The mind of a personal being has the power of freely exerting and directing its own energies. It is a causal force. The power of personal mind is a free power. Were the mind's choice caused by some force outside itself, then the choice would not be that of the mind, but rather that of the outside causative agency. A choice carries in it necessarily the idea of freedom. A choice necessitated by force differs in no respect from any other effect in the world of necessity. A choice is a result of a cause within and not without the mind; and it is always made in the light of obligation in the presence of certain rational ideas, such as that of the right, the perfect, the good, thereby differing from all effects in the impersonal realm. Self-active mind is a causative power. How it causes its own choices cannot be illustrated, because it has no analagon in nature. It is sui generis.

In this brief outline of man's mental constitution we observe that while the soul is a single conscious unit, or Ego, it is nevertheless, complex in its activities. It is power perceiving; power retaining, recalling and reknowing its possessions; power apprehending rational truth;

power analyzing, comparing, generalizing and classifying; power desiring, hoping and loving; and power self-directing its energy in the light of moral obligation.

"The powers I have been speaking of rush on to their ends instinctively and blindly. The native power goes on to action, the appetite claims indulgence, the dominant passion claims its object, each according to its nature. But these activities and propensities are often inconsistent the one with the other. The intellect would set out on high pursuits, but is opposed by some grovelling appetite, or the man would wish to acquire fame, but, in doing so, finds that he cannot accumulate property as he might otherwise do. Is man condemned to be the slave of these appetencies, yielding to the one which happens to assail him, or obeying the strongest when they are competing or clashing? It is probable that this is the condition of the brute creature, and would be the state of man did he not possess a higher power. That power is the will.

"Properly speaking, the will does not furnish the incitements, inducements, or motives; these come from the appetencies which we have just been considering. It is the province of the will, seated above them, to sanction or restrain them when they present themselves, and to decide among them when they are competing with each other for the mastery. We have seen that the characteristic property of emotion is attachment or repugnance, with associated excitement. The distinguishing quality of will is choice or rejection. Inducements being held out, the mind, in the exercise of will, sanctions or refuses. It assumes a number of forms, in all of which there is the element of choice. If the object is present, we positively choose it or adopt it; if the object is absent, we wish for it; if it is to be obtained by some exertion on our part, we form a resolution to take the steps necessary to procure it."[3]

Choice is the will's determination, among many motives or feelings, as to which one shall be gratified. A man feels under obligation to pay a debt; *conscience* pleads for its payment, *his cravings* for strong drink

[3] McCosh, Intuitions of the Mind, 246.

plead for gratification at the same time. His money is insufficient to gratify both. Which feeling shall be gratified, conscience or thirst? To settle this is the work of the will. The will decides which feeling shall be gratified by the will's action. By its inherent power of self-exertion and self-determination it decides which feeling shall have its aid, and then by voluntary exertion it proceeds to the act of gratifying that one. It is not the motive or feeling that determines the will's choice, but it is the will's choice that determines which motive or feeling shall prevail and procure what it craves. It is the combination of Intellect, Sensibility and Will in one spiritual entity that constitutes personality. *"A person is an individual, endowed with reason, susceptible to rational motives, conscious of free-will, and also conscious of personal identity through all his varied experiences."*

Now what are the realities in the realm of mind that regulate these several powers of this personal being, viz.: his power to know, his power to retain and recall his knowledge, his power of imagination and his power to choose? We will consider those realities regulative of his power to know and to choose, as illustrations of law in its primary meaning in the realm of personal spirit.

Laws of Thought, as Law in Its Primary Sense.—First there are the rational intuitions, regulative of the mind's power to think. They are called the laws of thought. As these fundamental realities operate within, and constitute law in the physical world, so they operate within and constitute law in the mental world. As we have already observed them to be the laws of things so now we observe them to be laws of thought. They are intuitive truths regulative of intellectual power.

First Law of Thought.—The mind can acquire no knowledge unless there is some reality to be known. Knowledge implies a subject that knows and a reality known, and in the absence of either knowledge is impossible. This has been called the first law of thought. Intellectual power may acquire knowledge of a multitude of existing objects and realities, under certain conditions, but in the absence of all objects and all realities to be known intellectual power is, of course, ineffectual. Reality is a condition precedent to knowledge. That the mind may know anything there must be some reality to be known is a self-evident, immutable and universal truth which regulates the very first effort of mental energy in its exertion to know. Without reality to be apprehended knowledge would be as impossible as it would be if there were no mind capable of apprehending. As fire cannot burn without something to consume, and as a person can not see a flower or a stream if there is no flower or stream to be seen, so the mind of man cannot know unless there is a reality or being of some kind to be apprehended. This self-evident truth determines what the intellectual power of man can and what it cannot do, and hence it has properly been called the *first law of thought.*[4] It is a fundamental truth or reality regulative of intellectual power, determining what that power can and what it cannot do.

Second Law of Thought.—Admit that some material object does exist, yet intellectual power is wholly unable to apprehend it except as being in space. Intellectual power cannot even in imagination posit a material object outside of space. It can apprehend such bodies in relation to space but not out of all relation thereto. Space is a reality and intellectual power cannot ignore it, but is compelled to picture objects in space relation, if it pictures them at all. That all objects must occupy space is an intuitive truth regulative of intellectual power, and is therefore a law to power in the true sense of the term.

Third Law of Thought.—If this self-active power of the mind, in its efforts to know a material object, observes it once, and afterwards observes it again, the idea of time comes necessarily into consciousness. By no possible exertion can the intellectual power of man separate itself from all connection with the past, the present and the future. Every event it contemplates must be contemplated as taking place now, or having taken place in the time past, or to take place in time to come. Mental power

[4] Porter, The Human Intellect, 62; Harris, Philosophic Basis of Theism, 10.

can no more over-leap the barriers of time than it can over-leap those of space. Time-relations hold intellectual power securely within their cast-iron grasp and permit it to exercise itself only within the limits which they establish. Time is a fundamental reality, and gives law to power in that it confines all its energies to the past, the present, or the time which is to come.

Fourth Law of Thought.—The intellectual power of man may think of an object as existing now, but as not existing in the past, but it is beyond such power to conceive of an object as both existing and not existing at the present time. That "a thing cannot both be and not be at the same instant" is one of those numerous self-evident and universal truths of reason, operative alike in the realms of both the personal and the impersonal. The intellectual power of man is wholly submissive to this law as a matter of absolute necessity. Hamilton calls this the "supreme law of thought,"[6] and it is supreme in the sense that is must be true to Reason always and everywhere.

Fifth Law of Thought.—"A thing either is, or it is not." One of these alternatives must be true. There can be no middle ground. To be, or not to be, are the extremes, but there is no mean position; hence this proposition is called the law of the "excluded middle." A proposition is true or it is not true; a cause of action exists or it does not exist; a murder was committed or it was not committed; a judge is corrupt or he is not corrupt; if any one of these propositions be true its corresponding alternative cannot be. The intellectual power of man cannot harmonize these contradictories, and make the absurd to be real. It may conceive the one as true and its opposite as false, but it cannot do both; hence this self-evident truth is a law to intellectual power.

Sixth Law of Thought.—"Whatever is predicated of a class of objects may be predicated of all that is contained in that class." This axiom is called Aristotle's dictum. It is self-evident, axiomatic and hence universally true. If it is asserted that one hundred acres of land are all

[6] Hamilton's Metaphysics, 526.

good and tillable, it must be true that each acre of the one hundred must be good and tillable. If the mind admits the first proposition it must admit the second. It is not a matter of choice but a matter of necessity. Intellectual power is subject to the all-regulative principles of logic.

Seventh Law of Thought.—The law of equality runs through all knowable objects. "Things equal to the same thing are equal to each other." This familiar axiom is not confined to numbers, but extends to all other realities as well. In physics, if the temperature of two separate liquids is equal to the temperature of a third, then the temperature of those two different liquids will be the same. This is a universal and necessary truth, and the intellectual power of mind is unable to draw any other conclusion. By no possible exertion of its energies can it think the contrary.

Eighth Law of Thought.—The law of attribution illustrates the same regulative nature of self-evident truth. "Every attribute implies a substance of which it is an attribute." The intellectual power of the mind can conceive and can know attributes—as extension, color, weight— but it cannot think of them except as attributes of some particular thing. There can be no color unless there is something to have a color. There can be no weight except there be something to have weight. There can be no motion unless there is a body to move; nor any power unless there is some being or thing to which that power belongs. The intellectual power is utterly unable to know an attribute without knowing at the same time that there must be some substance to which the attribute attaches.

It is not pretended that the constitutional characteristics of personal spirit and the self-evident truths which regulate its intellectual and voluntary powers which have now been enumerated are all the fundamental features or regulative principles of the finite mind. These that have been mentioned are only specimens of those original truths of reason which taken together make up the real code of genuine law in the realm of finite personal existence. They have been mentioned and illustrated principally to show the real nature of law as that which regulates power, and to correct the false but common impression that law if not creative is at least an active agency of universal control. The tendency of modern scientific discussion has been to deify law, and by attributing all change in the universe, if not all actual creations, to this potent agency it has been vainly supposed that the existence of an intelligent Creator was thereby rendered unnecessary. Laws are passive realities, not active forces. Laws regulate by their passive presence, and forces are regulated in their efficient activities.

Laws in a Secondary Sense.—But besides these fundamental realities and truths which are regulative of all power, physical and mental, there are in the realm of personal spirit, as in the realm of impersonal nature, certain generalized facts and orderly and uniform sequences, which we call laws. One thought follows another as day follows night; one feeling is followed by another as season succeeds season; a certain emotion follows a particular choice as regularly and as certainly as light attends the rising sun. Thoughts and emotions and choices are not lawless. The mind is not a pandemonium filled with irrational thoughts, frantic feelings and lawless choices, all in a bedlam of confusion; but thought suggests thought feeling inspires feeling, and choice confirms choice. Thus we may predict with a fair degree of certainty how certain men will act and how they will feel and what thoughts will be suggested to their minds under any given set of circumstances. We may make predictions as to the thoughts that will arise in the human mind under certain conditions, somewhat as we can predict when certain stars will arise above the horizon and appear in the heavens.

If I should throw twenty apples into the air they would all fall uniformly to the ground; so we say that gravitation acts uniformly, but if I should place a gold sovereign before each of twenty men and say that they could have them as their own, there would probably be a uniformity of action on their part quite as exact and undeviating as that of gravitation. Of course, it would not necessarily be so. If I should speak the word "mother" to an audience of a thousand thoughtful people, the thought and likeness of her who bore each one respectively of that assembly would come to those respective minds, and with the face would come a whole group of thoughts and memories of childhood. This result too would not follow necessarily. If a good man does a noble deed, there follows that act a feeling of self-approval; and just as regularly and certainly, if under stress of temptation he does a mean, ignoble deed, there follows it a feeling of self-loathing. With men as a general rule, emotions of approval follow right choices and emotions of self-denunciation follow wrong choices, with as great a uniformity as day follows night.

Philosophers have spent much time endeavoring to discover, formulate and classify the laws of the human mind, but it is never safe to say in our present state of knowledge that any enumeration is exhaustive. Among those generally admitted as primary laws of association are the following, which are called by President Porter "general facts or laws." [7]

Generalized Facts as Law.—Among these laws, in this secondary sense, is first, that of resemblance. Should one person see another bearing a marked resemblance to a friend of his, the thought of that friend would arise in the mind of the observer. Not that it must necessarily do so, but it would uniformly do so; and many times the slightest point of resemblance is sufficient to effect the association. If in his travels in foreign lands one sees a tree or mountain peak similar to one in his own neighborhood he will think of that in his own country. So, too, in middle life or in old age, if one hears a melody familiar to him in his childhood, he will recall the scenes and associations connected with it.

A second law is that of contrast. The thought of the very rich has a tendency to suggest to the mind the abjectly poor. The coldest days of winter will suggest the hot days of summer. The sight of a dwarf will often

[7] Porter, Human Intellect, 282.

suggest the idea of a giant, and if one contemplates time he will find the idea of eternity appearing to his mind.

A third law is that of contiguity in time or place. If one stands upon the lofty mound in the center of the battle-field of Waterloo, he will think of Napoleon and Wellington. It is safe to say that no one familiar with the history of that battle could visit the historic spot without recalling to his mind the two warriors who battled there. To the thoughtful American the recurring anniversary of the day of Independence revives in his mind the Declaration of the Revolution. So the thought of a person, in some manner associated with another, will uniformly recall that other before the mind. The thought of Wilkes Booth suggests the thought of Abraham Lincoln, as the thought of Guiteau suggests that of President Garfield.

The Secondary Laws of Association.—Then there are certain other laws of association of which President Porter says: "The secondary laws have been enumerated and propounded as follows: (1) Those objects are more likely to be recalled, other things being equal, which occupy the mind for the longest period of time; (2) those also which are apprehended most vividly; (3) those which are brought most frequently before the mind; (4) those which are most recently present; (5) those which are the most free from entangling relations; (6) those which are contemplated with the greatest strength of emotion; (7) those which are viewed with favoring circumstances of bodily health; (8) those which are coincident with prevalent habits; (9) those to which the original constitution of body or mind predisposes us with the greatest interest or aptness."[8]

It is unnecessary to examine particularly these so-called laws of association. They are laws in the secondary sense of the term. They simply state the general fact that the thought of one thing, connected under certain circumstances with another, will be followed in the mind by the thought of that other; and that in recalling certain past thoughts those that have been held in the

[8] Porter, Human Intellect, 286.

mind under certain specified conditions will be most easily recalled. These so-called laws of association are fixed facts, laid down and established, and unalterable in the human mind. They present what we may call an established order of the mental world.

It is contended by President Porter that the primary laws and some if not all of the secondary laws of association may be reduced to the one "general fact" or law, "that the mind tends to act again more readily in the manner or form which is similar to any in which it has acted before, in any defined exertion of its energy."[9]

Orderly Sequences.—As in physical nature so in the mind there are certain orderly sequences, or antecedents and consequents, between which there seems to be a causative connection. As in the world of matter the seed deposited in the soil bursts forth into "the blade, then the ear and after that the full corn in the ear;" so in the world of mind a truth apprehended by the Intellect affects the Sensibilities, which in turn incite the Will to a free choice, and succeeding the choice are certain emotions whose character is determined by the quality of the choice that precedes it. The fact that a friend is in distress being known by the Intellect may cause feelings of pity and excite a sense of obligation to go to his rescue, which feeling influences the will to determine and put forth an effort to minister assistance, which act being performed may be followed by the emotion of self-approval and gladness. When one is to choose between two courses of conduct, one of which is right and the other wrong, if he selects the right the emotion of self-approval succeeds, and if he chooses the wrong there follows the emotion of self-condemnation. The emotion of joy follows a knowledge of good news, as a feeling of sadness follows that of evil tidings; the emotion of beauty follows the apprehension of a perfect production or scene, and the emotion of triumphant joy follows the discovery and demonstration of some great truth. These orderly sequences prevail throughout man's emotional nature. They are laws in the secondary sense,

[9] Porter, Human Intellect, 282.

and they constitute a part of the established order of rational life.

Uniform Expression.—But besides these there are certain other uniformities worthy of consideration. The members of the human family are all endowed uniformly with certain emotions and desires, and these emotions and desires have certain uniform modes of outward expression. In every race of men we find existing "joy, grief, affection, fear, rage, and wonder, and each has a characteristic expression * * *. There must be some deep connection in the human frame between the inward states of consciousness and the physical or corporeal activities to produce results so uniform throughout the human race."[10]

There are also found in every human soul the desire for property, the desire for society and the desire for knowledge. No normally constructed person is without them. They may differ in their degrees of intensity according to the peculiarities of the individual or the race, and also according to the degree of civilization attained, but the germs of these instinctive desires are in every human spirit. They are very largely the impelling forces in man's progress from barbarism to refinement. They supply the motives to action.

Now, respecting all these emotions and instinctive desires which are uniform characteristics of finite persons, they have a uniformity in their modes of outward expression. Every emotion of the soul has its characteristic sign in the outward form. The countenance of a person writhing in pain is never mistaken for a countenance expressive of joy; the features of a child terrified by some frightful object are never mistaken for those of a child rejoicing in the possession of a new toy. Joy animates the whole person; grief depresses and weakens it. Fear draws the blood from the face and throws a pallor over the whole countenance, while hope animates and suffuses the face with radiance. Rage sends the blood coursing through the face and arms till the whole person is bristling with antagonism. and assumes an

[10] Int. Ency., Vol. V. p. 412.

attitude of defiiance. Wonder has its peculiar manifestations,—the eyes protrude, the mouth unconsciously opens, and surprise rests upon the brow. And so it is that every emotion of the mind has its characteristic expression in the face, the posture of the body, or in gesture. We never mistake the countenance of him who is pleased for the countenance of him who is angry. The uplifted brow and the smile are characteristic signs of the former, while the corrugated brow and closely closed lips are the unmistakable signs of the latter, the words of the former are filled with hilarity; the words of the latter with scorn and resentment.

These are characteristics slightly varying perhaps, but generally uniform throughout the entire length and breadth of the realm of finite mind; they are among its uniformities; they are part of the established order of the human race; they are fixed, laid down and unalterably established. We do not say that these are laws in the true sense of the term, but as all the uniformities in the physical world are fixed and relative to man, are to a certain extent regulative of his power so all these uniformities in the human mind are equally fixed, and relative to man are regulative of his power in dealing with his fellow beings. I cannot make a man smile and rejoice by stinging his soul to resentment and anger. I cannot fill him with revenge and hate by bestowing on him precious gifts and exercising towards him acts of love and affection. It is beyond my power to make a man hate me by helping him in disaster and cheering him in sorrow. These uniformities even are therefore laws in the true sense of the term, in that they determine what man can do as a mental force or power and what he cannot do.

Mental Order as Law.—As in the physical world so in the mental the orderly sequences, where thought suggests thought, where emotions of self-approval follow right choices and emotions of self-reproach follow wrong ones, where intelligence of good to come will awaken pleasure and that of evil to come will awaken pain, and where anxiety follows guilt as uniformly as mental rest and composure attend the guiltless spirit, are fixed and relative to man are changeless elements in the mental constitution of the finite soul. Man can no more change his mental constitution than he can change the constitution of physical nature. The orderly sequences in the one are as irreversible by man as the orderly sequences in the other. And as a personal power in this dual universe of mind and matter man must produce his results in harmony with this order and not in antagonism to it.

The mental order as a reality determines what mental power can and what it cannot accomplish. If one would secure a particular choice from a fellow man he can reach his will in but one way. He must impart such knowledge to his intellect as is calculated to and does arouse those feelings which appeal to and influence the will to make the choice desired.

Laws of Choice.—Having considered primary or self-evident truth as law of thought, and having also considered the laws of association and others of a secondary character in reference to intellectual power, the question next arising has reference to the rational intuitions as law to will power. The will, though free, is not lawless. It is under law in two senses at least.

First: The fundamental principles of intuition can not be changed, enlarged or diminished, or annulled by will power. In this particular they are law to the will in the sense that they set limits to its action. Will power can accomplish results in harmony with self-evident or primary truth, but it is powerless to produce results which they forbid. In this these first principles are law to the will in the same sense that they are to the intellect; they determine what it can and what it cannot accomplish.

Second: Law of Obligation.—But all the fundamental principles of self evident truth and all the necessary inferences that can be drawn from them are law to the power of free-will in a most important and vital sense. When any or all of these truths are brought to bear upon a free-will they do not command what it must choose, but in the light of moral obligation they inform the will what it ought and ought not to choose. It is possible for a free-will to choose a course of action antagonistic to these fundamental principles, and thus choose to realize an absurdity; but such choice is prohibited by the moral intuition that "a rational being ought to act rationally." To choose conformity to truth is rational, to choose non-conformity to truth is irrational. A person has immediate or intuitive knowledge that he ought to choose rational ends instead of irrational ones—that he ought to act rightly instead of wrongly. Here we come to a new realm, the realm of moral law. It may be said that when these primary or self-evident truths are brought to bear upon free-will they will then constitute moral law. They then operate upon a power which is free, not upon a power under necessity as is the case with physical or intellectual power.

When these primary truths regulate physical forces they are known as the laws of the material world, and are often called the laws of matter; when they regulate intellectual forces they constitute the laws of thought, and the first principles of logic are examples of this class; and when they are brought to bear upon will power they then become moral law. In the world of matter these principles determine what physical force can and what it cannot accomplish. It can change matter from place to place, but it cannot annihilate it. In the world of intellect they determine what intellectual force can and what it cannot conceive. It can conceive of two bodies at different points in space, but it cannot conceive of them as occupying the same space at the same time. When bearing upon the free-will of a personal being they determine, not what it can and cannot choose, but what it ought or ought not to choose to accomplish by its self-exertive and self-directive energy. These principles are, therefore, moral law in the sense that they are known to man as principles which he is under moral obligation to observe in the exercise of his free moral agency. When as a body of principles they are considered as regulative of physical power they constitute the physical order of the universe, when regulative of intellectual power they constitute the intellectual order of the universe and when they are considered as regulative of rational beings or free-will power they constitute the moral or rational order of the universe. Man knows intuitively that he ought not seriously to employ his energies in the fruitless effort to accomplish a known impossibility. A person might choose to waste his life in the vain and absurd effort to build up in himself a perfect moral character by violating every law involved in the process. But, constituted as he is, that he should do so without being conscious of self-condemnation is nearly inconceivable.

CHAPTER IV.

Laws Relative to Personal Beings.—Continued.—Individuals.

MORAL LAW.

In the last chapter we considered some of the laws and orderly sequences peculiar to the human mind; but of one important law we purposely omitted the consideration, that it might be duly emphasized by a separate and more extensive treatment. So far in the consideration of finite persons but slight reference has been made to man as a moral being. In what man's moral nature consists, and the peculiar characteristics of the moral law can now be better understood.

So far in this inquiry into the nature of law in general it has been contended that all the universal and self-evident truths of reason are laws in the true sense of the term, as they are regulative of power of all kinds. And it has also been observed that when the immutable principles of reason are brought to bear upon free-will power they then become moral law. As man lives in a physical and rational so he lives in a moral system. As a personal power man abides in a world of changeless realities which regulate his will power, in the sense that they determine what he ought and ought not to choose. Among the rational and moral intuitions which speak to the will in terms of authority are the following.

Conscience.—Man's power to know generally is called the intellect, but when the intellect knows self-evident truth it is called Reason, and when it knows moral truth it is called by some Moral Reason, by others Practical Reason and by still others Conscience. The power to know is a single power of the mind engaged in knowing three different classes of truth. It is one power employed in three ways and known accordingly by three names, as a person trying causes in court is called a lawyer, when sitting on the bench he is known as a judge, and when writing learned treatises on jurisprudence he is called a jurist.

But Conscience has also an emotive side. The term not only embraces the mind's power to know moral truth, but it also includes the mind's feeling of obligation. Standing at the beginning of two lines of action, one of which is known to be right and the other wrong, Conscience on its intellectual side knows that the will ought to choose the right and on the emotive side it feels that it ought to so determine. Conscience in its broader sense both knows and feels obligation. The intellectual apprehension by man that he is under obligation to obey the changeless laws that prevail about and within him is also uniformly accompanied by certain moral sentiments. Preceding every choice made between two courses of conduct one of which is known by him to be right and the other wrong, there is ever present a peculiar feeling prompting and inciting man to choose the former and reject the latter, and there uniformly follows the choice a feeling of approval or disapproval according as the choice was in accordance with or in violation of law. Not only does man intuitively know himself as under obligation to law, but that knowledge is ever re-enforced by what may be properly called the feeling of obligation. This feeling is an incitant to right and a deterent from wrong. It pleads for the former and dissuades from the latter. It urges the will on to obedience and restrains it from disobedience. And after the choice is made or the act is done, then springs up spontaneously in the soul the joys of self-approval, self-respect, or merit, in case the right prevailed or the pain of self-reproach, self-loathing, or demerit, if the wrong shall have triumphed. This power to know and capacity to feel obligation in the presence of known right and wrong is a fixed constitutional characteristic of man. It is a permanent, immutable and essential element in personality.[1] As a rational being

[1] See Carter's "Law, its Origin, Growth and Function," page 151, where the author considers the nature and authority of Conscience. See also Wilson's works, vol. 1, chapter 2.

man both knows and feels that he ought to act rationally. This knowledge is immediate and the rational or intuitive principle is generally stated by Intuitionalists as follows: "A rational being ought to act rationally," or as Professor Hibben expresses the truth, "Whatever is true to the reason becomes a law to the will."

Law of Obligation.—Man knows himself as subject to law in the physical, the intellectual, and the moral realms. The fundamental principles of reason are involved as law in the constitution of the material universe; and in the constitution of rational beings, being everywhere and always regulative of physical and intellectual power.

When these principles are brought to bear upon free-will power, they are also moral law in that they determine what persons ought and what they ought not to choose. In the presence of these truths, man knows them as law to his will. They speak to him in tones and words of authority. They say to physical and intellectual power, "you can," and "you cannot," but to will power they say, "you ought" or "you ought not."

The mind of man is so constituted that, when in the presence of these truths, he sees in their light, his obligation to conform his choices and his conduct to their demands. As a rational being he knows that he ought not to choose or act irrationally. Man ought not to spend his time and energy in the futile attempt to realize the absurd and impossible. This knowledge of obligation is intuitive. This doctrine has been clearly expressed in the following words: "The ethical idea of right and law arises in the rational intuition that I ought to act reasonably, that is, in accordance with the truths of reason; or, more generally formulated, 'a rational being ought to obey reason,' or, 'what is true to reason is a law to the will,' In this intuition the person comes to the knowledge of a new reality which is expressed in the word *ought* and to which the nouns corresponding are obligation, duty, law. This new reality is that he exists under law; that the universal principles and the necessary inferences from them, which he knows as truths, are laws which he is under obligation to obey. Like other intuitions this one is practically operative on his action before he formulates it in reflective thought or even recognizes it as a judgment. But as he reflects he finds that what he knows as true to his reason he knows to be a law to action; he finds himself saying, I ought, and learns the significance of obligation and duty; he finds himself approving some actions because conformed to principles which he knows as true; and this common quality of these acts he calls right, and the contrary quality he calls wrong. Thus the ideas of right and wrong rise directly from rational intuition. Without rational intuition man could never have known the difference of right and wrong or had any idea of law, duty and obligation."[2]

Authority.—Intuitional philosophy also teaches that these primary or intuitive truths, including this moral intuition, are eternal in the divine Reason. They are not laws above or outside of God, imposed upon Him, but as the absolute and unconditioned Being these truths are constitutive elements in His eternal reason. These rational principles are involved in and belong to the Divine Mind. They have their seat in God. They are law to the eternal will. These truths of reason, when addressed to a free will speak to it in tones and words of authority. Reason is authoritative. It says to physical and intellectual power, "Thou must," and to voluntary power it says, "You ought," or "Thou shalt." God's reason and not His will is the seat of final authority.

"All principles in the divine Reason are law to every rational being. So the ultimate ground of the authority of law and of moral obligation to obey it is eternal in God the Absolute Reason."

Some claim that the ground of authority and obligation is in the "constitution of things." This can only be true in the sense that the constitution of things is but the expression of God's mind. Back of the constitution of things are the eternal principles of Reason which, when applied to things, compose their constitution. Final authority is found in the original principles themselves.

[2] Harris: Phil. Basis of Theism, 187.

Others say that the ground of authority is found in the "rational and moral constitution of man." This too can be true only in the sense that man is but a likeness whose original is God. The rational and moral principles composing the constitution of man are those original truths eternal in the divine Being. The fountain head of all authority is back of all created things. "Authority is the right to declare and enforce law." Reason does this by its own right.

As we have already observed, primary or self-evident truths are intuitively or immediately perceived by the mind of man through his reason. Whenever these fundamental truths are brought to bear upon a free will, they are known as law to that will. Man knows them as regulative of power; he knows them as law to action. These principles are rational in the sense that they are involved in the constitution of rational beings. To act rationally, means to act in harmony with them; to act irrationally is to antagonize and attempt to override them.

Thus implicated in a world of changeless principles, man recognizes himself as under obligation to act rationally. This ability to recognize his obligation to obey law, his ability to know and feel obligation in the presence of imperative and immutable truth, characterizes man and separates him from other finite creatures, and classifies him as a moral being. This idea of obligation takes man into a new realm of thought and motive and purpose. Through this idea he enters into a moral and spiritual world, abounding in new visions of truth, where moral rights and duties to man and God, and where moral freedom and moral ideals and the possible moral perfection of his being dawn upon his spirit. This moral intuition, "That rational beings ought to obey reason," is the fundamental fact, or principle, in the moral and spiritual universe, as gravitation is in physics. It is self-evident.

To say that a rational being ought not to obey reason, ought not to obey the laws of its own nature, but is under obligation to violate them would be as contradictory to reason, as a statement that a thing can exist and not exist at the same instant. It would be equivalent to saying that a rational being ought to be at once rational and irrational; or that an adding machine calculated to register the right sum, should always register the wrong one.

This intuition has been stated in various forms, all expressing the same idea. As man is a rational being, it may be said that, "Man ought to act rationally." As to act rationally means to obey reason, it may be said that "Man ought to obey reason," and, as Reason in its absolute sense is equivalent in meaning to the word God, it may be said that "Man ought to obey God."

The reality of ultimate truth expressed in these various forms is intuitively discerned by conscience. Conscience knows by original insight; by immediate perception, that rational beings ought to obey reason. In this truth man sees and knows his moral obligation. At this point and in this discovery his moral life begins.

Conscience says, "obey law;" comply with the principles of reason which are law, comply with the principles of mathematics and logic and mechanics, and metaphysics generally, because they are the standards or tests of right and wrong in the concrete transactions of mankind.

The multiplication table is involved in all the daily affairs of human life in computing interest upon a debt. in determining the acreage of land conveyed, in ascertaining the price of articles sold, in estimating the cost and disbursements in actions and suits in legal controversies. And the principle of mechanics are to be applied in the construction of every kind of machinery and in every piece of mechanism, in the construction of bridges and buildings of every description. The navigator must have recourse to his logarithms, and the surveyor to the principles of geometry. The principles of logic and the syllogism are involved in every human effort to ascertain truth through reasoning and argument. They appear in political discussion, in financial controversies, in legal contentions, and wherever differences of opinion and conflicts of interests are sought to be reconciled through rational debate. And all the deeper principles of self-evident truth are assumed and employed everywhere and by everybody in the settlement of all questions arising in the complex affairs of human life. No transaction is too trifling to involve their application, whether on the farm, upon the street, in the shop, behind the counter, in the office, in the bank, in the court room, in the halls of legislation, or in the church.

These universal, immutable and imperative principles of primary law have a moral aspect, in the sense that they are standards and tests of right and wrong. The will ought not to disregard them in determining courses of conduct to be pursued, nor should it reject their demands in practical affairs. In the sale of two jewels worth one hundred dollars each, the sum of their values cannot be more nor less than two hundred dollars. Self-evident or mathematical truth is the test as to the correct sum of their values. Any dispute concerning their aggregate worth is referred to that test. To reject the result would be irrational and morally wrong, because such rejection would in principle plunge all human transactions into a chaos of perpetual confusion. It would transform the rational order into irrational disorder and make civilized life and moral progress impossible.

A rational being, then, ought to obey reason.

What Reason Commands.—If it is true that men ought to obey reason, the next important question arising is, what specific thing does reason command men to do? Reason commands men, as rational beings, living in a universal rational system, to choose and seek their highest good, or well-being; to make the most of themselves; to choose and seek for themselves that which is absolutely the best.

But the perfect is the best. The best body is a perfect body, the best intellect is a perfect intellect, the best memory is a perfect memory, the best imagination is a perfect imagination, the best will is a perfect will, the best spirit is a perfect spirit, the best disposition is a perfect disposition. the best moral character is a perfect moral character. "Be ye therefore perfect," is the command of reason to men. The perfection of his body, his mind, his susceptibilities, the perfection of his entire being physical, intellectual, moral and spiritual, constitutes man's highest conceivable good. Nothing else can compare with it in value.

Persons as Ends.—This command, "Be ye therefore perfect," is addressed to persons. Reason always addresses her commands to persons and not to things. The ultimate and true end for which all human effort is rightly made is some rational being. Persons are ends and not means.

The state, like the Sabbath, was made for man, not man for the state. Schools are established for children; children are not raised in order that there may be schools. Churches are organized and cathedrals are erected for the elevation of man's character; men were not created that there might be churches and cathedrals. The sculptor does not chisel out the statue from the block of marble for the sake of the block, but for the sake of some person, either himself or others, or both, who, looking upon the form of beauty, may experience some pleasing emotion or catch some holy inspiration. The painter does not produce his work of art for the sake of the canvas on which it appears, but for the sake of some person, who, beholding it, may experience some noble and worthy emotion. The author does not produce his work of fiction for the sake of the bound volume, but for his own gratification, or for the sake of others, who reading it, may in some way be affected by its sentiments. Nor does the projector of a transcontinental line of transportation construct it for the sake of the rails and the road-bed, but rather for his own sake, or that of his associates, or the people to be benefited thereby, or perhaps for all of them.

Persons—men, women and children—are ends in themselves, and they are never merely means to be owned and used as tools for the attainment of some other end beyond; or at least they should never be so used. Wendell Phillips was wont to say, "Our trade, our labor, our learning, our science, our religion and our law are only the scaffolding wherewith to make a man."

Humboldt said, "The fairest fruit the earth holds up to its Maker is a man." "The worth of a state," said John Stuart Mill, "is the worth of the individuals composing it." Lowell has said, "Democracy in itself is no more sacred than monarchy. It is man who is sacred." And Ruskin expressed the same opinion regarding man's value when he said, "The final outcome and consummation of all our wealth is in the producing as many as possible full-breathed, bright-eyed and happy-hearted human creatures."

Kant writes upon this subject as follows: "Man, and generally any rational being, exists as an end himself, not merely as a means to be arbitrarily used by this or that will, but in all his actions, whether they concern himself or other rational beings, he must always be regarded at the same time as an end. All objects of the inclination have only a conditional worth, for if the inclinations and the wants founded upon them did not exist, then their object would be without value. But the inclinations themselves, being sources of want, are so far from having an absolute worth for which they should be desired, that on the contrary it must be the wish of every rational being to be wholly free from them. Thus the worth of any object which is to be acquired by our action is always conditional. Beings whose existence depends not on our wills but on nature's have, nevertheless, if they are rational beings, only a relative value as means and are, therefore, called things, but rational beings on the contrary,are called persons, because their very nature points them out as ends in themselves, that is, as something that must not be used merely as means."

Much is gained in this world when we regard our fellow-men as spiritual beings to be loved and served and improved. No higher aim can be sought than their perfection equally with our own.

Perfection and Happiness Their Aim.—The law, "be ye therefore perfect," is not only addressed to persons, but it carries with it the ideal attainment to be sought for by them—the perfect. The perfection of man's nature, physical, intellectual, moral, and spiritual, is the supreme excellence. There is nothing beyond. Nothing better can be conceived or hoped for. The perfection presupposes a law and action exerted in accordance with that law. A perfect steam engine can be produced only when the mechanic complies with every law of mechanics involved in the construction of a steam engine. So a perfect character, spiritual or moral, can be attained only when the person complies with all the moral and spiritual law involved in the production of such a character. The same is true of intellectual and physical development.

Man has a four-fold nature, and in each we find a force operating under a specific law. The vital force of the body operates under the laws of the physical organism, such as respiration, digestion and gestation; the intellectual power under the laws of thought; the power of the will under the moral law, "Thou shalt love thy neighbor as thyself;" and the will power also operates under the spiritual law of man's nature, "Thou shalt love God with all thy heart, mind, soul and strength."

Perfection of man's entire nature, then, is possible only by obedience to the laws involved in his entire being. Only by obedience to the laws of his nature can the perfection of his nature be realized.

But the perfection of one's nature does not comprise the whole of the Supreme Good which man is to seek for himself and others. There is inseparably connected with the orderly process toward the perfection of the mind and body, a certain satisfaction, pleasure and joy. Happiness or enjoyment always attends the harmonious workings of the forces of human nature in harmony with the laws that regulate those forces. Each of the four distinct natures of man has its own peculiar desires, and a susceptibility to its own peculiar pleasures. The body has its desire for food and drink; the intellectual nature has its desire for knowledge; the moral nature its desire for approval and self-approbation; and the spirit craves divine protection and spiritual companionship.

Each nature has also its own peculiar emotional elements. The body experiences the satisfaction of gratified desire and the numerous pleasures and pains incident to a physical organism. The intellectual nature experiences the joy of intellectual triumphs, such as Newton and Franklin experienced upon making their great discoveries. The moral nature experiences the feelings of self-approval or disapproval, of self-respect, or self-loathing, of self-complacency or displacency; and so the spirit experiences the emotions of spiritual peace and joy and reverence for the Divine Being, or fear and torment according to the attitude it has assumed towards God.

Happiness and unhappiness are incident to man's entire nature. It is a prominent factor in the Highest Good of man. It cannot be ignored. But happiness may be either worthy or unworthy. The happiness incident to sinful action such as that experienced by the drunkard and debauchee is unworthy. It is tinctured with the virus of sin which spoils it. But the happiness incident to righteous action is worthy. It is befitting a rational being. Happiness is incident to wrong action as well as to right and it cannot therefore be the final standard of action as the false philosophy of the Utilitarian or Hedonist asserts. We cannot say that because a certain action gives us pleasure, therefore it is right. A bank robber might be delighted over his successful plunderings and escape from detection, but that fact would not prove him to have acted rightfully.

Whether a person experiences happiness in perpetrating a wrong upon his fellow men depends upon his moral character. In no event, therefore, can happiness be the test of right and wrong action. *Law* is the standard by which actions are to be tested. If the action accords with the laws of man's moral and spiritual nature it is morally right; if not, it is morally wrong.

Every right action as we have observed has persons, God or man, as the end for the sake of which the act is done. Then the question arises, what is the highest good to be attained by man for himself and others? What is the most worthy and valuable acquisition which man can secure? The answer to that question is, that *the perfection of his entire being, and the happiness inseparable from it,* constitute that most valuable acquisition. This compound of perfection and happiness constitutes the true good which man is to choose for himself and for his fellow-men. It is something to be acquired, possessed, enjoyed, as the most valuable and worthy attainment of human effort.

Hamilton says, "The value of ends is absolute—the value of means is relative. Absolute value is properly called a good; relative value is properly called a utility. Of good, or absolute ends, there are for man but two—perfection and happiness. By perfection is meant the full and harmonious development of all our faculties, corporeal and mental, intellectual and moral; by happiness, the complement of all the pleasures of which we are susceptible. Now I may state * * * that human perfection and human happiness coincide, and thus constitute in reality but a single end. For as, on the one hand, the perfection or full development of a power is in proportion to its capacity for free, vigorous and continued action, so, on the other, all pleasure is the concomitant of activity. * * * To promote our perfection is thus to promote our happiness. * * * Perfection (comprising happiness) being thus the one end of our existence, in so far as man is considered either as an end unto himself, or as a means to the glory of his Creator, it is evident that * * * studies and sciences in common with all other pursuits should be judged useful as they contribute, and only as they contribute, to the perfection of our humanity—that is, to our perfection simply as man."[3]

To the same effect Janet remarks, "If pleasure always accompanies action, if each function has its own peculiar pleasure, it follows plainly that every development of our activity, consequently every development of perfection in man, is accompanied by pleasure, whether we wish it or not. Nature has not troubled herself to inquire whether it will suit abstract philosophies, but has decreed that each of our faculties, the highest as well as

[3] Hamilton, Lect. on Meta., Lecture 11.

the lowest, shall have its own peculiar pleasure by the very fact of being exercised. Hence the perfection of being cannot be acquired without gaining also the feeling of this perfection, the joy of possessing it. Now this feeling, this joy, is what we should call happiness, inseparable, as we have seen, from perfection itself. Good, then is indissolubly composed of perfection and happiness."[4]

Doctor Harris carries the same idea of the true good somewhat further: "The essential good of a person is the perfection of his being; his consequent harmony with himself, with God the Supreme Reason, and with the Constitution of the Universe; and the happiness necessarily resulting. * * * Man's acquisitions are not merely of external goods to be consumed for his enjoyment or used as instruments in accomplishing his ends. There are also excellencies constituting the perfection of his being, which are to be acquired by his own action. This perfection is what he must primarily seek to acquire as the true good. * * * The attainment of perfection must begin in the acquisition of right moral character." * * * But "Besides right moral character the good consists in the perfection of all the powers and spiritual perfection. * * * And it can be realized only by action in accordance with the law of love. Should a person propose to himself his own perfection as the great object of acquisition and should he seek it only for his own aggrandizement and enjoyment, he would be serving himself supremely, not God and his neighbor; he would miss the perfection which he proposed to attain, and instead of its grandeur and blessedness would find himself shrivelled in selfishness and his whole sphere of interest and action, the whole firmament and horizon of his life shrunk within the bounds of what he can clasp within his own arms and hug to his own bosom. * * * But "There is no absolute perfection to a finite being, but only its perfection in its own kind and under its own necessary conditions. But man, endowed with reason and free-will, is capable of progress. While his moral

[4] Theory of Morals, p 72.

character at a given point of time may be right, he is in culture and capacity capable of continual growth. * * * His perfection, therefore is not a resting in any attainment as a finality. The very fact of resting in knowledge or power acquired or good works done as a finality and satisfying sufficiency would involve the cessation of activity, and the resting would be a rusting in routine, formalism and cant. The perfection of man involves continual growth. The growth is the perfection and harmony of the rational being and the happiness indissolubly united with it."[5]

To the same effect is the conclusion of Professor Paulson, "Such modes of conduct and volition are good as tend to realize the highest goal of the will, which we may call welfare. I mean by it the perfection of our being and the perfect exercise of life."[6]

That the perfection of man is the end of his being is also taught by the ripest science of the present day. Professor Fiske in his volume entitled "Through Nature to God" uses the following language bearing upon this topic: "Our historical survey of the genesis of humanity seems to show very forcibly that a society of Human Souls, living in conformity to a perfect moral law, is the end toward which ever since the time when our solar system was a patch of nebulous vapor, the cosmic process has been aiming * * * toward the spiritual perfection of humanity the stupendous momentum of the cosmic process has all along been tending, * * * that spiritual perfection is the true goal of evolution, the divine end that was involved in the beginning. When Huxley asks us to believe that 'the cosmic process has no sort of relation to moral ends,' I feel like replying with the question, 'Does not the cosmic process exist purely for the sake of moral ends?' Subtract from the universe its ethical meaning and nothing remains but an unreal phantom, the figment of false metaphysics." Science and philosophy both testify that the perfection of man is the ultimate end toward which the cosmic forces are ever tend-

[5] Harris, Phil. Basis of Theism, 271, 272, 273.
[6] System of Ethics, 223.

ing, and that man's own forces, when rightly directed, are ever tending to the same end.

And finally it has been tersely said: "But if we persist in having a world-goal, we can find a sufficient one only in the moral realm, a community of moral persons obeying moral law and enjoying moral blessedness is the only end that could excuse creation or make it worth while."[7]

The fact that man has been groping in uncertainty for ages, seeking the ultimate end toward which all his forces should be directed, need not shake his confidence in the correctness of his final conclusion that the perfection of his being is that true and ultimate end, because the deeper the truth or the more fundamental the law the more difficult the task of discovering, comprehending and accurately formulating it in human language. The law of gravitation was operative in the universe before the time of Newton, though not until his arrivel did any man accurately formulate and express it. But what intuitional philosophy has substantially claimed from the earliest days of metaphysical discussion, namely, that the perfection of man's being constitutes his "*Summum bonum,*" is now being, as we have seen, corroborated by cosmic philosophy and scientific deductions. The spiritual perfection of man is the goal toward which all the cosmic forces, including the powers of man himself rightly directed, are tending. Man recognizes this goal as the fixed and unalterably established end, and that end being fixed in the very nature of reason itself becomes the *supreme law* to all rational beings. It is one of those realities which, being unalterably fixed, becomes regulative of man's powers, in that it determines what he ought and what he ought not to choose as the final goal of all his efforts. This law says to man, "Make the most of all the powers with which you are endowed. Let the choice of the will be ever in harmony with the immutable laws under which you live." Man, recognizing this law of his being, knows and feels that he ought to comply with it. As between a superior and an inferior good man knows

[7] Bowne, Theism, 231.

intuitively that he ought to prefer and choose the former. He also knows intuitively that a perfect character is superior and preferable to an imperfect one. And he further knows intuitively that in the rational and moral system within which all personal beings exist each individual ought to act rationally toward all other individuals.

Physical, intellectual, moral, and spiritual perfection, and the happiness that flows from it, is then the highest good that man can attain.[8]

The perfection here demanded is not, however, that unattainable thing which consists in absolute completeness. Man can never become perfect in the sense that he cannot still grow in the power of intellectual and moral discernment and knowledge: but perfect in the sense that his will is ever in harmony with its law—perfect in essence, though capable of indefinite enlargement. The perfection demanded by the law is that state of well-being which it is possible to attain in the finite universe,—perfect as a child, but capable of indefinite development into a mature person.

Law of Service.—If then, reason declares that it is persons upon whom all human energies should be focussed, and that the perfection and happiness of man constitute his proper object and aim in life, then the next question arising is, in what manner, or according to what law shall that perfection and happiness be sought? Shall each seek his own highest good irrespective of others, or must each individual in society have regard to the good of others equally with his own?

How shall man's duties to persons be distributed?

[8] Mr. Carter, in "Law, its Origin, Growth and Function," p. 132, says, "Going back to fundamental principles we find happiness to be 'our being's end and aim'. But in what line of conduct is our happiness to be found?" He seems to adopt in his answer to this question Mr. Spencer's claim that "the largest and completest life must be the nearest approach to pure happiness." But it may be asked in what line of conduct is the "greatest and completest" life to be found? Our answer to that question would be—it is to be found in the completest obedience to all the laws of our physical, intellectual, moral and spiritual natures.

Perfection of character is the result of obedience to law, and such perfection is attended by satisfaction, or happiness. Perfection is the end, happiness the incident.

What service shall he render to himself, what to his neighbor, and what to God? Reason points out the object of life, does it also declare the *law* by which that object can be secured?

It has long been recognized that the highest well-being of each individual is involved in the highest well-being of all. In seeking his own supreme good, each person must regard the rights and interest of others equally with his own. So intercommingled and interrelated are the interests of mankind in the rational and social system that mutual services are a necessity. The highest perfection and greatest happiness of individuals in society are possible only by a proper balancing of egoistic and altruistic services. Each must serve others as well as himself. Universal egoism or universal altruism would work the universal destruction of the race. Each is born to minister and to be ministered unto. Such is the constitution of human society that it is only as each serves his neighbor that the highest good of self and others is possible.

If a laborer agrees to work for his employer a year for a specified sum, he can attain his own highest good only by faithfully and fully performing the work, if he is able, according to the terms of the agreement, and the employer can attain his own highest good only by compensating the laborer fully and promptly as he has agreed to do. Each serves the other. Each receives a benefit and in the same transaction bestows one. In society, each is intimately related to others. Each is so dependent upon others that mutual helpfulness becomes a necessity. But by what general principles is the individual to determine his duty to others?

As through rational intuition man knows that he ought to obey reason; and knows also through intuition that reason commands him to perfect himself physically, intellectually, morally and spiritually, so he also knows through intuition that, being related to others in a rational system he and all men are on the same level, each owing duties to all others, and that, "in all his actions bearing on another rational being he ought to consult the rights and interests of the other as really as his own." As he must work for his own highest good, so he must work for that of his neighbor. The best attainment he can acquire for himself is the perfection of his nature, so the best attainment he can help his neighbor to acquire for himself is the perfection of his entire nature.

Man is an object to be served, not a thing to be possessed and used as a tool. Persons are ends in themselves; they are never means to be employed for the attainment of some end beyond. Things may be sacrificed for the sake of persons, but persons cannot rightfully be sacrificed for the sake of things. As persons are the highest beings known to exist their claims are superior to all others, and their interests are to be promoted before the interests of any inferior beings. To serve persons then is the highest and hence the most imperative duty man has to perform. Man is under obligation to serve himself, to serve his fellow-men and to serve his Creator.

When man awakens to the fact that he exists in a rational system, bound by mutual and reciprocal rights and duties to other persons, he recognizes that he ought to regard the interests and welfare of others equally with his own. As it has been stated by another, "When a man finds his own action affecting the interests of another person and recognizes the fact that he and the other exist together in a rational system, he knows intuitively that he ought to respect the rights of the other equally with his own." *That man ought to serve his neighbor as himself is the great law of human service.* And it is equally true and equally recognized by man, that as the Personal Creator is embraced within the rational system in which finite human beings exist, the highest conceivable service of which he is capable is that which he can render to his Maker. *To serve God supremely, and to serve one's neighbor as himself is the supreme law of human action.*

First, under this law man is to serve himself. He serves himself when conforming his action to the laws of his physical nature he develops and perfects his physical constitution, when by conforming his action to the laws of his intellectual nature he acquires mental vigor, accumulates knowledge, cultivates his reasoning faculty, strengthens his imagination and invigorates all his intellectual forces, when by conforming his action to the moral law he quickens his moral sense, habituates his will to right choices, increases his self-respect and otherwise ennobles and harmonizes all his moral powers, and when by conforming his action to the spiritual law of love he gains truer conceptions of God, attains a more constant trust and acquires a purer reverence, a greater peace and holier purposes. And besides these services, by which man attains his own personal development, he may by the exercise of industry, frugality and economy amass a fortune of wealth in its varied forms, and by complying with the conditions of financial, political and ecclesiastical preferment he may attain commanding and honorable positions in the realms of commerce, statesmanship and the church. In these and other commendable ways man may serve himself. He may seek his own physical, intellectual, moral and spiritual perfection, and aspire to and attain positions of influence and power, all to the end that with these various instrumentalities of power he may the more efficiently and successfully serve his neighbors in their effort to attain for themselves a fuller life of development and power.

Second, man is to serve others. But in order to serve them he must first serve himself, not selfishly nor supremely but rightly. As man may serve himself by cultivating and developing all his physical and mental powers by perfecting his whole nature, so he can serve others by helping them to do the same. But it is evident that before man can impart knowledge to the ignorant he must first gain the knowledge himself; before he can teach man the science or art of correct reasoning he must himself have first mastered that science or art; before he can impart moral inspiration to others he must himself possess it; before he can awaken a holy zeal for divine things in others he must have experienced it within his own life; and before he can give food to the hungry, clothes to the naked, drink to the thirsty, shelter to the exposed, homes to the homeless, and before he can erect libraries, build and equip hospitals and endow universities for the public he must first amass the wealth necessary to such beneficence. Before a person can give a dollar to the needy or a book to the ignorant he must of necessity get the dollar or the book. As man can serve himself by making the most of himself so he can serve others by assisting them to make the most of all their powers and talents. Men can perform all their duties to their neighbors, and then their neighbors will have all their rights; and men may go far beyond this demand of justice and do deeds of beneficence, cherish toward others the spirit of benevolence and perform all other acts involved in the general law that men ought to serve one another equally with themselves. Men are so constituted and the solidarity of human society is such that one person can procure his own highest welfare and greatest happiness only as he performs his duties to other members of society and conscientiously regards the interests of all. The prosperity and growth and moral and spiritual well-being of others are involved in the process by which each individual seeks his own well-being.

Fulfilling his obligation to others is the means by which man attains his own supreme good. By the steps of justice, benevolence, veracity, gratitude, mercy and loyalty to others, man ascends to the exalted plane of his own perfection and happiness. Each individual, under the law, is to choose his neighbor as an object of loving service. In a rational system he is to look out for the rights and interests of others, helping thus in the great work of universal progress and the public welfare.

Each right thinking individual wishes to be a factor in the great work of human advancement. In the Universal uplift of mankind the individual sees a work worthy of his greatest energies of body and spirit. To have no share in this world-object is unworthy. Only as man sympathizes with all the practical movements and means adopted for its accomplishment, sympathizes with the material, educational, political and religious betterment of all mankind, and engages, to some extent, in efforts to realize the same, can he attain his own broadest development and highest self-respect. Like the elevator boy, man goes up with those he elevates, and goes down with those he lowers. The perfection and happiness of all mankind is the inspiring vision that most deeply stirs the soul conscious of its relation to God and His children.

"Thou shalt serve (love) thy neighbor as thyself," is the moral law.

Spiritual Law.

Service to God.—As the Supreme Source whence all things proceed, the fountain head of all finite being, and power, life, intelligence, order, and perfection, man owes particular duties to God.

As the Absolute Reason, Creator, Father, seeking in all the ways infinite wisdom suggests or permits to perfect the finite rational spirits of men, they owe to Him the duty of obedience, of trust, thanksgiving, praise and adoration. As absolute, independent, experiencing no want, man's service to God must consist primarily in submission and conformity to His will.

The law of service or love to God, which is commanded, consists radically in an act of the will, in a choice of God as an object of service, and requires obedience to His law however expressed, whether in the self-evident truths of intuition, in the constitution and laws of the physical Universe, or in the constitution and laws of finite rational life.

We have seen how intuitive truths reign supreme as law throughout the physical and spiritual realms and are involved in all the activities of material and mental forces, how human relations and the solidarity of the race are such that by mutual services only can individuals attain their highest well-being, thus disclosing the law of service as the supreme law of moral conduct; and as these laws are expressive of God's will, it is only as man conforms his will and his action to them, that it is possible for him to serve God. We serve him whose will we obey. Only as we obey orders are we faithful servants. So by conformity to these universal laws, man attains his own and his neighbor's highest welfare and happiness, and in doing this he is securing the very good which God is seeking for every individual. By obedience, therefore, man enters into the plan of God and becomes a co-worker with Him in the establishment of the kingdom of righteousness upon the earth. He is attaining the very good which God is Himself seeking for man.

In this conformity and obedience, then, man is engaged in the services of his Lord, serving at once himself, his neighbor and God. This rational principle that a *rational creature ought to obey his Creator constitutes the supreme law of human action.* This command that man shall serve (love) God supremely stands first in importance. It is the supreme law of the spiritual realm. It does not, however, as some have contended, constitute the whole law. Love to man is as imperative. The two laws together constitute the law of service to persons. Such are the relations of man to man, and man to God, that only as an individual serves man from a motive to obey God can he realize his own highest well-being.

It is theoretically possible for a person to be highly, if not perfectly developed physically, intellectually and morally, and yet know little, if anything, of spiritual life. He may be a Hercules in physical strength, an Apollo in physical form, a Plato or a Shakespeare in intellectual and poetic genius, and a John Stuart Mill in moral conduct, and yet be a spiritual dwarf. Robert Ingersoll was a man of fine physical development, having a powerful and well-trained intellect, and, so far as I know, he was a moral man, in the sense that he met his moral obligations to his family and to his fellow men; yet, no one would claim that he was a spiritually minded man. He himself would probably have resented any such claim made on his behalf.

There is then, a higher and a distinct nature in man; where we find a law different and superior to all other laws of his being. As the moral law commands the will to love and serve man, so the spiritual law commands the will to love and serve God. The moral law has for its object man, the spiritual law has for its object God.

Man's will power, regulated by the first and great commandment constitutes man's spiritual nature.

Man may, and often does, love his fellow men, work for their comfort, their general good, and for their intellectual and moral well-being; while, at the same time, he ignores the claims of this supreme law, which commands him to love God with all his heart, soul, mind, and strength. In such cases a person may develop his body, discipline his intellect, become as great a moralist as Marcus Aurelius or Seneca, and yet, because he has never recognized the existence of his spiritual nature, has never acknowledged the reign of the Supreme Law of love within his soul, has never entered into and cultivated his highest self, he is spiritually benumbed, if not spiritually lifeless.

Man, then, has his four natures, each fully equipped with its power and its law, its peculiar desires and its peculiar pains, pleasures and emotions.

Of these four the spiritual is the highest—highest in the sense that the law which reigns there is the Supreme Law of man's life. The law of love to God is a constitutional provision. It is supremely authoritative. It applies to all the finite souls in the universe. No other law has any validity in reality if it violates this one.

Man's spiritual nature, then, is not only distinct, and superior because the essential law reigning there is the supreme law of the spiritual universe, but because the person to be loved under that law is the Supreme Being, the Eternal Father. In the moral realm we are to love ourselves, and our neighbors as ourselves; but in the spiritual realm we are to love God, serving him in all the ways our minds can devise, with all the enthusiasm our heart's affections can inspire, and with all the strength of our mental being.

As we have already seen, man's moral nature consists primarily of his will-force acting under the law, "Thou shalt love thy neighbor as thyself." Now, a man becomes morally developed, disciplined and perfected just in proportion as that will force chooses and acts in harmony with that law. When by habitual practice the will comes to always obey the law and becomes changelessly confirmed in that habit, then that person has become morally perfect.

So we have seen that man's spiritual nature consists primarily of his will-force acting under the law, "Thou shalt love the Lord thy God with all thy mind and heart and strength." Now also, a person becomes spiritually developed, disciplined and perfected just in proportion as that will force chooses and acts in harmony with that law. When, by habitual practice, the will comes to always obey that law, and becomes changelessly confirmed in that habit, then that person has become spiritually perfect,—not perfect in the sense that the spirit cannot still grow in the power of spiritual comprehension and blessedness; but perfect in the sense that its will is ever in harmony with the demands of its law, and hence, ever in tune with the will of God—perfect in essence, though capable of enlargement.

Spiritual progress, then, consists in the habituating of the will to obey the Supreme Law of love to God. As that habit becomes more and more firmly established, the soul of man becomes more and more godlike, and hence more and more spiritually inclined, and spiritually stable, and spiritually confirmed in godliness; and all the spiritual emotions of the soul become more keenly alive.

Man must take the initiative in securing spiritual progress, just as he must in securing physical, intellectual or moral development. In other words, he must take the initiative, so far as to comply with the necessary conditions of spiritual progress. Before he can have the advantage of the sunlight, he must open his eyes; before he can have the assistance of electricity he must make his connections; before he can have a harvest, he must sow the seed; and so, before he can experience the gracious and regenerating influences of the Divine Spirit he must comply with the first and great law of the spiritual world.

Now, as man progresses toward physical, intellectual and moral perfection by exercise and practice, so he progresses spiritually in the same maner. He must make a fight for it. He must make it his chief business. He must work for it every conscious moment. The prize fighter spares no pains or effort in preparing his body for the ring. Intellectual equipment can be secured only by untiring exertion. The moralist can acquire the habit of applying the rules of right conduct only by resolute effort and self-denial. So, in this highest realm, that of spiritual discipline and equipment, excellence and progress toward spiritual perfection can be attained only by making it the chief business of life. Persons become spiritually minded when they are willing to pay the price of self-denial which it involves.

Man must serve God, not simply man. If a starving fellow being ask me for bread, and, without any idea of God in my mind, or care for God in my heart, or reverence for God in my spirit, I give to the hungry one the bread he needs, through pity or human compassion, I do a good and a moral act; but I have not performed a religious act, nor have I complied with the supreme law of my spiritual nature. I have acted on the moral plane alone. I have not ascended to the high privilege the occasion affords me. But let me see in that poor, starving man, a child of God, a finite spirit in the image of its Maker, a struggling soul whom God loves with an infinite tenderness, and one whom God wants me to help; and one whom he has commanded me to help; and, out of loving obedience to God, as well as out of pity for the starving one, I feed him and help him; I have then ascended to the plane of spiritual activity; and my sense of God's presence is quickened, my spiritual desire to please God is satisfied, my conscience approves the act, and an upward movement of my soul toward the state of habitual obedience has been realized.

My recognition of God is the cause, my spiritual uplift is the effect. Putting God into all the transactions of daily life, as the controlling motive, is a condition, necessary for spiritual progress.

Again, only as we keep the spiritual nature of man distinct in our thought, can we see the true significance of religious education.

As we have seen, a person may train his body to the highest degree of strength and development, as do many of the pugilists, giving no special attention to his intellect or to his moral or spiritual natures; or, one may train his body and his intellect, disregarding the higher claims of his moral and spiritual life; or even, one may train his body, his intellect, and his moral sense, but give no thought to his religious life, as is frequently the case in schools of the world today. But no such person has entered into the largest privileges of life. No such person has learned where true education begins, for, while it is possible to train our body and intellect and moral nature to a high degree, to the exclusion of the spirit, it is not possible to train the spirit and neglect our three-fold nature below it. A person may be moral and not religious, but he cannot be religious and at the same time immoral, or intellectually and physically indolent and neglectful. The law in our spiritual nature, demands obedience to God's will; and the moral law, and the laws of the intellect and body are expressions of God's will. Those laws are God's laws. To serve God involves obedience to all His laws whenever they are brought to bear upon the voluntary power of man.

It is God's will that man should obey the laws of his body, and the laws of his intellect and moral life, for they, too, are His laws. So man's religious education involves the symmetrical development of his entire fourfold nature. Only in this manner can man gain the end of his existence, to-wit: the perfection of his being, and the happiness incident to and inseparable from that perfection.

"Thou shalt serve (love) God supremely," is the controlling law in the spiritual world.

Summarizing the whole moral law then, *the best* language that can be employed is that of the great teacher:

(1) "Be ye therefore perfect even as your father which is in heaven is perfect."[9]

(2) "If thou wouldst be perfect * * * thou shalt love (serve) the Lord thy God with all thy heart, and with all thy soul, and with all thy mind * * * and thou shalt love (serve) thy neighbor as thy self."[10]

Regarding the relation of these two laws it has been said: "We now see that the two great commandments of the law are complemental; neither can be obeyed in its full significance without obedience to the other. They are two aspects of one and the same law, the law of universal love. In the history of the Christian church we discover tendencies to overlook this unity and to give preponderant attention to one with comparative neglect to the other. The inadequate attention to either is practically dangerous and cripples the individual and the church in their character, work and influence. If the fact that love to God must manifest itself in loving service to men is overlooked, the tendency is to regard religion as consisting exclusively in the worship of God; then the tendency is to seek highly wrought feeling, to retirement and meditation in the life of worship, to asceticism, to mysticism and fanaticism, to superstition, to the pharisaic and self-righteous multiplication of rites and rules, and punctiliousness in observances. If, on the other hand, the fact is overlooked that there can be no true and normally effective love and service to man which is not vitalized, inspired and guided by love to God, the tendency is to a godless and shallow humanitarianism, which seeks to better man's condition from the outside by changing his circumstances, by enactment and enforcement of civil laws, by caring for his physical wants, without seeking the spiritual renovation of the man himself, and in disregard of the principle of Christian progress, 'Make the tree good and the fruit will be good also,' and without recognizing man's relation to God and the true significance of right character and the attractive motives to it involved in that relation. * * * This one-sidedness in the conception of the two aspects of the law of

[9] Matthew, 6-48.

[10] Matthew, 19-21, and 22-37 and 39.

love and the consequent misapprehensions and misapplications of the law are rebuked by Christ. In his person and life, as well as in his teaching, he reveals the inseparable unity and interdependence of love to God and love to man, as two aspects of obedience to one and the same law. * * * He teaches that all true love to God issues in love to man. Thus he declares the inseparable unity of the two great commandments of the law; obedience to one is never genuine and complete without obedience to the other. He presents them in unity as the principles under which all human duties to God and to man are summarized, and from which all duties in detail are to be unfolded and defined. It will be an epoch in the advancement of the kingdom of God and the renovation and progress of human society when the inseparable unity of religion and morality, of love of God and love to man, is acknowledged in its full significance and importance and the lives of all Christians are in conformity with the law of love in both its aspects."[11]

Moral Law, Continued.

We have now seen in what the spiritual law consists. Thou shalt love (serve) God supremely. We have seen its relation to the moral law, thou shalt love (serve) thy neighbor as thyself. The two are often spoken of as one, and that is called the moral law. We prefer to treat them separately, because men often exhibit moral virtue and observe the rule of moral conduct, without having any spiritual culture: and moreover it is upon the moral law, service to self, and to one's neighbor, that the great systems of positive law which we are to consider are chiefly based.

This law of man's interest in man was early recognized and has appeared as an accepted principle all along the history of the race.

It is not claimed that this law is known, in rational intuition as formulated and expressed by the Great Teacher, but philosophy has recognized the essential element of the law from the remotest days. Men find

[11] God, Creator and Lord of All, 2d vol. pp. 348, 349.

themselves in a rational system so related to one another in society that their highest welfare depends upon mutual helpfulness. Nowhere is man in a state of complete isolation. The family, the tribe and the clan are aggregations of individuals who from the very first have recognized themselves in a system of reciprocal rights and duties. The sympathies and affections of men have ever bound them in smaller or larger groups, and they have recognized that absolute selfishness, where each looked alone to his own pleasure, would work the utter extinction of the race.

Of the early recognition of this law of service Buckle says: "There is unquestionably nothing to be found in the world which has undergone so little change as those great dogmas of which moral systems are composed. to do good to others, to sacrifice for their benefit your own wishes; to love your neighbor as yourself; to forgive your enemies; to restrain from passions; to honor your parents; to respect those who are set over you; these and a few others are the sole essentials of morals, but they have been known for thousands of years, and not one jot or tittle has been added to them by all the sermons, homilies and text-books which moralists and theologians have been able to produce." [12]

Long before men constructed systems of philosophy and gave accurate expression to the laws embraced within those systems the laws themselves were recognized upon occasions in experience and habitually obeyed by mankind. The law of gravitation was recognized of necessity from the earliest days in human history, but never until Newton's time did anyone formulate and give it accurate expression; and so the law of service, which demands that men should not live in utter selfishness but should recognize and respect the rights and necessities of others and should unselfishly exert themselves in their behalf, was operative in human society centuries before philosophers and teachers ever gave it expression in human language. That man ought to perform his duties by respecting the rights of others, that he ought to choose

[12] Hist. of Civilization, Vol. 1, p. 129.

for himself and others good instead of evil, is recognized intuitively by man's reason, upon those occasions in his experience when he is called upon to choose one or the other.

To emphasize the practical character of this law of service I quote the following eloquent words: "Political economy, the science of business exchanges, which is founded solely on enlightened self-interest, coincides with Christian ethics in this respect. Its fundamental principle is, that every legitimate exchange is the exchange of equivalent services; it is coming to accept the word 'service' as best expressing whatever is exchanged."

"Legitimate business is in its prosecution a service, because it is productive, and supplies human wants. The farmer raises food for man and beast, and material for clothing. The mechanic and manufacturer fit the raw material for use. The merchant transports products and makes them accessible to those who want them. The peoples of the world serve each other by their productive labor—the Asiatic serves the European, and the European serves the Asiatic. Over all the world men are industriously serving each other, producing what meets human wants. Thus viewed, the creation and circulation of products through the world, beneficent as the circulation of air and water, rises to the sublime. The circulation of the products of all countries, passing in white-sailed ships over the ocean, millions of wealth always in motion from mart to mart, a circulation so noiseless that the products of the other hemisphere flow daily through the streets unnoticed as the wind, and so equable and complete that you have only to step across the street and the product of any country is stored ready for your hand, and the table is daily spread with the products of every quarter of the globe—this circulation, all pervading as the flow of blood in the body, binds all nations in the unity of a common interest and life." [13]

This law of love, both to God and man, appears in the religion, philosophy and literature of nearly every civilized race of ancient times. To regard the rights and

[13] Kingdom of Christ on Earth, p. 153.

interests of others is not peculiar to Christianity. Far back in the days of Confucius, we find the doctrine that one should do to others as he would have them do unto him. Buckle says in the "History of Civilization," that the "system of morals propounded in the New Testament, contained no maxim which had not been previously enunciated, and that some of the most beautiful passages in the apostolic writings are quotations from pagan authors is well known to every scholar; and so far from supplying, as some suppose, an objection to Christianity, it is a strong recommendation of it, as indicating the intimate relation between the doctrine of Christ and the moral sympathies of mankind."[14]

Budha taught that religion is the faculty of love. Plato recognized the relation of God to man and the universal moral order when he said, "The ruler of the universe has ordered all things with a view to the preservation and perfection of the whole. * * * Everything that comes into being exists for the whole, that the whole may be blessed. You exist for the whole, not the whole for you."[15]

Epictetus comprehends and states the same great truth, "He then who has observed with intelligence the administration of the world, and has learned that the greatest and supreme and the most comprehensive community is that which is composed of men and God, and that from God have descended the seeds not only to my father and grandfather but to all beings which are generated on the earth and are produced, and particularly to rational beings, for these only are, by their nature formed to have communion with God, being by means of reason conjoined with Him, * * * why should not such a man call himself a citizen of the world * * * a son of God?"[16]

He also recognized the great truth that the highest goal of man could only be attained by self-sacrifice—service to others. "Speak good of your brother, never claim in opposition to him any of the things which are inde-

[14] His. of Civilization, Vol. II, p. 129-130.

[15] Laws Book X 903.

[16] Book 1, Chap. 9.

pendent of the will, but readily give them up that you may have the larger share of what is dependent on the will. For see what a wonderful thing it is, in place of a lettuce (trifle)—you gain for yourself goodness of disposition. How great is the advantage."[17]

And Marcus Aurelius recognized the solidarity of the race in his saying: "We are working together to one end, some with knowledge and design, and others without knowing what they do."[18] And again he says, "Adorn thyself with modesty and simplicity, and with indifference toward the things which lie between virtue and vice. Love Mankind, Follow God."

Approving the sentiments of Plato, Cicero says, "But (as has been strikingly said by Plato) we are not born for ourselves alone, our country claims her share of us; and, as the Stoics hold all the earth produced is created for the use of man, so men are created for the sake of men, that they may mutually do good to one another."[19]

Terence voiced the same sentiment, "I am a man and nothing which is human can be alien from me." Augustin, bishop of Hippo, in the fourth century, said, "Every man is most closely connected with his fellow men, nor should any distance of relationship enter into consideration where there is a common nature."[20]

The Persians also expressed their faith in this law, which requires good to be bestowed upon even our enemies. The verse of Saadi says: "Confer benefits on him who has injured thee," and Hafiz writes in the same strain:

"Learn from yon Orient shell to love thy foe,
"And store with pearls the hand that brings thee woe."

Cicero also recognized a distribution of duties, "In society there are degrees of duties by which every man may understand what belongs to himself. The first is owing to the immortal gods, the second to our country, the third to our parents, and lastly to others through different gradations."

[17] Book 1, Chap. 10.

[18] Epictetus 1, Chap. 10, Note, Meditations p. 190.

[19] Offices, Book 1, Chap. 7.

[20] Offices, Book 1, Chap. 10, Note.

The moral law is rooted in the very constitution of man and of human society. It is the fundamental principle from which is developed all the rights and duties of mankind.

Rights and Duties.—The rights and duties of persons are all developed fundamentally from the one all-comprehensive law of service or love, namely, "Thou shalt serve (love) thy neighbor as thyself." Persons are to serve themselves. They are to perfect themselves. But self-perfection involves the performance of duties to others.

If I owe a person money which is due and payable, and I have or can procure the same, in order to secure my own highest good or well-being, I must perform my duty to my neighbor by paying the debt. It is my duty to pay and his corresponding right to receive payment. If I have contracted to sell and convey to my neighbor a particular farm on a certain day for a specified sum of money in order to attain my own highest good, I must sell and convey the farm to him according to the terms of the agreement. It is my duty to convey and his right to have the conveyance.

If I agree to work for my neighbor for the term of one year for a specified sum of money, in order to attain my own highest welfare, I must, if able, perform the labor fully and faithfully. It is my duty to perform the work and his right to have it performed. If I negligently injure my neighbor, in order to attain my own highest well-being I must, if able, duly compensate him for the injury he has sustained. It is my duty if I am able to compensate him and his right to receive compensation. If I am selling my neighbor a machine for a particular purpose, and there is in it a latent defect, in order to attain my own highest good through the transaction, I must if I know it inform my neighbor of the defect. It is my duty to inform him and his right to receive the information. The same law of love or service which commands me to perfect my moral character commands me to perform my duties to my neighbor in all the affairs of life and at the same time confers upon my neighbor a right to the discharge by me of those duties.

It is in this outward world of concrete affairs that persons find the opportunity to realize their own self-completion or self-perfection, and to secure the happiness which is inseparably connected with right conduct.

It is by justice, and benevolence, and veracity, exercised by one person toward another in the varying relations and necessary transactions of life, that persons attain the true end of their individual existence. If one would attain his own perfection and happiness he must obey the law of social service; and, if a merchant, he must give full weight and measure to his customers; if a laborer, he must perform faithful services to his employer; if a physician, he must exercise his utmost skill in behalf of his patient; if a teacher, he must instruct, inspire and in every possible way improve and encourage his pupil; if an attorney, he must employ his best judgment, knowledge, and skill in the interest of his client to the end that justice may be secured. And, on the other hand, the customer, the employe, the patient, the pupil and the client are under equal and corresponding obligations to reciprocate to the full extent demanded by this law of service.

Rights and duties are not abstractions. They are necessarily involved in the application of the moral law. If I would attain my own highest excellence under the law of service, I cannot ignore my duties to the poor, the unfortunate, the depraved. Whatever, under any particular circumstances, my duty to them may be, only by the full discharge of that duty can I meet the rights which they possess. It may be my duty to give, without hope of reward, to the sick and the helpless. Benevolence is often a duty.

Persons also have a right to the truth. If, when I am about to sell my neighbor a farm, he asks me the number of acres it contains, if I know, it is my duty to inform him. He has a right to the truth. If I would gain my own highest good, I must meet all the demands of his right by performing my duty. So in all the transactions of life, persons must, under the law of service, satisfy the rights of others by the performance of their own duties to those others. Otherwise, one does not love himself as the law requires.

This law of service is fundamental. It is the one all-comprehensive moral law. It is generic, of which all moral precepts and rules of human conduct are but the species.

While one must, under this law, perform duties to others, he also has rights which under the law they must respect.

If persons are themselves ends, or beings to be served, and the perfection of all their powers and susceptibilities is the greatest service that can be rendered them—the "greatest good" to be attained for self or conferred upon others—then the law of service imposes upon man the duty to seek his own and his neighbor's highest well-being—their perfection and happiness. It imposes upon man the duty of enlarging and perfecting all his powers and susceptibilities,—physical, intellectual, moral and spiritual. This is the end of man's being and at the same time a law to his action, and in so far as it imposes upon man the duty to perfect himself, it accords to him a right to the means necessary to the performance of that duty. "A man will have a right to everything that is essential to the attainment of the end for which he was made."[21] It cannot be one's duty to accomplish the impossible, and that is impossible for the attainment of which there are no means. It cannot be the duty of any one to cross the American continent in an hour, because there are no means known to man by which such an act can be accomplished; and it is equally clear that when the law imposes upon one the duty to do a specific thing it guarantees to him a right to the means essential to its accomplishment. The same law which imposes the duty confers a right to the means necessary to its performance. If it is made the duty of an officer of the law to see that the peace is kept, the same law which imposes that duty confers upon the officer the legal

[21] Hopkins, Lectures on Moral Science, p. 254.

right to command the assistance of other persons if necessary to the performance of his duty; and whenever anything is required by civil law to be done, and it is found impossible to do that thing unless something else be done which is not expressly authorized by that law, then the right to do that necessary thing must be held to exist by necessary implication. So the law of man's highest well-being, which makes it his duty to educate, expand and perfect his intellectual, moral and spiritual powers, accords to him the right to his life, his liberty and the products of his own industry as means absolutely necessary to the attainment of that end. These natural rights then are grounded in man's constitution; they are inherent in the very frame-work of his personal being. They are not rights created by any civil enactment, but they exist prior to civil enactment and but for their existence civil enactments would have no significance. Beings without rights and duties are not persons, but they are impersonal beings like animals. It is here in the moral constitution of man that we find at once the law, the duty it imposes, and the rights it confers upon him. The duty of self-perfection, the right to life, to liberty and to the products of his own industry, and the right to defend himself against the unwarrantable and violent assaults of others are found to be constitutive elements in personality.

A Right Defined.—We may therefore define a right as a claim one has to anything accorded him by law. If accorded him by civil law the right is a civil one, if accorded by natural law the right is a natural one. A person is said to have a legal right to occupy his dwelling-house because the positive law recognizes his claim to do so and will restrain other persons from interfering with such occupation. A person is said to have a natural or moral right to defend himself against the unprovoked and violent assault of another because the natural law of instinctive resentment accords him that right and warrants such defense. And so a person is said to have a natural or moral right to a sum of money due under a contract that is outlawed because the moral law accords him that right, though the law of the land will not enforce it. A right, then, implies the existence of a law; and the natural or moral rights of man are the claims accorded to him by natural or moral law.

If then man has a right to the means essential for his development and perfection the question arises as to what are those essential means.

Life.—Foremost among those essential means of self-perfection is physical life. Man has a right to his body. Without knowledge man cannot improve his mental condition, and all his knowledge begins with impressions made through the medium of the senses. The five senses are the avenues of approach from the external world to the internal spirit. It has been said by another, "this body is the necessary means of his development. He is developed by the body. He learns through the eye and the ear, the hand and the foot, the activities of the physical organization. Is he blind, one element of his development is cut off; is he deaf, another element; is he deprived of his sense of touch, a third element. With these all gone some development may be carried on, but generally speaking it may be said that the body is necessary to his development. By the very discipline he receives through his body, his soul is moulded and shaped. He is educated through the physical organization. Then he comes into the second stage in which this body becomes the necessary instrument of his activity. It is the power by which he operates upon the world without. His lungs, his heart, his stomach keep the machine in order while the machine is being used to impart to other lives. Because he has hands which are themselves tools, he makes tools as no handless animal can. Because he has eyes he can produce color which otherwise he could not produce. With his tongue he speaks and communicates his thoughts to others. His body is the necessary instrument of his activity." [22]

If as a finite person man is to develop his powers of mind, enlarge the scope of his mental vision, strengthen the wings of his imagination and grow into perfect man-

[22] Abbott, in Outlook for March 27th, 1897, p. 842.

hood, if this is his duty, if this is the end to be attained by his earthly pilgrimage, then he has a claim, a right, to his body as an indispensable means to that exalted end. Deprive him of the means and the end is unattainable. It follows, therefore, that, if self-perfection is enjoined under the laws of reason, man must have a right to his life, his liberty and to the product of his own industry which are the means necessary for his own perfection, and also the means necessary for him in his efforts to aid others to a like perfection of their being. A person's physical constitution conditions all his possible growth and development in human society; hence the right to life is properly regarded as the most sacred of rights. The law which commands me to work for the perfection of my neighbor as well as for my own also commands me, by necessary implication, not to deprive him of physical life, or of his physical liberty, or of anything pertaining to his physical perfection. This law was as imperative before the announcement of the decalogue as it was afterwords, and it would be as imperative today in the absence of positive law forbidding the same as it is in the presence of such law. The fact that a legislature of men says, "Thou shalt not kill," does not make it any more obligatory upon man to respect his neighbor's life than it was before. In all his efforts for his own and his fellow-man's well-being man ought to act conformably to all the laws of the moral system in which he lives.

The test of the means man may employ for the attainment of his end in life is law itself. He is to seek his own and his neighbor's good or well-being *according to law.*

Liberty.—Only in freedom can man attain his highest well-being. Liberty is a means necessary to man's perfection. He cannot perfect himself while in bondage. He must have the free use of his body. If confined in prison, what knowledge can man gather from the world in which he has been placed? When he is shut in, the world to him is shut out. The thoughts it suggests, the inspiration it imparts and the broadening effects upon man of his communication with nature are denied him just in proportion as his liberty is circumscribed. Nearly the same observations regarding man's liberties can be made as those that were made regarding his life. To attain the end of self-perfection man must be free. Only in the free use of his powers can man perfect them. Next to the importance of physical life as a condition of self-culture is the condition of physical liberty—freedom to execute those choices which a person makes for the accomplishment of the true end of his being. So long as man is under command to attain his highest well-being he has a right to all the means essential thereto, and freedom is one of those means—freedom of body, freedom of speech, freedom to carry out in human affairs those enterprises calculated to secure his own and his neighbor's good. Man must have liberty to act as he chooses so long as he does not interfere with the like liberty of every other person. Man has a right to liberty as a means to attain the end which he is under obligation to attain.

Property.—We find also among the means necessary for man's perfection the product of his own industry. Man must have houses and clothing to protect his body, books to inform his mind, churches in which to worship, and accumulations for the purposes of leisure wherein he may investigate the truths and laws of the world in which he lives. As a means for the attainment of self-development man has a right to property. "Thou shalt not steal" was written in the constitution of the race long before its announcement from Sinai.

My right to life, liberty and property is a law to all other persons in that it commands them to respect that right. The rights of each are laws to all others in the sense that those others ought not to violate or disregard those rights. These natural rights are fixed and established facts in the realm of personal existence, and as such they are regulative of human conduct, in that they determine what man ought and what he ought not to do. With these we might include the right to reputation, the right of free speech, the right to contract, the rights growing out of domestic relations, and many others, but they are all laws, some in the primary and others in the secondary sense of the term, in that they are regulative factors, declaring what man ought or ought not to choose or to actually do.[23]

We might carry this analysis of rights further, but those which form the basis of positive jurisprudence have been already considered. As the perfection of man's being is the prime duty to himself, as seeking the perfection of the being of others is his prime duty toward his fellow-men, it follows that he has the right to all the means which will best enable him to accomplish those ends.

Intellectual and Moral Order as Law.—The intellectual and moral order of personal beings is a fixed, and relative to man, a changeless reality. That order can no more be changed by human power than the phenomenal order of the physical universe. Man finds himself implicated in that order. His intellectual and moral constitution, his intellectual powers, desires, and emotions; his moral intuitions, desires and asprations are all as fixed and real as the nature and orbits of the planets and stars. That order is a reality and determines what man can and what he cannot do; and also what he ought and ought not to choose. One can secure intellectual and moral results only by complying with the intellectual and moral nature of man. One can become learned only by complying with the laws of thought, of memory and imagination. One can impart knowledge to another only in the same manner. One can become morally sensitive and resolute only by complying with the provisions of his moral constitution and the laws of his moral nature. If an attorney wishes to secure a certain verdict from the jury, or an orator wishes to secure the passage of a certain resolution by his audience, or the preacher wishes

[23] With these rights to life, liberty, property, and to free speech, to contract and to trade, human laws are chiefly concerned. To protect persons in the exercise of these natural rights is the function of constitutions, legislation, and judicial action. These inherent rights are constituent elements in personality. They precede human law as man himself precedes human law.

Wilson's Works, Vol. I, page 275. Vol. II, page 309.

to secure some definite action by his church, he can do so only by imparting to them information calculated to arouse such desires, emotions or passions as are likely to induce such a choice as the speaker desires. He cannot compel such choice. The intellectual and moral order forbids that. By complying with the demands of that order he may procure the result or obtain the object he wishes. The order confronts him. He may comply with it and succeed, otherwise he must fail.

CHAPTER V.

Laws Relative to Personal Beings, Continued.—Society.

SOCIOLOGICAL LAWS.

In the last two chapters we have seen how the individual is subject to the laws of thought; to the laws of association; to moral and spiritual law, and to a phenomenal order that prevails throughout the universe; and now, we wish to enquire whether Human Society—the entire aggregation of individuals—is also subject to invariable and uniform laws, and if so whether those laws, or some of them, have been discovered and reliably formulated so that there may properly be said to exist at the present time a Science of Sociology.

Is human society subject to law in its primary meaning, as we have seen physical nature to be, and have social affairs also such a fixed order of sequence as we have found to prevail throughout the realm of matter?

If there is such a phenomenal and definite order of sequence, if the movements of society, the successive stages to civilization, have all taken place conformably to certain uniform laws, then this order and these laws are, of course, the subject of scientific investigation, and to discover and formulate them is to found the Science of Sociology.

That human society has progressed from simplicity to an almost incomprehensible complexity there can be no question. In language, in government, in music, in art, and every other line of social development, progress has been from the homogeneous to the heterogeneous, and that this progress has taken place conformably to law, rather than by chance, is also generally admitted.

But the disputed question relative to human progress has been whether the law of causation reigns supreme and universal throughout the realm of social phenomena. Are human choices necessitated, so that they must be what they are? Are human choices bound by the law of necessity? Do they take place according to a fixed order, subject to fixed laws, as bodies of all kinds tend toward the earth, under the influence of gravitation?

It is stated by some that the law of causation is universal, that if it has ever in any one instance been violated, we may be excused for taking up with the theory of chance; and so it is asserted that all the vast bodies in the siderial universe move on for untold ages in their orbits in strict conformity to law; that in conformity to law, the solar system in all its complexity, has grown out of a homogeneous nebula, that the earth's crust has cooled and condensed, that organic life has arisen, and that man has been created in accordance with law; that his thoughts chase each other along definite paths and contiguous channels marked out by the laws of association; that never and in no place is law interfered with—that yesterday, today and forever the effect follows the cause with inevitable and inexorable certainty. And hence, we cannot believe that in one particular corner of the Universe, upon the surface of one little planet, in a portion of the organism of one particular creature there is one special phenomenon called volition, in which the law of causation ceases to operate.[1] And consequently, those who hold this view of causation contend that social phenomena are all subject to natural law, that human choices are determined by the established order, and that the science of sociology comprehends within its jurisdiction every social phenomenon of every kind and character whatsoever.

This materialistic view reduces man to a child of fate, swept on by the current of human events as helpless as the log that floats upon the river. Whatever reasoning and subtle philosophizing those who hold this view may indulge in, they have never yet convinced any considerable number of the human race that man has not a free will and that he is not the creator of his own moral character.

[1] Cosmic Phil. 2d vol., 171–2.

It is useless to argue against the instinctive beliefs of the race. No one can be convinced by argument, however plausible, that there is no God, that the soul is not immortal, and that man is not free in the exercise of his will power.

Can there, then, be a science of sociology? Any pretended science which denies or ignores unmistakable facts cannot be a true science. Upon this point it has been said: "Sociology will never reduce human action to the exactness of mechanical laws. This is impossible for the simple reason that man is not a machine, but a person. Free will is a power above mechanism and chemical affinity. And it is inherent in the very essence of free will that it can disobey law. Hence the actions of particular persons or communities cannot be foretold with unerring accuracy. The man who was a blasphemer in the morning, may be a penitent at night. The young man who till yesterday has abstained from intoxicating drink, may drink to drunkenness today; a community quite under despotism this year, may be in armed revolution the next. In the Duke of Alva's time a Protestant fleeing from an officer of the Inquisition crossed a frozen lake. His pursuer broke through the ice and was likely to drown. The fugitive, hearing his cries, returned and rescued him from death. Then the officer seized the unarmed and defenceless man and delivered him up to the Inquisition. No person, probably, would have predicted that a man would make this return to one who had voluntarily come back to him and saved him from death.

In all calculations as to the probability of human action the moral character of a person or of a community, acquired by free choice, must be taken into account. The very same agencies that move one person or community to righteous and benevolent action, will move a person or community of different moral character to unrighteous and selfish action."[2]

The assumption that there is a law underlying all social phenomena, including the voluntary choices of man, which absolutely determines these choices, and determines

[2] Phil. Basis of Theism, 404.

the course of human progress, and necessitates the flow of human events, as the force of gravity necessitates the current of the river towards the sea, is unwarranted and contrary to the facts of consciousness.

We are not to infer, however, because the choices of man are not subjected to the law of necessity, that there is no such science as sociology. Such a science has a legitimate sphere, and there are certain well defined sociological laws, consistent with man's moral freedom.

Society, as an aggregation of individuals, possesses power, performs acts, applies means to the attainment of ends, and is subject to law as truly as is the individual himself. There are certain things that it can, and certain other things that it cannot accomplish.

That Humanity, or Society, in its broadest sense, should have divided itself, politically, into the Japanese, Chinese, Germans, Italians, Turks, Russians, Austrians, French, Spanish, English, the various American Nationalities and others, so that each should occupy just the position it does, within just such territorial limits upon the globe, possessing the form of government it possesses, and has made just the history for itself it has made, and that too, by mere accident, is to accredit human progress to chance and deny the existence of a directive intelligence in the affairs of mankind.

But, on the other hand, if a directive intelligence has superintended the course of history, and "hath made of one blood all the nations of mankind, to dwell upon the face of the whole earth, and ordained to each the appointed seasons of their existence, and the bounds of their habitation," then a uniformity of process, and an orderly sequence of events would be expected in the history of man as truly as it is found in the evolution of matter. In examining it with reference to the laws that prevail therein, we find society subject to law both in the primary and secondary sense of the term.

Primary Truth as Law.—All the primary or self-evident truths previously considered are regulative of social forces as truly as they are of physical and mental power. They are law to Society as they are to individuals, and in the same sense that they determine what society can, and what it cannot effect.

Society cannot produce something from nothing; no Parliament or Congress can make a dollar out of fifty cents, nor reduce a pound sterling to a dime; no nation can cede its dependencies to another and at the same time retain them; nor can society elude, modify, or annul the Moral law, or change the phenomenal nature of the physical or mental systems in which it is implicated and under which all social forces are exercised. Reason speaks to society in the same imperious terms of authority that she uses in addressing individuals.

All primary truth and the inferences arising therefrom are law to all the social forces of mankind. They are rigidly regulative of the forces of any community, of a nation, of a state, and of humanity as a whole, just as truly as they are regulative of the physical or mental powers of the individual.

Generalized Facts as Law.—But here, as in the realm of physical nature, there are certain generalized facts, certain processes, certain uniform courses of phenomena which are dignified by the distinguishing title of Law. It is our purpose to enumerate a few of the more common ones sufficient to illustrate their existence and general character; and we will first consider the "Law of Human Progress." Humanity is capable of and destined to, unlimited progress and development.

There is in the human mind an ineradicable desire for knowledge. This desire incites man to observe the world in which he lives, to seek the causes of the phenomena which he beholds, and to discover the laws that insure order and system throughout the universe. This desire for knowledge is implanted in every finite mind. In children we call it curiosity. It manifests itself in an early age in the young of every tribe and class and race of men. It is as natural for the mind to be curious and inquisitive, as it is for the sun and stars to shine. This inborn desire of the mind is a certainty. Concerning its existence there is no doubt, and by its naturally diverse tendencies great variety of human knowledge is insured.

One mind tends toward the study of the earth, another toward the study of the heavens, another toward the study of natural history, another toward the study of human history; while others desire a knowledge of the human mind, knowledge of metaphysical truth, and others a knowledge of God. So in these diverse mental tendencies a sure provision is made for advancement in knowledge.

Influenced by this desire, men have observed the phenomena of the finite mind, and penetrating in behind these phenomena, they have discovered the laws that regulate them. They have observed the phenomena of nature, and going behind them, they have found the grand system of natural law. Unsatisfied with these, men have sought the deepest truth of all, and there have found the cause and the original constitution of the universe. So men have come to know something of God, something of nature, and something of the finite mind, which are the only objects of human knowledge. God nature and the finite mind are the three great continents open to man's investigation. They comprise the entire sphere of human knowledge. Therefore, under the influence of this desire implanted in the human mind, the human race has already made excursions into many realms of truth, though it has merely begun its rich accumulation of facts and its thrilling discoveries of law. What it has done is but prophetic of what it will do. What progress it has made in knowledge is but a promise of what it will make.

But as deeply fixed in the human mind as the desire for knowledge, is the further desire for power. Man is not content with knowledge. He desires to produce results. He desires to make his power known and felt and acknowledged. He desires to combine the forces of nature, to control their results, and to conquer them. From the mere child commanding his toys up to Alexander commanding the world or Franklin commanding the lightning, all are fascinated by achievement and inflamed by victory. Men are not satisfied with a knowledge of steam power, but they must enslave it, chain it to a car, drive it around the world. Men are not satisfied with a knowledge of electrical force; they enslave it; they make it carry humanity's burdens, herald humanity's thoughts, illumine humanity's habitations. Men are not satisfied with a knowledge of atmospheric power, but they throw themselves across its pathway and make it waft them over the sea and spirit their white-winged ships from ocean to ocean. No principle in physical or mental science is more universally recognized and acknowledged than this human desire for power.

Not only is there a desire for knowledge and a desire for power, but equally deep in the human mind is planted the desire for property. Man naturally craves those things which minister to his sustenance and his comfort. This desire is a fixed and ineradicable constituent of the finite mind. Without it the wheels of human progress would cease to revolve, as quickly as would the wheels of an engine without steam. Property, and an individual right to its use and control, is an indispensable condition to civilization. This desire for property and desire for power have been regarded by some writers as identical, because wealth augments one's power. But whether one or two distinct desires, they constitute together an incitation to progress in civilization. The two are correlated. With wealth, a man is more powerful than without it. With it he can attain results which without it are unattainable; with it he can exercise control where without it he would be powerless.

These desires, with other active and moral powers of human nature stimulate industry, economy, prudence, and insure progress in the varied forms of civilization.

Not only is man possessed of these desires for knowledge, power, and property, but there is in man's nature a radical impulse to put forth all his mental powers in action. This radical impulse is deeply fixed and instinctive in the human finite mind. This instinctive propensity toward the exercise of all man's intellectual and voluntary powers is at the bottom of all human progress. This tendency of the human mind to put itself forth in action is a constituent element of the mind. And we find in this instinctive, deeply fixed impulse to action the moving element in the law of human progress.

In this impulse and in these desires, and other constitutional powers provision is made for continuous progress.

The motive forces of human progress, so to speak, having been considered, the next question naturally arising is, "According to what law or laws does society progress?" A partial answer to this question was given by Herbert Spencer in the April number of the Westminster Review for the year 1857. In an article entitled, "Progress; its law and cause," the law that progress is from the simple to the complex is illustrated by numerous and most striking examples, and there, that law according to the author, finds its first full and coherent statement.[3]

The Germans had recognized the fact, at that time, that the series of changes in the progress of individual organisms, as in the development of a seed into a tree, or an ovum into an animal, constitutes an advance from the homogeneity of structure to the heterogeneity of structure. In its primary stage every germ consists of a substance that is uniform throughout, both in texture and in chemical composition. The first step in its development is the appearance of a difference between two parts of its substance; of (as the phenomenon is described in physiological language) a differentiation. "Each of these differentiated divisions presently begins itself to exhibit some contrast of parts; and by and by, these secondary differentiations become as definite as the original ones. This process is continuously repeated—is simultaneously going on in all parts of the growing embryo; and by endless multiplications of these differentiations there is ultimately produced that complex combination of tissues and organs constituting the adult animal or plant. It is settled beyond dispute that organic progress consists in the change from the homogeneous to the heterogeneous."

Then the author asserts that "this law of pro-

[3] But see First Principles, p. 284 note.

gress is the law of all progress. Whether it be in the development of the earth, or the development of life upon its surface, in the development of society, of Government, of manufactures, of commerce, of literature, of language, science, art, this same evolution of the simple into the complex, through the process of continuous differentiations, holds throughout. From the earliest traceable cosmical changes, down to the latest results of civilization, we shall find that the transformation of the homogeneous into the heterogeneous is that in which progress essentially consists."

According to the Nebular Hypothesis, the nebulous mass, nearly homogeneous, through concentration, consolidation and varied velocities, increased its differentiations in number and extent until there was evolved "the organized group of sun, planets and satellites which we know now— a group which presents numerous contrasts of structure and action among its members."

The earth too, has been becoming more and more heterogeneous by the multiplication of its strata, in its variety of rocks caused by the heat within, in the varied elevations of its mountains, in its change of climates and in numerous other particulars.

Coming then to the plants, and to animals that live upon the earth's surface, each organism has been developed out of the simple seed or ovum, then it has progressed from the simple to the complex; but whether the earth's Flora and Fauna as a whole have become more heterogeneous is more difficult of proof.

But in the case of man, it is claimed that during his existence upon the earth, the human organism has gradually become more and more heterogeneous; and that the species as a whole has been made more complex by its multiplication of races, and the differentiation of those races from each other."

Language too has progressed in accordance with the same principle of development. Language began with exclamations, with single sounds, the simplest kind of speech; but later the noun and the verb appeared, followed by the adverb and the adjective, the conjunction and all the other parts of speech; and the moods and tenses, written as well as unwritten language, prose and poetry and all that goes with them to make up the languages of the earth as they exist at the present time. Painting and sculpture are no exception to this order of development.

Mr. Spencer says further, "On passing from humanity under its individual form to humanity as socially embodied, we find the general law still more variously embodied and exemplified. The change from the homogeneous to the heterogeneous is displayed equally in the progress of civilization as a whole, and in the progress of every tribe and nation; and is still going on with increasing rapidity."[4]

In his later works, however, Mr. Spencer regards the transformation from the homogeneous to the heterogeneous as the most conspicuous part of the secondary redistribution in Evolution, rather than Evolution itself, giving greater attention to the integration of matter and dissipation of motion, and finally states the law as follows: "Evolution is an integration of matter and a concomitant dissipation of motion, during which matter passes from an indefinite, incoherent, homogeneity to a definite coherent heterogeneity and during which the retained motion undergoes a parallel transformation."[5]

Recognizing this law of Evolution, Mr. Fiske in Cosmic Philosophy, considers the evolution of society, and endeavors to discover and formulate the law of social evolution. The prime factors in social progress he finds to be "the community and its environment." It is unnecessary for our purpose to follow his argument. It is enough that we state his law, which is as follows: "The evolution of society is a continuous establishment of psychical relations within the community, in conformity to physical and psychical relations arising in the environment; and during which, both the community and the environment pass from a state of relatively indefinite, incoherent homogeneity to a state of relatively definite coherent heterogeneity, and during which the con-

[4] First Principles 122 id. 145. [5] First Principles 407.

stituent units of the community become more and more distinctly individual.''[6]

Mr. Fiske also undertakes to state more fully than the author himself, Comte's law of human progress. It is as follows: "The progress of society is a gradual change from anthropomorphic to positive conceptions of the world, and from military to industrial modes of life; and the latter change is determined by the former.''[7]

The law of human progress is stated by Charles Sumner in his renowned oration on the "Law of Human Progress,'' as follows: "Man as an individual is capable of indefinite improvement. Societies and nations, which are but aggregations of men, and finally the human family, or collective humanity, are capable of indefinite improvement. And this is the destiny of man, of societies, of nations, and of the human family.''[8]

In order to understand fully the significance of any of these so-called laws of human progress as it lay in the mind of the author, a thorough study of his arguments leading up to the generalization, is necessary. But for our purpose it is sufficient to notice that the law as stated in the various definitions is simply a statement of the steps by which, or the manner in which, society has advanced from the simplest beginnings to its present stage of complexity. It is a general statement of the process by which society goes from the homogeneous to the heterogeneous. The law simply states how society advances. The simple fact that man individually and collectively has the capacity of indefinite improvement, and that such improvement is his destiny, constitutes the essence of the law as stated by Sumner. His is not even the statement of a process, but the statement of a capacity and a tendency. This is a law in the secondary sense of the term—a mere general fact or truth called a law.

In discussing the distribution and development of mankind, Prof. Guyot frequently applies the word, Law, to the important general truths, which he emphasizes in his lectures upon "Earth and Man.'' We have recognized,

[6] Cosmic Phil., 2d vol., 223.
[7] Cosmic Phil., 2d vol., 240.
[8] Works of Chas. Sumner, Vol. 2 p. 115.

he says, "in the life of all that develops itself, three successive states, three grand phases; three evolutions identically repeated in every order of existence; a chaos, where all is confounded together; a development where all is separating; a unity where all is binding itself together and organizing. We have here observed," he says, "that here is a law of phenomenal life, the formula of development, whether in inorganic nature, or in organic nature."[9]

After numerous illustrations of this law, he proceeds to note the differences between the development or progress of man toward a state of perfection, and that of the rest of the animal kingdom.

Besides the law of human progress, working from the simple to the complex in structure, function and government, mankind seems to be distributed over the earth and mentally and morally developed according to a generally recognized and established order, which Prof. Guyot formulates and calls the "law of distribution and development."

Considering the animal kingdom, he finds the Arctic Fauna is the least highly developed, the species are fewer in number, more uniform in figure, and darker in color. This region is inhabited by the white bear, the reindeer and the whales, which are the lowest in rank of all mammals. From this region, down through the temperate to the torrid zone, there is a regular increase in the development of animal life. The fauna of the temperate zone is more varied than that of the arctic, and the fauna of the torrid is still more varied in form, more brilliant in color, more numerous in species than that of the temperate zone. In this region, animal life is stronger and more highly developed. The types are improved; there is greater intelligence, and here the animal form approaches more nearly to that of the human figure.

The regular gradation in animal development, from the arctic to the torrid regions is thus formulated as a law. "Nature goes on adding perfection to perfection from

[9] Earth and Man p. 100.

polar regions to the temperate zone, and from the temperate zone to the regions of the greatest heat."

But man forms an exception to this rule. While all the types of plants and animals are increasing in perfection from the polar to the equatorial regions, in proportion to an increase in temperature, "Man presents to our view his purest and most perfect type at the very center of the temperate continents, at the center of Asia—Europe, in the region of Iran, of Armenia, and of the Caucasus; and departing from this geographical center in the three grand directions of the lands, the types gradually lose the beauty of their forms in proportion to the distance, even to the extreme points of the southern continents, where we find the most deformed and degenerated races and the lowest in the scale of humanity."[10]

He states the law as follows: "In man the degree of perfection of the types is in proportion to the degree of intellectual and moral improvement, and to the physical conditions favorable to physical and moral improvement."[10]

The author then proceeds to say that "this law of development is the law of man, the law of the human race, and the law of society."[11]

Customs.

Having noted the general fact of human progress, which is sometimes called its law, and also the law of social evolution, and the law of distribution and development of organic life in general and of man in particular, we come now to consider the further question as to whether society as a whole exhibits orderly sequences, and uniformities of social conduct, similar or analogous to those which obtain in the physical world.

Are there social laws, and if so, do we find them formulated in the social sciences? Are there in human society, as there are among impersonal beings, rules of action uniformly observed, and to which uniformity, the term law is applied?

[10]Guyot, Earth and Man, p. 250. [11] Earth and Man p. 265.

Answering affirmatively, we will consider a few of these so-called laws, and examine their nature. As in the physical world bodies unsuspended in the air uniformly tend toward the earth, and as in the animal world there is a uniform tendency towards self-preservation, so, in human society, there is a constitutional and uniform tendency on the part of the individual to preserve life; acquire property; exert power; and to meet the demands of their other common and instinctive appetites, affections, and desires; and groups of persons also uniformly contend for prolonged existence, and struggle for the acquisition of wealth, and for the possession of power. There is, in these particulars a general uniformity of conduct. What individuals and groups of persons will do relative to self-preservation, and to the acquisition of property and power can be predicted with a fair degree of certainty.

Besides these tendencies to uniform conduct based on the instinctive, active and moral powers of man, customs and usages of various kinds and character appear throughout human society as a natural product of social life. Society is not lawless. As naturally as leaves appear in the forests, and grasses spring from the soil, so, as naturally general and local customs spring up, imperceptibly but inevitably, among the different tribes and races of men, providing a code of unwritten laws which insure harmony of action and supply a kind of natural government, where other law and government have not yet been consciously provided by mankind. This spontaneous generation of customary rules of conduct in society is undoubtedly the oldest form of law-making among mankind.

When, where, and under what circumstances the first custom arose among men, is, of course, as uncertain as the date and place of man's origin; or the year, the month, and the day when organic life first made its appearance upon the globe; but the existence of these regulative agencies in the family and in the tribes of ancient peoples, as well as among the nations of the world generally, and at all times, is a part of their accepted history.

A custom has been described as "any usual method of action, defined and enforced by the tacit consent of the community, or of the class to which it belongs." "They are the earliest and simplest products of the organic tendency in society. They arise, in a large measure, unconsciously, preceding all forms of conscious constructions, preparing the way for them and accompanying them. Custom is the cellulose tissue of the social body, occupying all vacant places, storing material, and ready to pass into more specific forms. Customs arise inevitably among social rational beings."[12]

Among those which have prevailed with the essential force of law, are the domestic and religious customs of various peoples, and they vary from time to time in the course of their history. The ceremonies attending marriage, the betrothal of children, the burial or other disposition of the dead, have generally been of a uniform character throughout specific tribes and communities. The number of wives allowable, the character of personal ornaments adopted in a community, and even the style of their huts in primitive and of their more pretentious dwellings in the higher stages of progress, have been largely determined by the regulating force of custom. Even the division of labor, whereby the wife in a savage state performs the drudgery of the domestic circle, while the husband engages in the hunt and in the common sports of the tribe, is sanctioned by the usage of the tribe, and in civilized communities such division of domestic duties is equally the result of a customary course of conduct.

These domestic customs, varying so widely with different peoples, and varying in the history of the same peo-

[12] Bascom Sociology, p. 11.

For an able and interesting discussion of Custom as Law, consult Carter's "Law, its Origin, Growth and Function." Page 173.

On page fourteen, the learned author asks the question, "What is Law?" He here refers to law as a rule of human conduct, and in the pages immediately following he gives the historic development of custom. On page 122 he says, "Custom is the uniformity of conduct of all persons under like circumstances." On page 173 he summarizes his conclusion thus, "Custom is not simply one of the sources of law, from which selections may be made and converted into law by the independent and arbitrary fiat of a legislature or a court, but law, with the narrow exception of legislation, is custom, and like custom, self-existing and irrepealable.

See also Wilson's works, Vol. 1, pages 88, 89, 429.

ple, are the law of the social circle, in the sense that they determine what is proper, right, or safe for the individual members of the group to do. For the wife and the mother in an American home to appear in the presence of the family attired in man's clothing, and to persist in such a violation of the customary rule of dress, could not be much more offensive to the family circle by the enactment of a positive statute forbidding it.

Where these domestic usages have become fixed rules of conduct, to act counter to them is to offend the feelings of the group among which such rules prevail, and consequently, such domestic customs become, in a sense, binding upon the individuals of the community, and to that extent they approach the essential character of a positive law.

Religious customs and usages have also exerted a potent influence upon the history of mankind. Religious rites and ceremonial observances stimulated by the sentiments of the human heart, have attended and largely determined the progress and development of every historic race; the recognition of the gods, customary forms of worship, the erection of altars, the establishment of priestly orders, the adoption of eccliastical vestments, the offering of sacrifices, and burning of incense, the setting apart of certain days for feasts and religious celebrations have found a prominent place in the religious history of the world. In later days, the customs of family devotions, the invocation of a divine blessing upon the daily meals, the customary attitude of kneeling in prayer have had among Christian people at different times and places the force and effect of divine Commandments.

To a congregation being accustomed to the kneeling posture while partaking of the emblems, a forced change of the custom to a standing posture would produce a revulsion of feeling approaching positive indignation, and awaken a sense of impiety.

Among the religious customs, that of animal sacrifices is at once the most common and universal. From its universality it is obvious that it arose from a common sentiment among people widely dispersed and variously constituted. From the common practice of sacrificing the choicest of the flocks and herds, the custom extended to the immolation of human victims, the bloody rites attending which, have darkened the history of both hemispheres. It is hardly possible that the offering of children to Moloch or Kronos could have equaled in extent or cruelty, the sanguinary offerings made by the fierce Aztecs of Mexico as late as the fourteenth century, upon whose bloody altars there were annually immolated, it is variously estimated, from twenty to fifty thousand victims; and whose every festival was closed with these loathsome and bloody rites.

Generation after generation, these religious customs are observed, until they obtain over the minds of those who obey them, the sanctity of a divine law.

The rules of social intercourse, likewise, and the behavior of persons in society generally, embraced within the term etiquette, are largely fixed by custom, or usage, and they become an important factor in the good order and social development of mankind.

The commercial and industrial worlds also exhibit uniformities of action or conduct attributable to custom. The usages of merchants, which developed into the Law Merchant of England, such as allowing "days of grace," in connection with commercial paper, is an example of the law-making power of society through custom.

The whole body of the common law exhibits, on a large scale, the tendency of society to supply itself with rules of action, anterior to the rules or existence of positive law, or the existence of courts for its enforcement. Illustrative of those usages of the people which ripened into the "Custom of the Realm" are those determining how land should descend, as where by general custom the eldest son alone was the heir of his ancestor, and, in case of three brothers, the eldest was the heir of the second, in exclusion of the youngest; and again, by the particular customs of certain boroughs, the youngest son should inherit the estate in preference to all his elder brothers, and the widow should be entitled, as dower, to all her husband's lands, instead of a one-third part, which was the general rule, and further, according to the custom of gavelkind, in Kent, all the sons alike succeeded to the inheritance, instead of the eldest son of the father. And under general customs again, property could be acquired and transferred by writing, a deed was of no validity unless sealed and delivered, a breaking of the peace was an offense and punishable by fine and imprisonment. And many similar rules were not created by statute, but their validity, as a law, depended entirely upon immemorial usage. And even the courts of the realm depended for their existence upon custom rather than positive enactment, as the four courts of record, the Chancery, the King's Bench, the Common Pleas, and the Exchequer; and even the Constitution of England and her form of government rest upon immemorial usage. And from these facts, we see that society possesses the inherent power of generating orderly and uniform courses of conduct even to the extent of providing courts, and constitutional governments. Originating in usage, by a kind of evolutionary process, the customs of the people, unconsciously adopted, develop into the consciously recognized and judicially enforced laws of the realm.

All these customs, or usages, to which reference has been made are but, "the usual methods of action, defined and enforced by the tacit consent of the community, or of the class to which they belong." They arise among the people unconsciously, and they precede all conscious attempts at law-making. But society does not outgrow its usage-forming or custom-making habit. Every nation and every community continues to evolve new customs as its changing circumstances and conditions demand. A large part of the regulative principles of every people consists of the usages and customs in business, and the uniform fashions, rules of etiquette, and the conventional regulations necessary for the good order and success of every social, literary, political, religious, or other organization.

From the foregoing facts, we observe that usages prevail in every group of human society, and that they constitute the spontaneously evolved rules of action which society unconsciously observes, and are among the first agencies regulative of human conduct, having nearly the effect of positive law; and some of which actually pass into the realm of Jurisprudence.

Just when a usage becomes a part of the positive law, it is difficult to tell. Many of them never do. When reasonable, certain, and prevalent from time immemorial, and by meeting other requirements, they may be regarded and treated as positive law by judicial recognition and enforcement.

"The state, through its delegates, the judges, undoubtedly grants recognition as law to such customs as come up to a certain standard of general reception and usefulness. To these, courts give operation, not merely prospectively from the date of such recognition, but also retrospectively; so far implying that the custom was law before it received the stamp of judicial authentication. The contrary view, supported by Austin, is at variance with fact. The element of truth, in his view, which has done good service, by bringing it into prominence, is that usage, although it may make rules, cannot, without obtaining for them the recognition of the State, make laws." * * * "When, therefore a given set of circumstances is brought into Court, and the court decides upon them by bringing them within the operation of a custom, the Court appeals to that custom as it might to any other preexistent law. It does not, *proprio motu* then, for the first time make that custom a law; it merely decides as a fact, that there exists a legal custom, about which up to that moment there has been some question, as there might about the interpretation of an act of Parliament. It then applies the custom to the circumstances just as it might have applied an act of Parliament to them." [13]

Custom, it has been said, was the first method of lawmaking in human society. "There can, in fact, be no doubt that customary rules existed among people long before nations or states had come into being."

Courts were established, governments organized, and

[13] Holland Juris. 57.

constitutions created, in part at least, through the agency of immemorial custom.

After the formation of the state, usage developed into positive law. Justinian says, "The unwritten law is that which usage has established; for ancient customs, being sanctioned by the consent of those who adopt them, are like laws."[14]

By judicial recognition and enforcement they become known as a part of the law of the land, and together with constitutions, statutory enactments, municipal charters, ordinances and all other rules of social conduct enforcible at law, they constitute the jurisprudence of the state.

Jurisprudence, then, is one of the social sciences, but as we are here examining the meaning of the term law in other than its legal sense, we shall not consider the rules of positive law in this connection.

Another of the social sciences which affords numerous illustrations of the use of the term law, applied simply to express the existence of a generalized fact or orderly sequence, is the science of political economy.

When we transfer our inquiry to the science of political economy, we find that law as here used, also signifies simply a general proposition, or a uniform order of events. If a certain state of things exist then as a matter of fact, a certain result will follow; if a redundant issue of paper money is put into circulation, then as a matter of fact, gold will cease to circulate. If the population of a state greatly increases, then we may reasonably expect that the price of land there will increase. If land is made to bear a heavy burden of taxation, then, as a general thing, the price of the land will decrease. If there is a rise in the rate of interest, then there will be a decline in the price of stocks. So, as has been said, "An economic law is nothing but a general proposition or statement of uniformity, more or less certain, or more or less definite." Such general statements appear almost without number in works upon the social sciences, but it is only when they are of unusual importance that they are severally dignified by being called laws.

[14] Just. 1. §2. 9.

An illustration of how a general proposition, or a statement of a general truth is termed a law, is found in Mr. Mill's "Three laws of production." After stating that Political Economy endeavors to investigate and teach the nature of wealth, and to discover and formulate the laws of its production and distribution, and adding that the requisites of production are labor, capital and land, or the Materials and the motive forces afforded by Nature, the author proceeds to discuss the three laws involved.

First: Of the law of "Increase of labor" he says, "The increase of labor is the increase of mankind or population. The power of multiplication inherent in all organic life may be regarded as infinite. There is no one species of vegetable or animal which, if the earth were entirely abandoned to it, and to the things on which it feeds, would not in a small number of years overspread every region of the globe, of which the climate was compatible with its existence. To this property of organized things, the human species forms no exception. Its power of increase in indefinite, and the actual multiplication would be extraordinarily rapid if the power were exercised to the utmost. * * * Population has the power of increasing in an uniform and rapid geometrical ratio."[15]

Second: Discussing the law of the increase of capital, the author says, "Since all capital is the product of saving, that is of abstinence from present consumption for the sake of a future good, the increase of capital must depend upon two things: the amount of the fund from which the saving can be made, and the strength of the disposition which prompts to it. The fund from which savings can be made, is the surplus of the produce of labor, after supplying the necessaries of life to all concerned in the production (including those employed in replacing the materials, and keeping the fixed capital in repair). More than this surplus cannot be saved under any circumstances, as much as this, though it never is saved, might be."[16]

Third: Considering the Law of increase of products

[15] Principles of Pol. Ec. 97-100. [16] Principles of Pol. Ec. 101.

from land, Mr. Mill states it in the following words: "After a certain and not very advanced stage in the progress of Agriculture, it is the law of production from the land, that in any given state of agriculture skill and knowledge, by increasing the labor, the produce is not increased in an equal degree; doubling the labor does not double the produce, or to express the same thing in other words, every increase of produce is obtained by a more than proportional increase in the application of labor to the land." He says further, "This general law of agricultural industry is the most important proposition in political economy. Were the law different, nearly all the phenomena of production and distribution of wealth would be other than they are now." [17]

This last proposition of Mr. Mill is also called, "the law of diminishing return," and Mr. Perry states it as follows, "Increase of agricultural efforts and expenditures on a given piece of land will secure a larger amount of produce, but as a general law, the increased amount will not be proportional to the increased expenditures."[18]

Mr. Marshall states the law as follows: "An increase in capital and labor applied in the cultivation of land, causes, in general, a less than proportionate increase in the amount of produce raised, unless it happens to coincide with an improvement in the arts of agriculture."[19]

The law of demand and supply has been formulated in the following language, "As the price falls, (other things remaining the same), the quantity demanded increases, and conversely, as the price rises, the quantity demanded decreases." [20]

Discussing the law of demand and supply, Mr. Mill says, "Demand and supply, the quantity demanded and the quantity supplied, will be made equal. If unequal at any moment, competition equalizes them, and the manner in which this is done is by an adjustment of value. If the demand increases, the value rises; if the demand diminishes, the value falls. Again, if the supply falls off, the value rises, and falls if the supply is increased.

[17] Prin. Pol. Econ. 109.
[18] Prin. Pol. Econ. Perry 154.
[19] Prin. Econ. Marshall 229.
[20] Prin. of Pol. Science 29.

The rise or the fall continues until the demand and the supply are again equal to one another; and the value which a commodity will bring in any market is no other than the value which, in that market, gives a demand just sufficient to carry off the existing or expected supply. This, then, is the law of value with respect to commodities not susceptible to being multiplied at pleasure.[21]

Discussing the same principle, Mr. Marshall says, "there is then, one law of demand, which is common to all demands, viz: that the greater the amount to be sold, the smaller will be the price at which it will find purchasers; or, in other words, that the amount demanded increases with a fall in price, and diminishes with a rise in price."[22]

The Law of Rent is one which has received much attention from economists, and is stated by Mr. Walker as follows: "Rent arises out of differences existing in the productiveness of different soils under cultivation at the same time, for the purpose of supplying the same market. 2d: The amount of rent is determined by the degree of those differences. Specifically, the rent of any piece of land is determined by the difference between its annual yield and that of the least productive land actually cultivated for the supply of the same market, under equal applications of labor and capital, it being assumed that the quality of the land as a productive agent is, in neither case, impaired or improved by the cultivation.[23]

The Law of international values has been concisely stated as follows: "The produce of a country exchanges for the produce of other countries, at such values as are required in order that the whole of her exports may exactly pay for the whole of her imports. This law of international values is but an expression of the more general law of value which we called the Equation of Supply and Demand. We have seen that the value of a commodity always so adjusts itself as to bring the demand to the exact level of the supply."[24]

In the subject of currency, Gresham's law is, that

[21] Prin. Pol. Ec. 272.
[22] Prin. of Econ. Marshall 175.
[23] Pol. Econ. Walker p. 207.
[24] Prin. Pol. Econ. Mill p. 358.

"Bad money drives out good money," and perhaps one of the most fundamental laws is that "An increase of the quantity of money raises the prices and a diminution lowers them," of which Mr. Nicholson says that it is the most elementary proposition in the theory of currency, and without it we should have no key to any of the others.[25]

Coming to the Science of Sociology as it is now being formulated, the elements of which are, in these days, being subjected to critical examination, we find the same use of the term Law, that we have found in the various specific sciences which we have before considered.

It is applied to not only the general truths well established, but also to "Approximations to general truths." In order to fully understand the real meaning, and to comprehend the full significance of those sociological laws which are to be considered, it would be necessary to follow the author's analysis and general treatment of the subject matter from which he makes his generalization. But for our purpose, the meaning of the propositions, or the laws, as stated by the different authors, will be sufficiently clear for us to recognize their general character as mere statements of fact.

A few illustrations may be taken from the "Elements of Sociology," by Mr. Giddings. He begins his "Elements of Sociology," by calling attention to the facts, among others, that natural societies are found in those parts of the globe, where the physical features of the land and the climate are favorable to the grouping of living beings: that the different groups or societies are increased either by the birth of new individuals or by the immigration of individuals into one group from groups located elsewhere: that these living objects are conscious individuals who think and feel, who have appetites, desires and passions, who form purposes in life, and try to achieve them: that there is usually a stronger sympathy among members of a family than among all the members of a nation; and stronger sympathy among Protestants than among Protestants and

[25] Nicholson, Prin. of Pol. Ec., Vol. 2, p. 113-118.

Roman Catholics taken together; and from these facts of sympathy the author deduces and formulates what he terms the "law of sympathy," viz: "The degree of sympathy decreases as the generality of resemblance increases."

Further considering the "crowd," the same author says it is devoid of the sense of responsibility, because, when lost in the mass, the individual loses his own feeling of responsibility. Like the savage and the child, the crowd is intolerant of anything interposed between its desires and their realization, and it always manifests a tendency to carry suggested ideas into action.

After considering these and other conditions favorable to sympathetic and impulsive social action, the author states the following laws:

First: "Impulsive social action is commenced by those elements of the population that are least self-controlled."

Second: Further he says, if starting from one individual the suggestion or impulse is communicated by him to a second there are immediately two centers of influence, and if each of these again communicates the impulse to another individual not yet reached, there are at once four centers of influence, and so on in a geometrical ratio; and the individual who started the movement was at the outset, subject only to the original stimulus acting upon his own mind: but when he has communicated it the emotional excitement of a second mind reacts upon the first, and when in turn they communicate it to two more, the emotional reaction of three minds has begun to act upon each of the four, and so on indefinitely: and hence, from these facts, the author deduces the second law, as follows: viz: "Impulsive social action tends to extend and to intensify in a geometrical progression."[26]

Third: The only restraint, the author proceeds to say, that can hold in check the tendency to impulsive social action is deliberation—critical comprehensive thinking.

Deliberation, however, must have become a habit of mind in order to exercise much restraint upon social impulse.

[26] Elements of Sociology 139-140.

Many of the most vital achievements in life depend upon indirect means, and the discovery of indirect means is possible only through reason and deliberation. If, under the stress of impulse, one's thoughts are diverted to some other matter than that which occasions the excited feelings, those feelings subside, so the law of Restraint is stated as follows: "Impulsive social action varies inversely with the habit of attaining ends by indirect and complex means."[27]

After discussing the difference between belief and knowledge, and noting how tradition acquires in society all the tremendous force of authority, the author states the laws of Traditional Control.

First: "Tradition is authoritative and coercive in proportion as its subject matter consists of belief rather than critically established knowledge."[28]

Discussing the "Laws of Social Choice," the author again says: "So long as the majority of men chiefly value the primitive virtues of power, independence, courage and ability in every form, it is evident that rational social choice must more often than not turn upon this particular object of social esteem. In like manner the least influential object in determining social choice is that rational self-realization which appeals only to the few. Consequently we have the first law of social choice, the law of preference of ends to be achieved, as follows: In all social choice, the most influential ideal is that of personal force, or of virtue in the original sense; the second in influence is the hedonistic or utilitarian ideal, namely the ideal of pleasure; the third is the self-conservation, or the Puritan ideal; the least influential is the ideal of self-realization or self-development. But if mental evolution continues, the higher ideals become increasingly influential."[29]

In a similar way the author proceeds to consider the facts and formulate what he calls the "Law of Combination of Means," the "Law of Development of the Social Composition," the "Laws of Liberty," and finally, the

[27] Elements of Sociology 139-140.
[28] Elements of Sociology 154.
[29] Elements of Sociology 168.

"Law of the survival of social interests and relations," all of which are but an enumeration of facts, generalized into the form of a comprehensive statement of the truth, as the author discovers it to exist.

Examples of sociological laws, sufficient to answer our purpose have now been given. Upon examination we find them belonging chiefly to what we have called law in the secondary sense of the term. They are, as will be observed, mere statements of general truth—or an approximation to the truth.

In the last three chapters we have considered some of the powers and laws of the human mind and of society. Here as in the realm of physical nature, we find the fundamental truths of reason operative as law. They set fixed and changeless limits to mental and social forces. The ideas of time and space, all the familiar axiomatic principles, such as the law of attribution, the law of equality, the law of excluded middle, the so-called Aristotle's dictum, and all the other self-evident principles, laws of logic, mathematical axioms, and the necessary inferences that may be drawn from them, are regulative of all intellectual, moral, spiritual, and social forces. The mind can never escape their presence, modify their demands nor annul their irresistible and regulative influences.

And besides these primary realities, there are in the realm of personal spirit, as in the realm of impersonal nature, certain generalized facts, and orderly and uniform sequences to which we give the name of law. We find one thought following another as day follows night, certain emotions following particular choices, as a feeling of self approval follows a choice of the right and a feeling of condemnation follows a choice of the wrong, under the law of contrast the idea or thought of the vastly rich tends to suggest a thought of the poor, and the coldest days of winter tend to suggest the hottest days of summer, the thought of success inspires joy, the thought of defeat inspires fear, pure thoughts ennoble the character, and impure thoughts debase it, the feelings of joy bring the smile, and the feelings of sadness bring the tear, and so throughout the mental realm we find a phenomenal order under which thought awakens feelings, feelings influence choices, and choices are succeeded by emotions varying according to the character of the choices themselves. These generalized facts and orderly sequences of the mind are not laws in the sense that primary truths are law, but the name law has been given to them. As all the uniformities and orderly sequences in the physical realm are fixed and relative to man are regulative of his power, so all of these orderly sequences of thought, and feeling, and choice, and emotion are equally fixed and relative to man they are regulative of his power in dealing with his fellow-men. They are facts to be considered and reckoned with in all human transactions. I cannot make a person smile and rejoice by stinging his soul to resentment and anger. I cannot fill him with revenge and hate by bestowing upon him precious gifts and performing for him acts of love and affection. It is beyond my power to make a person hate me by helping him in disaster and cheering him in sorrow. All the uniform successions of thought, ideas, feelings, choices, and emotions that compose this phenomenal mental order are laws in the true sense of that term in that they determine what a person can and what he cannot do. Man can produce his desired results only in harmony with this established intellectual, moral, spiritual and social order and not in antagonism to it.

CHAPTER VI.

Teachings of Intuitional Philosophy.

We began our brief survey of physical nature in search of those fixed and invariable realities which, regulative of power, constitute the true laws of the material world. The general properties of matter, which are simply self-evident truths applied to physical bodies, first engaged our attention, and finding them immutable realities, we pronounced them laws of matter in the primary sense of the term. We observed also that the whole system of self-evident and irreversible truths, and all the necessary inferences that can be drawn from them, operate throughout the finite universe, regulative of its physical forces; and consequently being changeless universal and imperative they are the fundamental laws of the material universe. In addition to these universal truths, we observed certain generalized facts and orderly sequences in the impersonal world, which are not eternal verities, yet regulative of power they are laws in a secondary sense. They belong to the finite and temporal realm. They had a beginning and we are taught by science that they will have an end. They all came into existence, continue in existence, and will finally terminate, if at all, in accordance with the universal truths or primary laws.

Coming to the realm of personal beings, we observed the universal prevalence of these same fundamental truths regulative of mental forces. They determine what intellectual power can and cannot conceive or effect. They are laws of thought in this realm as they were found to be laws of things in the realm of matter. They set the limits within which intellectual power may acquire knowledge, they guide the reasoning power through all its processes of ratiocination and they speak in authoritative commands to the will declaring what it ought or ought not to attempt. They constitute law in the deepest and truest meaning of the term in the realm of mind no less than in the realm of matter. In this region of mental forces we also observed generalized facts and orderly sequences which have acquired the name of law, but which are not self-evidencing and imperative. Like the general facts and observed uniformities in the physical world, they are laws relative to man in the sense that he has no power to change their established order, and they determine what he can and what he cannot accomplish. But the facts and processes of the finite realm of material and mental forces lack universality, immutability, and imperativeness that characterize the primary principles of reason.

Those first principles, such as, "every change or beginning must have a cause," and, "every complex of causes always produces the same effect," persist unchanged through all the changes, upheavals, convulsions, reconstructions and dissolutions of material or spiritual existences; and, in fact, it is in strict accord with these fundamental principles that all these changes occur. The finite universe including all its general facts and orderly sequences—laws in the secondary sense—comes into existence under the superior and regulating influence of these primal realities. We have detected the prevalence of the first principles in both the region of mind and matter. They are primal. They regulate all power. They are law in its true sense, and they are of such importance that their distinctive characteristics should be observed.

Tests of Intuitive Truths, Self-evident.—The most generally recognized test of intuitive truth is its self-evidence. Whenever upon an occasion in experience one of these rational intuitions comes out into the light of consciousness the mind at once recognizes its self-evidencing character. If one sees two parallel lines, as for example, the two rails upon a railroad track, and the possibility of their meeting is suggested to his mind, he knows immediately that those two lines cannot be made to meet so long as they remain parallel. This truth is seen at once. No proof can make it plainer. The moment these truths are announced in terms which are understood their validity is instantly recognized. Should a child of even tender years be asked if he can take a knife out of his pocket, when there is no knife there, he would give an immediate and correct reply. And if he is asked further if something can ever be taken from a place where there is nothing, he would give an answer equally correct if he understood the terms employed. From one example he sees the truth just as clearly as he can ever afterwards discern it. A multiplication of examples does not make the truth more convincing. When once the mind comprehends a self-evident truth, it demands no other proof of its validity than that which the truth carries within itself.

Universal.—These truths are also universal in the sense that they are constituent elements in the minds of all rational beings, but not in the sense that they are formulated principles in the minds of all men. Infants and savages do not have these self-evident truths clearly formulated, and even many intelligent and highly educated people may never have given these metaphysical truths sufficient attention to have a clear and extended knowledge of them. Yet the capacity to know them is there, and whenever the circumstances or occasions in experience are such as to suggest the truth, it will then be seen in all its self-evidencing clearness and in this sense these truths are universal. These fundamental realities are also universal in another sense. They are not only truths of reason, but they are laws regulative of all things, and hence they are universal in the sense that they are everywhere applicable as regulative factors throughout the universe. And they are also universal in the sense that they are without exception.

Necessary.—Again, these truths are necessary in the sense that the opposites of them cannot be conceived. By no possible exertion of mental energy can the mind conceive of something being made from nothing, that a proposition should be both true and false is equally inconceivable. That "everything that begins to be must have a cause," is a necessary truth in the sense that the opposite of it is unthinkable. The multiplication table is true throughout the whole universe, not only on this earth but on every planet and star and sun. So all self-evident truth is necessarily true always and everywhere because it is truth. The same truth cannot be true in one place and false in another, any more than gold on the earth would cease to be gold if taken to the moon.

These fundamental principles are not true because the mind of man is so constituted that it cannot conceive of them otherwise than they are. The nature of the finite mind is not the cause of these primary truths, but these primary truths, existing as realities independent of finite mind, do themselves regulate the intellectual powers of man so that he cannot over-leap their bounds. The multiplication table is not what it is because the finite mind recognizes and accepts it as true, but the finite mind recognizes and accepts it because it is true and real and so limits the intellectual power of man that it cannot conceive the relations of numbers to be other than in reality they are.

These truths or principles then are among the things that are fixed and irreversibly permanent. If "law" in all languages carries in it the idea of fixedness, then we may properly regard as among the realities that are thus fixed and permanent these self-evident universal and necessary truths of reason. If we ask what among all the transitory and fleeting forms of time can be found that is changeless and eternal, we can safely say that these self-evident and fundamental principles of reason are absolutely and irreversibly fixed, so that by no possible energy of mind can the slightest variation in any of them be either calculated or even imagined. Their opposites are unthinkable. Here then, in our search for things that are unchangeable, do we find the most permanent and immutable realities that the finite mind has ever discovered. If those realities which are firmly fixed and unchangeably established are laws, then these rational principles must constitute the eternal laws of the universe.

Having observed the primary truths prevailing in the

physical and mental realms, and having found them ever regulative of power, we are naturally led to make the venturesome inquiry whether they extend up into and operate throughout the Infinite Mind, which from logical necessity we are obliged to place back of the finite world. While not abandoning our search for the true essence and character of law, we may venture to question intuitional and theistic philosophy in order to ascertain if possible whether these primary laws in our finite world prevail throughout the untraversed and boundless zone of the Infinite that surrounds our temporal and limited sphere.

Theistic philosophy teaches that as we find man, in this finite universe of effects, an intelligent, rational and free moral being, it must logically follow that the Creator of man is an intelligent, rational and free moral Being, for the reason that the cause must always be adequate to the effect. The effect cannot be greater than the cause. The stream cannot rise higher than its source. The personal cannot spring from the impersonal. A stone without life could not create a tree with life. The Creator cannot impart what He does not Himself have. If He has imparted to man life, intelligence, reason, moral sense and the power of free-will, it follows of necessity that He possesses those powers. Man, the effect, is a personal being endowed with reason. God, the Creator, must then have had reason with which to endow him. It is the office of reason to recognize self-evident or primary truth. Man, the effect, possessed of reason, recognizes those truths as operative in his own mind and also operative as law throughout the physical world; so God, the cause, possessed of reason, recognizes the primary principles as fundamental realities, not above and separate from Himself, but as constituent elements of His own eternal reason. In the First Cause must exist potentially all that actually appears in the effect. These fundamental principles, these necessary universal truths or realities, pervade and operate as law throughout the entire finite universe; so, it is contended that in the Eternal Creator Himself these fundamental realities exist and are law to His eternal will. Otherwise, it is said, He would not be a moral being.

From this reasoning the conclusion is reached that these first principles or primary truths which we have recognized as universal laws in the physical world and in the minds of personal beings were operative as law in the Eternal Mind before the creation of the finite universe, and in obedience to, or in accordance with them the worlds were made and their inhabitants created. In this view of the case, theistic philosophy teaches that these primary truths are the supreme laws of the finite universe. Before the worlds were, they were law to the Eternal Creative Energy; and in accordance with their permissions and prohibitions all finite things were constructed.

This philosophy reaches the conclusion that personal beings, endowed with reason, conscience and freedom, must have been created by a being as highly endowed, at least, as the creatures which he has made. As life comes from life, so personality must come from personality, and such has been the opinion of many of the world's most thoughtful and profoundest thinkers.

Carlyle, sharing the belief of Frederick the Great, said, "Atheism truly, he never could abide; to him, as to all of us, it was flatly inconceivable that intellect and moral emotion could have been put into him by an Entity that had none of its own."[1]

That these intuitive truths are operative in the Infinite and Eternal Reason has been contended for as follows: "Theism teaches that the principles and laws of reason are not external to or independent of and above God, also that they are not caused by His will or dependent on it, but are eternal in God the Absolute Reason. * * * Therefore these principles and laws of reason are not independent of God and external to Him. They are not mere abstractions. They are concrete as constituent elements of Absolute Reason, the guiding lights of the Divine Intelligence and action, and are real with all the reality of God. * * * While the truths and

[1] Carlyle's Works, Vol. VI. p. 501.

laws of reason are eternal, immutable and uncreated in God, they are the laws in accordance with which, in the exercise of his almightiness, he freely determines to direct his action in constituting the universe. * * * God creates matter and endows it with its interacting forces so that it is real being and is capable of real interactive energy in the chain of causes and effects which we call the course of nature. This constitutes the physical system. God also creates personal beings. Each of these is a real individual being, a sub-creative center of intelligence and energy. * * * As thus constituted, the universe has a dependent but not actual reality in itself, * * * it is the objective reality on which God exerts His power, the plastic medium in which He expresses His thought, and by using its energies He progressively realizes in it the ideals of His wisdom and love. The principles and truths of reason are the laws of nature in the true meaning of that phrase. Because physical things and powers in nature have no choice, its construction according to the principles and laws of reason insures in it continuity and uniformity of sequence. * * * The true laws of nature are inherent in the physical system, and are the principles eternal in God, realized and revealed in nature. Because rational persons are free agents, the moral law does not insure the certainty of their uniform obedience to it. In a life of selfishness the person puts himself in opposition to the constitution of the universe and to the principles and laws of Absolute Reason. There is no place nor time in the universe in which a person may realize his perfection and well-being in a life of selfishness. The law of love is in the spiritual system analogous to the law of gravitation in the physical. Thus the laws both of the physical system and of the spiritual are eternal in the Absolute Reason and are the constitution of the universe."[2]

It is also claimed by the theist that as rational and moral intuitions are found operating as law in the mind of the creature they must also be operative as law in the mind of the Creator. These truths or principles are con-

[2] God, Creator and Lord of All, Vol. 1, p. 147-154.

stituent elements in the Divine Nature, and hence are eternal. Doctor Lidden comments upon this phase of the question in the following words: "Why the 'Eternal' Law? This question can only be answered when we reflect upon the nature of moral truth. Moral truth is not like the laws and facts of the physical world; it is not something which might have been otherwise than it is, had God so willed. God was under no necessity to make either one or a million suns or planets, or to furnish them with a particular temperature and particular inhabitants. Why not? Because there was nothing in his necessary nature which constrained him so to do. * * * He might have created otherwise; he was free not to have created at all. But could God ever have sanctioned you or me in saying that that which we know to be false is true? Why not? Because, in sanctioning us, God would be contradicting, not a law which He might have made other than He made it, but a necessary truth of His own Eternal Nature. A moral truth is like a mathematical axiom, we see it intuitively and we do this because it is necessarily true, and, as being necessarily true, is also a truth of God's Eternal Nature. Can any reasonable man, for instance, without destroying and uprooting the very constitution of the mind which God has given him, conceive that under any possible circumstances it could ever have been true that things which are equal to the same thing are not equal to one another? If not, then here we have an eternal truth. And if this be an eternal truth, it is, as such, a real part of God's Eternal Nature; since if this be denied, we must admit that there are eternal truths independent of God, and existing eternally apart from Him. Would not this in effect be a denial of His solitary self-existence? Either God does not exist, or all that is eternal is God. But if pure mathematical truth, as being eternally true, be thus Divine, moral truth is not less so. If we cannot believe that a lie was ever right, this is because veracity is an eternal law of the Divine Nature; and this applies to the whole moral law, which is, in reality, the Divine Nature, formulated into rules which suit the conditions of creaturely existence. Thus, given the parental relationship, it never could have been right to dishonor a father or a mother; given human life, murder could never have been any other than criminal; * * * given the idea of personal rights, of property, and stealing is necessarily condemned. And thus it is that sin does not contradict a rule which God has made of one kind, but which He might have made of another; it contradicts a rule which, in its principle, is necessary and eternal; a rule which does not depend even upon the will of God Himself, since it embodies and expresses His Divine and unchanging Essence; a rule which, accordingly, it is impossible to contradict, without running counter to, and, so far as we can, setting at naught and destroying the very Being and Nature of God Himself."[3]

SUMMARY.

Having thus pursued our investigation from the material bodies that surround us up through the universal realities, generalized facts and orderly sequences of both the impersonal and the personal realms, finding them law at every step either in its primary or secondary signification, we have reached at length by a process of justifiable inferences, generally acceptable to the inquiring mind, the eternal law that reigns supreme in the Divine Nature. According to this philosophy, all the primary truths of reason which we have found at every turn in the world of matter and in the world of finite mind, regulating every physical and mental force, are eternal realities reigning as law to the Eternal Will of the Creator, and constituting the *supreme constitution* in accordance with which every thing was made that was made. We have found orderly sequences, uniform processes, generalized facts, and certain general properties of matter as existing and fixed realities in the physical world; and we have observed also orderly sequences, uniform processes, generalized facts and certain constitutional characteristics fixed and abiding as realities in the human mind; to all of which we may properly apply the term "law," in

[3] Lidden, Some Elements of Religion, 151.

its secondary sense,—law pertaining to finite and temporal things and beings, law pertaining to things that have been created and which processes and sequences could not have been law prior to their creation: hence they are temporal, not eternal. We have also observed that the primary transcendent and universal principles of reason are regulative of things in the world of matter and regulative of thought in the world of mind, and according to theistic philosophy, regulative of the Eternal Will itself. To those changeless and imperative rational and moral principles the term "law" applies in a special sense. They are primary, universal and eternal law. They constitute the *"Supreme Constitution"* of the universe, in the sense at least that in accordance with and obedient to them the finite universe and all its processes, orderly sequences and uniformities, called laws, have been created and established.

This theistic conception of the universe, briefly referred to in the foregoing quotations, places Spirit before matter, and in Spirit it places these original principles of reason as constituent elements. It is in the power of rational spirit to recognize these original realities and also to recognize their irreversibility and their authority as laws regulative of mental power. These truths of reason give law to the Divine Will, and hence all created things were brought forth not in violation of but in perfect accord with them. This conception of creation regards the Eternal Energy whence all things came as the God of the universe, and pictures Him as projecting His creations into space in strict compliance with these eternal principles. The universe came into being, not spontaneously, in violation of the law of causation, but obedient to it. God was Himself the cause. He spake by the might of his power and the worlds appeared in perfect harmony with these truths of His reason. The half of everything He has created is less than the whole of the same thing, the shortest distance from Mars to Venus is a straight line and not a broken one, nowhere among all His creatures can be found a being that is both rational and irrational, that is both animate and inanimate, that is both a solid and a liquid, that is both round and square, that is both good and evil, that is both sound and unsound, that is both perfect and imperfect, at the same instant; and nowhere has He posited a world outside of space, nor created a world that is both luminous and non-luminous perpetually; nowhere has He placed two neighboring mountains without a valley between them, nowhere do highlands appear unaccompanied by lowlands, and nowhere has He created a being who is both free to choose and at the same time irresistibly constrained so to do, but everywhere all created things have come into existence and arranged themselves in an orderly and harmonious universe obedient to these original principles resident in the Eternal Mind of their Creator.

Law, therefore, is not a product of God's will, but it is an inherent element in His reason. Regulative truth is law. Reason is legislative, giving law to the universe; will power is executive, creating and arranging things *according* to law. These fundamental realities in the Eternal Reason, regulative of the Eternal Energy, constitute the eternal laws to which impassioned reference has been made by statesmen, orators and poets from the earliest times. These original truths are supreme, they are themselves unconditioned, while they condition all created things; power is regulated by them, but it is not possible for power to ever annul or modify them. These principles are changeless, universal and all-controlling; they "regulate both thought and things, and they persist unchanged through all changes and convulsions, through all production and all dissolution, and all changes must accord with them. No action of power, even though Almighty, ever interrupts their operation." They are the primary principles that regulate, and power is the thing that is regulated. They are thus laws to power. *A law, in its true and primary sense, then, is truth regulative of power; and as these fundamental laws are supreme, eternal and irreversible, in pursuance of which all finite things have been created, we may properly style them the Supreme Constitution of the Universe.*

CHAPTER VII.

RIGHT, LIBERTY AND JUSTICE.

Accepting the theistic view of the universe, we have as the *Supreme Constitution,* in harmony with which all finite things have been created, all the fundamental and immutable principles eternal in the Creative Mind. They are universally regulative. To their authority all power must submit, and in harmony with them all things have been fashioned. They constitute the primal and supreme law.

The second system of law is that operative throughout the physical and impersonal universe, consisting as we have seen of the general properties of matter, generalized facts, such as the orbits and orderly motions of material things, and the uniform sequences which everywhere abound throughout the physical world; and in addition to these the principles of the Supreme Constitution extending down, as we may say, into and operative throughout the entire material and impersonal realm.

The third system is that operative in finite personal spirit. It includes all the laws of association, the laws of memory, imagination, reasoning, the law of moral obligation, and all those orderly processes abounding in man's intellectual, moral and religious nature; and here too we find the principles of the Supreme Constitution constantly operative, giving us the laws of thought.

Thus we have a triple system of Law—laws of the Divine Nature, laws of physical and impersonal nature, and the laws of finite personal nature. This triple system of law constitutes "the nature of things," so often referred to.

The immutable principles operative throughout the realm of the impersonal, and the established order and uniform sequences prevailing there, constitute the "nature" of impersonal things; and likewise the immutable principles operative throughout the personal realm, and the established order, intellectual, emotional and moral, prevailing therein, constitute the "nature" of personal beings, and consequently when we say that a certain event can or cannot happen from the "very nature of things" we mean, if we speak intelligently, that such event is possible or impossible under the existing laws of this triple system.

As every citizen of an American city lives under a triple system of human law, composed of the Federal Constitution and Statutes, the Constitution and Statutes of his state, and the Charter and Ordinances of his municipality, so every person lives under this triple system of natural law which antedates all civil institutions and whose commands and prohibitions are binding upon all civil government. Hence, our study should not stop with the common law of the land, nor with the constitution and statutes of the state and nation, nor even with the broader rules of international conduct; but above and beyond all these human enactments and compacts are the superior principles of that great triple system of natural law, whose regulative influence, as we shall hereafter see, plays a most important part in the administration of justice in the conflicting affairs of human life.

Right and Wrong.—It is in view of this triple system of law that we are now in a position to see clearly the significance of right and wrong as qualities of action. Law is the test or standard of right and wrong. Right is applied to any action which conforms to law, and wrong to any action which does not so conform. Until we know the law in any given instance we are unable to tell whether the action is right or wrong. The mother who sacrifices her child to appease the wrath of an offended deity believes that the law demands it, and subjectively the mother's act is right; but whether the act is objectively right depends entirely upon what the law actually demands. The physician who ministers a certain drug to his patient believes that certain favorable sequences will certainly follow under the established order of the patient's physical constitution, and subjectively his act is right, for what is true to man's intellect becomes a law to his will; but whether that act is objectively right depends upon the established order of nature, and whether as a fact the drug will be followed by the favorable sequences anticipated, whether the act is objectively right depends upon the law operative within the patient's physical constitution. The statesman who advocates a tariff upon foreign imports believes the highest welfare of his country demands it, and his advocacy of the measure is subjectively right; but whether the highest welfare of his country will, as a matter of fact, be promoted in the long run by such a measure depends upon the law regulative of international traffic, and if that law permits or demands such a measure the act is objectively right, but objectively wrong if such law forbids govermental interference. The difficulty of the problem arises from man's present inability or failure to discover the law applicable to the case, and to convince the world of its immutable and imperative character.

Right and wrong imply law. Independent of law they have no significance. Law therefore is primal. The quest for law is man's mission, both in the world of mind and of matter. Only as we discover and learn how to conform our action to it is human progress and civilization possible. By the term "the right" is meant agreement with law. The term has no intelligible meaning independent of law. The ground of "right" or of "the right" is not the will of God, as some theologians have claimed, nor happiness, as some philosophers contend; but law itself, the fundamental and abiding truths or realities in the realms of personal spirit and impersonal nature, is the ground of right. Law exists first and right and wrong afterwards. When we apply the term right to a moral act we mean simply that the act is in agreement with moral law, and if the act is in agreement with positive law, we say it is legally right. But the term is applied to any act that is in harmony with any law.

Liberty.—In view of this triple system, we can also see the true meaning of liberty. Liberty is freedom to do right, or freedom to act in accord with civil law, natural liberty to act in accord with natural law. Man is unrestrained when there is no law forbidding what he is doing. The law does not forbid any action in harmony with itself. Man is at liberty, so far as law is concerned, to do anything the law allows. This is the only liberty known to rational beings. Law stands opposed to all who would violate it. Man was never at liberty to advance five years into the future, nor to run back five years into the past, nor was he ever at liberty to add one cubit to his stature, nor to be true and false at the same time in a single act, nor to possess a good and a bad character at the same time, nor to both love and hate his neighbor continually. Man was never at liberty to break an immutable law. He may choose to do so, but he cannot. He is at liberty to conform his action to law, that is, to do right. Hence the only liberty man ever possessed was the liberty to do right. In every other effort the law opposes him. As paradoxical as it may seem, there is no liberty without restraint. Every finite rational being is restrained by his own limitations, as well as by the immutable laws of the universe. If a man could find a spot on earth where no human law prevailed, yet even there the laws of thought and moral obligation and others would reign. He can never escape beyond their jurisdiction. A person is always free to act lawfully. If one keeps within the permission of the law in this triple system there is nothing to oppose him, but as soon as he attempts to violate or override it or to accomplish ends contrary to the provisions of the law he finds the whole rational system opposing him. They confront him, they defy him, they thwart his purposes, they antagonize him at every point.

Living within this rational system of law, all the liberty of which we have or can have any knowledge must be such as is consistent with this system. We are living in a system of rational and moral order, and nowhere in it is there unrestrained license. No one can do as he pleases unless he pleases to do right; and when we come to the realm of positive law we shall also find that civil liberty consists in one's freedom to act obediently to that law. Within the limits of law one is free, but to break over those limits he is not free. If he attempts it the law opposes and restrains him. Its sanctions threaten him.

Justice.—We are now in a position to see, also, in what Justice consists. Many definitions may be found in the numerous works upon Ethics and jurisprudence, but that of Justinian is, perhaps, the most simple and accurate. "*Justitia est constans et perpetua voluntas jus suum cuique tribuendi.*" Justice is the constant and perpetual wish to render every one his due. But even in this definition Justinian confines himself to subjective justice alone. He says justice is the constant and perpetual "wish" to render every one his due, implying that he would be a just man who *wished* to render everyone his due, whether he were able to actually render it or not. Wishing to do a particular thing, and actually doing it are two separate acts. A person may wish to pay a debt, but be wholly unable to do so, in which case he would be subjectively just; but objective justice would not be realized. Objective justice consists in the outward act of rendering to persons that which is due them. Justice, therefore, presents two distinct aspects; the inward wish, and the outward act, and in considering the matter with reference to jurisprudence, this distinction becomes important because courts of justice attempt only to control external conduct.

Subjectively considered, justice consists in the will's consent to the law, and to its demands. He is a just person whose constant and perpetual purpose is to accord to every one his due. His inability to perform the outward act does not alter his inward will or purpose. His will still consents to the law which demands the performance of duty. The law of obligation demands the discharge of duty so far as ability will permit, but no farther. Duty ceases where ability fails. One cannot be morally bound to do what for him is impossible. To this law of moral obligation the will of the just man cordially consents, and to realize its demands to the extent of his power, is his constant and perpetual wish.

Justinian has given us a faultless definition of subjective justice. It consists in the "constant and perpetual wish to render to every one his due."

Should A purchase of B a precious stone, agreeing to pay him on a certain day, a specified sum of money for the same, there would arise upon the completion of the bargain, certain reciprocal moral rights and duties. To pay the stipulated sum on the appointed day would be the duty of A, and B would have a corresponding right to the money at the same time. The duty of A and the right of B are correlative. As we have already observed, the law of moral obligation demands of A full payment of the money upon the specified day, and the same law confers upon B a right to the actual possession of the money at that time.

Objective justice consists in the actual extinguishment of B's right by the actual performance of A's duty. The transfer of the money cancels both A's duty or obligation, and B's right. B no longer under this transaction has any right to money from A, and the duty to pay money to B no longer rests upon A. Their respective rights and duties have been adjusted by the performance of the outward act agreed upon. Objective justice consists in the outward adjustment of the rights and duties of persons. As we shall see hereafter, objective justice may be secured by the assistance of courts of justice, irrespective of the defendant's willingness to perform his duty. Objective justice may be secured, though subjective justice be wanting.

As we have already observed, an action which conforms to law is right; so we say that an act which conforms to law, as when A pays the debt he owes to B, is just. Is there then no difference between rightness and justice? While the term "right" may properly be applied to any act in agreement with law, the term "just" is properly confined to those acts only which acknowledge or deny the rights of some person or persons. If the government should take one man's property and give it to another, the act would be both wrong as contrary to law, and unjust as an infringement upon the rights of him whose property was taken. But if the government should enact a statute providing that the sum of ten and ten should equal thirty, the act would be wrong as contrary to a mathematical law, but no citizen could complain of any injustice resulting to him. Injustice consists in depriving some person of his natural or legal rights. Natural justice consists in according a person his natural rights, as legal justice consists in according him his legal rights. The denial of these rights is injustice.

That natural justice consists in according to persons their moral rights is discussed by John S. Mill in his essay on Utilitarianism.

"In our survey of the various popular acceptations of justice, the term appeared generally to involve the idea of a personal right—a claim on the part of one or more individuals, like that which the law gives when it confers a proprietary, or other legal right. Whether the injustice consists in depriving a person of a possession, or in breaking faith with him, or in treating him worse than he deserves, or worse than other people who have no greater claims, in each case the supposition implies two things—a wrong done, and some assignable person who is wronged. Injustice may also be done by treating a person better than others; but the wrong in this case is to his competitors, who are also assignable persons. It seems to me that this feature in the case—a right in some person, correlative to the moral obligation—constitutes the specific difference between justice, and generosity or beneficence. Justice implies something which it is not only right to do, and wrong not to do, but which some individual person can claim from us as his moral right.

No one has a moral right to our generosity or beneficence, because we are not morally bound to practice those virtues towards any given individual. And it will be found, with respect to this as with respect to every correct definition, that the instances which seem to conflict with it are those which most confirm it. For if a moralist attempts, as some have done, to make out that mankind generally, though not any given individual, have a right to all the good we can do them, he at once, by that thesis, includes generosity and beneficence within the category of justice. He is obliged to say, that our utmost exertions are *due* to our fellow creatures, thus assimilating them to a debt; or that nothing less can be a sufficient *return* for what society does for us, thus classing the case as one of gratitude; both of which are acknowledged cases of justice. Wherever there is a right, the case is one of justice, and not of the virtue of beneficence; and whoever does not place the distinction between justice and morality in general where we have now placed it, will be found to make no distinction between them at all, but to merge all morality in justice."[1]

There is also a sentiment of justice—a feeling that prompts man to demand his own rights, and to sympathize with another whose rights are violated.[2] When the rights of any person are denied him there is a universal feeling among men that the wrong-doer should be made to suffer for the injury he has inflicted upon him whose rights he has violated. This sense of justice is not satisfied by anything less than the punishment of the wrong-doer or a complete restoration to the injured party of all that has been wrongfully denied him. This sentiment is a fixed element in the moral constitution of man. It demands a perfect and complete adjustment of all the rights and duties of mankind. It is satisfied only when all men perform all their duties, for then all men will have all their rights. This fixed and universal reality or element in man's moral constitution constitutes the "principle of justice," inasmuch as it is regulative of free-will power telling it what it ought and ought not to choose. Free-will power which chooses to perform individual duty thereby accords to every one his corresponding rights, and justice being secured the universal sense of justice is satisfied. As natural justice rests upon the natural rights and duties of personal beings it is desirable that their constitutional nature be further empha-

[1] John Stuart Mill, Utilitarianism, 118-120.

[2] Carter's "Law, its Origin, Growth and Function." Page 155. "Justice considered as a sentiment is the sense of what ought to be done by one to another."

sized, and to that end I quote the words of President Porter as being especially clear and forceful:

"The extent and authority of these rights is emphasized by the adjectives natural, universal, and inalienable. They are called natural, because they are founded in the natural capacities and requirements of all human beings, and are entirely independent of any artificial or changing capacities or circumstances. They spring directly from the constitution of man as man; from his entire nature, be it observed, as personal, social, sympathetic, and moral. They are called such in contrast with those which are artificial, limited, temporary, and adventitious; such as are constituted by statutes which may be repealed, by fashions which may change, by institutions which may be abandoned, by relationships which may be dissolved, and yet which, while they exist, may enforce sacred obligations of duty. The nature from which they spring, and on which they are founded, is human nature.

"These rights are also universal. Being derived from the nature of man, they extend as widely as universal manhood. They are limited to no race, color, or citizenship, but are co-extensive with the human family. Being founded on an assumed similarity or community of endowments, and sanctioned and consecrated by that conscience which makes the whole world kin, they include as receivers and givers all those to whom the capacity of being blessed and the obligation to impart a blessing can reach. By this is not intended that every member of the human race, under all conceivable circumstances, is entitled to the actual security or enjoyment of these so-called universal rights. Some men may forfeit their claims by crime; others may be debarred the actual enjoyment of the blessings in their gift, under the pressure of circumstances that refuse them a developed and normal manhood. It is intended, however, that, so far as a common manhood is concerned, it avails for all alike whether these rights are claimed or waived; and that the claim is always responded to at the court of conscience and of unperverted public opinion.

"These rights are also inalienable. They are incapable of being rightfully parted with by their possessor, or being taken away from him by any act of personal violence or arbitrary decree. By this is not intended that a man may not expose himself to certain death to save the life of his friend or to defend his country, or voluntarily subject himself to the external conditions of personal slavery for benevolent or moral ends, or from similar motives abandon all private ownership of property, so far as this is possible. It is intended, however, that no act of an individual man or of society can deprive a single individual of any of these descriptions of rights, except for reasons or by processes which apply to all men alike.''[3]

In harmony with the position taken that justice consists in the consent of the will to the demands of the moral law respecting the performance of duties and the satisfaction of rights, the same author further says: ''If 'rights' are used to signify what are generally known as the natural or universal rights of man then justice is interchangeable with the benevolent recognition of these natural rights, and the duties which these involve.''[4]

And to the same effect are the following words of Dugald Stewart: ''In the case of justice, also, there is always a right on one hand corresponding to an obligation on the other. If I am under an obligation, for example, to abstain from violating the property of my neighbor, he has a right to defend by force his property when invaded. It therefore appears that the rules of justice may be laid down in two different forms, either as a system of duties, or as a system of rights. The former view of the subject belongs properly to the moralist, the latter to the lawyer. It is in this last form, accordingly, that the principles of justice have been stated by the writers on natural jurisprudence.''[5]

[3] Porter, Elements of Moral Science, 401.

[4] Porter, Elements of Moral Science, 413.

[5] Active and Moral Powers of Man (Walker), 362.

CHAPTER VIII.

Ethical Basis of Jurisprudence.

We have already observed in Chapter IV that the moral law manifests itself under three distinct forms among others, those of Justice, Benevolence, and Veracity.

As the clover seed sends up its single shoot, which, as a stem, unfolds at the top into three distinct leaves, so this single moral law presents to us three distinct aspects, justice, benevolence and veracity. They are not three separate moral principles, but only three different manifestations or aspects of one principle.

This one law of love or service requires man to seek his highest good, but in order to attain his highest good, he must perform duties to others. The same law requires him to work for the good of others as well as his own; and such are our human relations that only by performing our duties to others can we attain our own self-approval and our own highest well-being.

Man attains his moral perfection largely by his conduct in the outward affairs of life. If he borrow money of his neighbor, he can attain his own highest good only by paying his neighbor when the money is due. If he has negligently injured his neighbor, he can gain his own highest good only by compensating his neighbor for the injury. If he has contracted with his neighbor to sell him a farm for a certain sum of money, he can attain his own highest good only by executing the contract according to its terms. If he has slandered his neighbor, he can attain his own highest good only by recompensing his neighbor for the injury inflicted. If he agrees to do a day's work for his neighbor, for a stipulated compensation, he can gain his own highest good only by performing the labor fully and fairly, according to the agreement. And, so, in all the possible instances of reciprocal services, each can attain his own greatest good only by rendering to the other that which is due him.

But all such conduct as this is what we call justice. The moral law, then, when applied in outward affairs appears in that form. Objective justice is but the outward manifestation of that one moral law.

Again, if man would attain his highest good, his perfect character, he must render gratuitous services in many instances to the weak, the ignorant, and the helpless. If he would attain his own good, he must, under certain circumstances, feed the hungry, clothe the naked and shelter the homeless. So this law of service manifests itself necessarily in the form of benevolence. He who would serve himself best; he who would live up to his moral ideals, cannot ignore his duties to those in distress. His highest good can only be secured by bestowing good gratuitously and benevolently upon his fellow men.

This basal law then manifests itself also in the form of benevolence.

But perhaps this law of service manifests itself in no other form so frequently and so constantly as in the form of veracity. Every human being needs reliable information from others. His need constitutes a right, and the right upon his part imposes a duty upon others. So under the law of service, a person cannot attain his own highest well-being, except as he performs his duties to others by conforming his communications with them to the truth. The importance of truthfulness in the affairs of human society is immeasurable. To secure it, the courts of justice resort to the oath. In his home, in business, in society, everywhere, he who would attain his own highest well-being must conform his words and his action toward others to the demands of truth.

Man's highest well-being begins in right moral character. This he can attain only by veracity. If, in selling a jewel, whose quality he knows but the buyer does not, the seller serves himself best by telling the truth to the confiding buyer. Instances arise daily in every life which illustrate this truth. Here also the law of service manifests itself in the form of veracity.

So necessary is veracity in social life that, without it, society would crumble into ruin and the administration of justice become impossible. Imparting knowledge of the truth to others is one of the highest forms of service to them, and, at the same time, one of the highest forms of service to self.

Now what relation does this one fundamental law of service, in its three-fold manifestation, sustain to jurisprudence? This is our question.

First: The moral law, which is coeval with rational beings, was first in order of time. Under the moral law, as we have seen, it is the duty of each to serve his neighbor, and the neighbor possesses a corresponding right to be served. In the concrete affairs of life, if A owes B a sum of money, the day it falls due, it is the duty of A to pay it, and the right of B to have it. The duty of one is always attended by a corresponding right in the other. Duties and rights are correlative. They exist as correlatives in the nature of the moral system. When man appeared upon the globe as a moral being, implicated in a moral system, he was subject to the moral law; just as when he appeared upon the globe as a physical being, implicated in the physical system, he was subject to the law of gravitation and the other laws of physics. Moral rights and duties precede, legal rights and duties follow. Jurisprudence is the product of ethical conceptions; ethical conceptions are not the product of jurisprudence.

Second: Besides being the first in order of time, the ethical conceptions of justice, benevolence and veracity called for legal assistance in man's struggle for life, for development, and for civilization.

From the dawn of human history, men have been contending for their moral rights against those who were unwilling to perform their moral duties; and from time to time a human law was announced by a despot, a monarch, a court, a king, or enacted by a tribe, a council, or a parliament, which, in some manner, secured to the individual his moral rights, in a certain class of cases, such as his right to life, his right to liberty, and his right to property.

And all those human laws, taken together, and in force in any particular state, constitute the Jurisprudence of that state. As the race has advanced, and as men have come from century to century, to recognize more clearly their moral rights and duties, they have multiplied human enactments, amended deficient laws, adopted improved systems of government, and enlarged the sphere of judicial action, so that the Jurisprudence of the world today is the mature product of centuries of evolutionary development.

The desires men have for the enjoyment of their rights ensure the construction of systems of human law, just as certainly as their desires for knowledge ensure the establishment of educational institutions, or their desires for national safety ensure the construction of coast defenses. As the moral consciousness of the race discerns more and more clearly its individual and collective rights, and duties, the Jurisprudence of the world must correspondingly develop and improve.

I have purposely singled out this basal law of Ethics, and have specifically illustrated its three-fold manifestation as justice, benevolence and veracity, because Jurisprudence chiefly concerns itself with these three forms of human conduct. Much that this moral law demands in the outward conduct of men toward one another, Jurisprudence also demands. The moral law demands that the individual pay his just debts to his neighbor; Jurisprudence insists upon the same: the moral law commands that those with ability shall feed the destitute, care for the sick, and assist the ignorant; jurisprudence also provides almshouses for the poor, hospitals for the sick, and schools for the ignorant and defective; the moral law demands that men shall speak the truth, one to another, in their communications; jurisprudence discountenances in severest terms deceit, and lying, and fraud in the outward concerns of human life.

The moral law of service says, " thou shalt not steal,"

and Jurisprudence repeats it, saying, "if you do, you shall be punished." The moral law says, "thou shalt not bear false witness against thy neighbor," Jurisprudence enacts the same principle and provides additional penalties for its violation. The moral law says, "thou shalt not kill," and Jurisprudence makes murder unlawful and inflicts its heaviest punishment upon the murderer, so wherever the moral sense of mankind, preceding, discerns man's rights respecting his life, his liberty, and his property, Jurisprudence, following, undertakes to secure to each individual the enjoyment of these rights.

The sanctions of the moral law were insufficient, in many cases, to secure its observance. So to those sanctions the state added others, enforcible by human courts, and calculated to secure obedience to that moral law, at least in the outward conduct of mankind. In this way Jurisprudence grew up on the foundation of the moral law, prohibiting what it forbade, and compelling what it commanded, within a certain range of human action. Jurisprudence, therefore, supplements Ethics. By its added sanctions it secures correct conduct, where Ethics left to itself, would fail. Ethics precedes, commanding men to be just, benevolent and truthful, and Jurisprudence follows, compelling obedience to this command within the practical range of outward observance. And hence, we may properly regard Jurisprudence as a branch of applied Ethics.

The Federal Constitution and the Constitution of every state in the Union declare that they are severally ordained and established, among other things, to establish justice and to promote the general welfare. Justice is the most conspicuous form of the moral law, which demands the attention of the state.

It is not too much to say that the administration of justice is the chief object of civil governments and human laws. Justice is the tap-root of Jurisprudence, upon which it rests, out of which it grows, and from which it draws its vitality. To see the true relation, however, existing between them, an analysis is necessary. As we have seen, justice appears in two forms; one subjective and the other objective. Subjective justice consists in the consent of the will to the demands of the law. Justinian's definition of justice has reference to this subjective form. He says, "Justice is the constant and perpetual wish to render every one his due." It is the constant and perpetual consent of the will to accord every one his due that constitutes subjective justice, or that constitutes one a just person.

An illustration may be permissible. If A owes B one hundred dollars for borrowed money, which sum is due and payable, and A has the money with which to meet the obligation, it is A's moral duty to pay the debt, and it is B's moral right to have the money. If under these circumstances, A, recognizing his duty, consents to the demands of the moral law to pay B, is willing to do so, wishes to do so, he is subjectively just. This voluntary consent upon his part to meet the demands of the law makes him a just man, subjectively considered. But up to this point we see nothing but subjective justice.

Now if A actually pay over the money to B, and B surrenders the note, if one, to A, then objective justice is secured. A's duty to pay and B's right to have the money, have both been met. A's duty is correlative to B's right. The outward adjustment of this right and duty by actual payment, constitutes objective justice. So we define objective justice to be the *outward adjustment of the rights and duties of persons.*

But again, if A, under the circumstances supposed, when the money is due, and he has it in his possession, refuses to pay B, then he does not consent to the demands of the law, and he is subjectively unjust. He is an unjust man. This unwillingness to meet the moral law's requirements constitutes subjective injustice. And the actual withholding of the money by A, from B, who has a right to it, constitutes objective injustice.

Now, suppose B sues A for this money, procures a judgment against him, has an execution issued; and the officer duly levies it upon A's land, sells the same and out of the proceeds pays over to B enough to fully satisfy the debt, and pays the balance, if any, after settling the costs, over to A. Then objective justice has been secured. The right and the duty of the parties have been adjusted. B no longer has any right to money from A; and the duty to pay money to B no longer rests upon A.

But it will be observed, that while objective justice has been secured by means of the court, yet A has remained unwilling all the time to pay, consequently he has remained subjectively an unjust man. This distinction between subjective and objective justice is essential in the consideration of our subject, because courts of law have to do with objective justice only. The courts enforce the outward adjustment of men's rights and duties, leaving the subjective justice and injustice wholly to the court of conscience.

In other words, Jurisprudence concerns itself with objective conduct and not with the subjective state of the human mind.

Jurisprudence will proceed to collect the debt, irrespective of A's consent or dissent to the demands of the law. From the nature of things, human courts cannot investigate men's mental states, consequently there is a great zone of ethical conduct which lies around and outside of the narrower zone of judicial redress. No court of law will issue a writ of mandamus to compel one to love his neighbor, nor will a court of equity issue a writ of injunction restraining one person from hating another. Until a moral law has been adopted, or taken up into jurisprudence by judicial or legislative action, its violations are left to the courts of conscience alone for recognition and redress.

But Jurisprudence does not deal exclusively with justice. Every civilized state recognizes its duty to the poor, the defective, and the insane. Human laws provide for their care and well-being. Enormous sums of money are raised each year by taxation for the comfort and improvement of the unfortunate.

The laws of the United States, by which lands are donated in large quantities to the respective states for educational purposes, the laws of the state exempting colleges and seminaries and churches from taxation, the laws of the state compelling certain persons to care for their destitute relatives, and providing for county, city, village and town systems of charity, whereby the poor shall be cared for,—all these laws, and many more of a similar character, are embraced within the term Jurisprudence, and they all recognize the duty of the strong to care for the weak and unfortunate. Volumes could be written upon the laws of civilized states and their interpretations by the courts, which have for their object a benevolent regard for the poor; and still more could be said about that multitude of laws whose object has been to secure donations for the church and other religious organizations. No small part of the world's Jurisprudence has recognized the duty of mankind to render gratuitous services in the form of tithes, donations, or taxes, to the destitute and unfortunate portion of mankind.

We need to give but brief consideration to the rules in both the systems of law and equity, which recognize man's duty to speak the truth to his neighbor. The maxim that, "Equity will not suffer a person to speak the truth when he wants to, if he neglected to speak it when he ought to," expresses the attitude of Jurisprudence upon this subject.

Fraud, which is generally practiced by untruthful words, deceitful conduct, or misleading silence when one should speak, constitutes one of the great subjects in the consideration of which both courts of law and equity spend much of their time and thought. The duty of one party to speak the truth, and the duty of the other not to mislead or deceive, appear in one form or another, in nearly every transaction in the business of the world. Without truthful witnesses, the administration of justice were impossible, and hence the oath in many systems of legal procedure.

The moral right, which the individual has to the truth in human transactions, is one which the courts are most frequently called upon to consider, and no species of injury is more vigorously redressed by them, than that which one party sustains by the fraud, the deceit and the lies of the other.

The moral law then, as it is manifested in the forms of Justice, Benevolence and Veracity, is the foundation of Jurisprudence. It is the tap root extending down into the rational nature of man, while, at the same time, its vitalizing and civilizing forces extend above into the body and into all the branches of Jurisprudence.

But while the moral law supplies the foundation of Jurisprudence there exists an important and interesting relation between Jurisprudence and the other systems of Natural Law which we have already considered.

The student of Jurisprudence is daily confronted by references, in judicial authorities, to certain systems of law, which exert a controlling influence in the administration of justice, while at the same time, the jurist would not admit that they constitute any part of the positive law of the land. What is the relation of Jurisprudence to those various systems of truth.

The courts take judicial notice of the well established and generally recognized laws of physical nature; requiring no proof of the well authenticated laws of causation, of gravitation, or of the ebb and flow of the tides, the time of the rising and setting sun; the instincts of animal life, as the instinct of self-preservation, and that of protection exercised by the parent toward the offspring. But this body of natural law is not regarded by the jurist as any part of Jurisprudence.

The courts also take judicial notice of that important body of self-evident truths including all the fundamental principles of mathematics which are necessarily involved in all mathematical processes or calculations, as in the estimation of legal damages, in the entering up of financial judgments, and in ascertaining the amount of fees, costs and disbursements incident to any particular litigation or judicial proceeding. While these mathematical principles are necessarily involved and applied in every judicial proceeding, hearing, or final process, yet, as a body of changeless principles the jurist does not regard or treat them as a part of the positive law of the state or nation.

Then there are the fundamental laws of human thought and of logic; the laws of association, and the generally recognized and well established principles of psychology, such as the power of the human soul to know, its capacity to feel, and its power to choose; and all of these too are judicially noticed by the courts of civilized nations, yet these laws of thought, of logic and of psychology, are not in the estimation of the jurist any part of state, national or international law. In their administration of justice, the courts, as we have said, often recognize and give effect to the laws of these various systems of truth which antedate all human enactments and judicial tribunals.

To know the generally recognized laws of the Universe is indispensible for him who would be profoundly learned in the laws of states and nations. Positive law presupposes the existence of moral principles and it is administered by our courts in the helpful light of all those physical and mental truths before alluded to.

A relation exists, therefore, between Jurisprudence and ethical principles that does not exist between Jurisprudence and the other system of law referred to. The system of self-evident truths, the laws of physical nature, of animal existence, of thought and of sociology, are all presupposed by Jurisprudence and, of course, they antedate it in time; but of ethical truths something more takes place. Many ethical or moral principles are practically re-enacted by either judicial or legislative action and in that way they are adopted into and become a part of positive law. Thou shalt not kill, thou shalt not steal, thou shalt not commit adultery, and the more general ethical principle, thou shalt not in any way injure thy neighbor in his person or property simply for the sake of injuring him, were all ethically prohibited long before they were forbidden by positive enactments. The sanctions of the moral law were insufficient in many cases to secure its observance. To those sanctions the state added others, enforcible by human courts, calculated to secure obedience to those re-enacted commands, at least so far as they pertained to the outward conduct and behavior of mankind. In this way Jurisprudence grew up on a foundation of ethical principles and by re-enacting the same, Jurisprudence supplements Ethics. By its added sanctions it secures correct conduct, where Ethics, left to itself, would fail. Ethics precedes, commanding men to be just. Positive law follows compelling obedience; and consequently Jurisprudence may be properly regarded as a branch of Applied Ethics.

While there is this intimate and special relation between Jurisprudence and Ethics, there are also important relations between Jurisprudence and each of the other systems referred to. The courts give effect necessarily to their respective principles, though we cannot say they execute those laws. If A claims a title to certain property from B and it appears to the court that B never had any title to it, the court must deny A's claim, not because the positive law says it must be denied, but because the metaphysical truth that "something cannot come from nothing," necessitates the denial.

Likewise in the realm of physical nature, the court gives effect to the known laws operating in that sphere. If in a cause to determine the parentage of a child it appears to the court that for a year or more immediately before the child's birth, the alleged father was continually in one country and its mother in another, according to the natural law of gestation the decision of the court must be that the alleged father could not be the actual father of the child. That law of physical nature renders necessary such a decision by the court.

And in the realm of finite mind, if in determining whether a person has committed a certain crime, it appears to the court that, at the time the act was committed, the accused was so insane that he did not know what he was doing, he must be acquitted of the charge, upon the fundamental principle of the mind that there can be no intent in a mind destitute of knowledge. Intention necessarily implies a knowledge of the thing intended.

I say Jurisprudence is a branch or part of applied ethics, because positive law is not co-extensive with morality. The courts of the state assume no jurisdiction whatever over the thoughts and feelings and secret purposes and motives of the individual, however wicked and vicious and immoral they may be. All of these unexpressed activities of the mind are within the exclusive jurisdiction of conscience. But when these inward impulses and immoral purposes find expression in outward conduct, in acts violating the rights of others, they fall within the jurisdiction of human tribunals, so far, at least, as legislation and judicial authority have included them within the scope of positive law. But here even not every immoral word or act will be a sufficient cause for judicial consideration. Jurisprudence covers but a part of the moral realm, even so far as outward behavior is concerned. Many incivilities and insults experienced in social life, while morally reprehensible, are ignored by the courts of the land.

For the lawyer to understand man's ethical nature, to understand the relation of Jurisprudence and its fundamental principles, and to know how the courts regard and give effect to the laws of the universe of both mind and matter, is of vital importance, would he aspire to the broadest conception of the sublime subject of Jurisprudence.

The courts, as I have said, take judicial notice of these systems of Natural Law. They give effect to them in the administration of justice. They judicially notice the well-known laws of physical nature, the principles of mathematics, and other primary principles of reason, the instincts of animal life and the laws of the human mind as well as the established principles of Sociology. The courts do not execute or administer them in the sense that they administer positive laws, but all through the text-books and judicial reports we find frequent illustrations of the court's recognition and application of them in the settlement of contested causes.

Among the many instances where courts have recognized the primary laws of reason and the phenomenal order of nature, may be mentioned the following cases:

That something cannot come from nothing (*ex nihilo nihil fit*), is one of the fundamental truths of reason, whose appearance, as a controlling fact, in judicial reasoning, is frequent and noticeable. Where a testator devised one portion of his real estate to a son named Joseph and another portion to another son named Medeef, and ordered, if either of his sons should die without lawful issue, that his share or part should go to the survivor, it was held by the court that the right of Medeef in the share devised to Joseph, during the lifetime of Joseph, was a mere naked possibility, which in law is no interest at all, and as a necessary consequence its assignment by Medeef to one Winter carried nothing to the assignee. If Medeef has nothing, he could assign nothing to another, *ex nihilo nihil fit.* [1]

And the principle is again illustrated where it was sought to introduce a void clause in a will to show the intention of the testator regarding a valid portion of the same instrument. The judge in his argument says: "Void things are as no things; as a void award is said to be no award. * * * Assuming that the clause is merely void it follows that it cannot be read for any purpose, and especially for the purpose of showing intention. *Ex nihilo nihil fit.*" Adopting the language of others, he says further, "The expressions which cannot have any meaning are rejected as if they had not been written, and do not hinder the others from having their effect." Quoting the language of the court in another case, the judge says: "The trust being void is as though it never existed. So we may say of this power it is as though it had never been written in the will. You cannot argue from it any more than from the history of Lilliput or Robinson Crusoe." And the court finally says: "The law has not divided zero into degrees. How am I to infer from what the law will not notice that there was any intention to create an authority?" How can an inference be drawn from nothing? How can a testator's intention be inferred from nothing? An inference cannot rest upon zero any

[1] Jackson vs. Waldron, 13 Wend. 221.

more than a conclusion can rationally be drawn from non-existing premises. *Ex nihilo nihil fit.*[2]

Of the same nature is the maxim, *qui non habet, ille non dat.* Where an heir previous to the death of his ancestor conveys by deed all his interest in the estate of his ancestor, and there is a judgment against the heir previous to the conveyance on which, after the descent of the property, a sale is had, the purchaser, at such sale, and not the grantee under the conveyance, takes the land, because says the court, When the deed was executed the grantor had no title or claim to the premises, and could therefore convey no right to them. *Qui non habet, ille non dat.* A grant by a person who has no estate cannot, of course, pass any estate to the grantee.[3]

To the same effect, Lord Coke says that where a son releases in the life time of his father the release is void, because he has no right at the time of making it. The father takes nothing because the son has nothing to give.[4]

The same principle assumes another form in the maxim, *Nemo plus juris in alium transferre potest quam ipse habet.* In the court of Exchequer, where one Dixon agreed to join his brother in making a promissory note for his accommodation, provided that B would also join, Dixon the brother accordingly signed an instrument in the form of a promissory note, a blank being left for the name of the payee. B refused to join; and Dixon, for whose accommodation the note was to be made, inserted the plaintiff's name as payee and represented that he had authority to deal with the note, when in fact he had no authority whatever. The money was advanced by the plaintiff, and when payment was refused, he sued the signer, and the judge said that where a party takes such an incomplete instrument he cannot recover upon it, unless the person from whom he receives had a real authority to deal with it. There was no such authority in this case and unless the circumstances show that the defendant conducted himself in such a way as to lead the plaintiff to believe that the

[2] Root vs. Stuyvesant, 18 Wend. 301.

[3] Jackson vs. Bradford, 4 Wend. 619.

[4] Coke on Littleton, 265 a.

defendant's brother had authority, he could take no better title than the defendant's brother had to give. The plaintiff could only take it as a note under the authority of the defendant's brother, and he had no authority consequently the instrument is void, as against the defendant. The maxim of law is, *Nemo plus juris in alium transferre potest quam ipse habet.* The instrument was a piece of blank paper not a note, and consequently the plaintiff received no note.[5]

Another illustration of the same principle arises when one attempts to grant goods which are not in existence, or which do not belong to the grantor, actually or potentially, at the time of executing the deed. One may "grant all the wool of his sheep for seven years," but he cannot grant "the wool that shall grow upon the sheep that he shall buy hereafter." In other words one has no grantable interest in a possibility upon a possibility, and where one grants goods which are not in existence or which do not belong to the grantor at the time of executing the grant, no title passes to the grantee, as the grantor had none to transfer. *Nemo dat, qui non habet.*[6]

Another primary law of reason is found in the expression that, "the same body cannot be in two different places at the same time," and this fundamental law of reason is illustrated in all those cases where, in criminal prosecutions, the defense of an alibi is interposed. If the defendant accused was in New York at the time the criminal act was committed in San Francisco, that fact would of itself constitute a perfect defense. The universal principle that a person or an object of any nature cannot be in two different places at the same time would be recognized by the court and given effect in the prosecution of the case. In the case of the People vs. Levine, the Supreme Court approved the following language of the court below: "One of the defenses in this case is called an 'alibi'; that is, that the accused was elsewhere at the time the offense is alleged to have been committed. If

[5] Awde vs. Dixon, 6 Exch. 869, 872.

[6] Lunn vs. Thornton, 1 C. B. 379; Chidell vs. Galsworthy, 6 C. B. N. S. 471, 478.

this is true, it being impossible that the accused could be in two places at the same time, it is a fact inconsistent with the charge sought to be proved, and excludes its possibility. * * * In considering the strength of the evidence necessary to sustain this defense it is obvious that all evidence tending to show that the accused was in another place at the time of the offense is in direct conflict with that which tends to prove that he was at the place where the crime was committed and actually committed it."[7] The conclusiveness of this defense when clearly proven is stated by the court in another case as follows: "The defense of an alibi sought to be set up, though very conclusive, if certainly, clearly and fully established, is one liable to abuse."[8] To the same effect is the language of others considering the "alibi."[9]

The primary truth that a thing cannot both be and not be at the same time must find its application in the realm of jurisprudence as truly as elsewhere. A contract cannot both exist and not exist at the same instant; there cannot both be and not be at the same time a valid consideration for a promise; a contract cannot be both valid and not valid, voidable and not voidable, legal and illegal at the same moment. A pleading cannot be both sufficient and insufficient, a firm cannot both exist and not exist, a corporation cannot be and not be duly created and organized, and there cannot be at the same time both a cause of action and not a cause of action existing against the same party, growing out of precisely the same set of circumstances, jurisdiction in the court either exists or it does not, the judgment of the court is either valid or not valid, the stock issued by a corporation is either valid or not so, and the criminal intent necessary to constitute the crime of which a prisoner is accused either does or it does not exist,—in all these instances and countless others familiar to the jurist there is involved the fundamental and self-evident principle under consideration. There cannot be both jurisdiction and no juris-

7 People vs. Levine, 24 Pac. R. 632.
8 State vs. Thompson, 5 Humph. 138.
9 People vs. Atman, 76 Ill. 149.

diction in the court. Jurisdiction exists or it does not; and all these and numerous other instances, abounding in the adjudicated cases, illustrate the primary truth of reason that a thing cannot be and not be at the same time.

In the case of Scovill vs. Thayer,[10] an incorporated company had issued certificates of stock in excess of the limit imposed by its charter. Such issue being without legal authority was void in the sense that the holder of such shares was not entitled to the legal rights, nor subject to the legal liabilities which attach to the holder of authorized stock. Inasmuch as the holder of this stock attended the meeting of the corporation at which the stock was voted and received and held the illegal certificates, it was contended that he was estopped to set up their invalidity as a defense to an action by creditors against him to recover the unpaid balance due for the said certificates. This over-issue of certificates of stock was illegal. There was no such stock. The so-called certificates were nullities. They were nothing. They constituted stock or they did not, and in view of this principle, holding the over-issue a nullity, the court allowed the defendant to assert his non-liability. To have held the unauthorized stock void, and at the same time to have held the defendant liable to pay for it, would have been in reality holding the stock at once void and valid—stock and at the same time no stock.

The principle is further illustrated in Stace and Worth's case,[11] where it appeared that there was an agreement for the amalgamation of the London Northern Insurance Corporation and the Life Investment Mortgage Insurance Company, and the two corporations to be formed into one, under the name of the corporation first mentioned. The corporation was to issue shares in exchange for those held in the company, and the amalgamated board was to consist of five directors of the corporation, and of seven of the directors of the company, to be selected by themselves. After the amalgamation, Stace

[10] 105 U. S. 143.

[11] Law Rep. 4 Ch. App. 682.

and Worth, it was alleged, received and accepted certificates for shares in the corporation in exchange for their shares in the company, and they with five others were appointed directors of the corporation. Afterwards a resolution was passed for voluntarily winding up the corporation, and the names of Stace and Worth were placed on the list of contributors. An application to have their names removed from the list was made to Vice-Chancellor James, who, after hearing the case argued, directed their names to be removed. This was done on the ground that the agreement for amalgamation was beyond the powers of the corporation, and therefore, void. In giving the reasons for his decision he said: "It is, however, contended that notwithstanding the agreement itself was ultra vires and void, yet there are personal acts and things personally affecting these two gentlemen which render them still liable as shareholders." These were the acceptance of shares by Stace and Worth, the fact that their names appeared on the register of shareholders, and that they had sat as directors of the corporation after the attempted amalgamation. But he declared: "This was a void agreement with a void acting upon it, a void recognition, and a void ratification by the acts which have been mentioned. It comes to an aggregate of nothings, and that aggregate of nothings is all that there is to fix these gentlemen on the list of stockholders."

Again, the "whole includes all the parts of anything," so if a person has title to a section of land he must have title to each quarter of that section, and in a negative form Judge Christiancy recognized judicially this principle when, in a case for damages the question of reasonable care arose, the court said that it was bound to know that when no care was used in approaching a danger, reasonable care could not have been used.[12]

Further illustrations of this principle are found in the case of contracts void because made in violation of the common law or of some statute. In many states con-

[12] L. S. & M. S. R. R. Co. vs. Miller, 25 Mich. 273.

tracts made on Sunday are declared by law to be void. Gambling contracts and contracts to do any act prohibited by law, and in some states contracts tainted with usury are void, and hence are nullities. Strictly speaking there cannot be a void contract, because a void contract, as that term is used, means no contract. The term void agreement more properly expresses the idea intended, because a void agreement is such an agreement of the minds as does not create any legal rights. When we speak, therefore, of a void contract, we mean an agreement destitute of legal effects. From the nature of things a contract cannot be attended both legal effects and with no legal effects. If any legal rights are created by an agreement of parties, to that extent they have made a valid contract. There can no more be a valid contract which is not a valid contract, than there can exist a planet which is not a planet. Consequently the courts in considering void contracts speak of them as "nullities." They have no "legal force or obligation." And of one it was said, "No repudiation by a formal act was requisite to render it inoperative," and "it has no partial validity, such as would make it capable of subsequent completion.' Speaking of a Sunday agreement the court said that the defendant could not ratify the illegal contract, because its want of validity did not depend in any degree upon his choice. The law annulled it and there was no subject of ratification.[13] The so-called void contract is no contract, and there cannot be a ratification of a contract unless there is a contract to ratify, nor can there be an "adoption" of a contract unless there is a contract to adopt.

It is, of course, equally true that a statute repugnant to the constitution cannot be a valid law and at the same time void. It is either a law or it is not a law. It cannot be and not be a law at the same instant. In the language of Justice Brewer, "an unconstitutional act is not a law; it confers no rights; it imposes no duties; it affords no protection; it creates no office; it is in legal contemplation

[13] Day vs. McAllister, 15 Gray 433.

as inoperative as though it had never been passed."[14] It is a nullity and consequently a Board of Commissioners assuming to exist under an unconstitutional act has no legal existence; it was an unauthorized and illegal body; their acts in subscribing for stock and issuing bonds in payment for the same were void. The act being void conveyed no rights, and to hold their action as valid would be to hold the act both void and valid at the same time.

The courts also judicially notice all mathematical truth. The self-evident needs no proof. They not only recognize and give effect to the fundamental principles of arithmetic, geometry and trigonometry, but all necessary inferences, logical consequences and accurate calculations based upon those principles they equally recognize and adopt. The almanac, based upon mathematical calculations has been held a part of the law of England. As far back as 1702 a defendant was convicted under a statute for embezzling yarn delivered to him to be woven. It appeared on the face of the conviction that there was no summons duly served upon the defendant, for he was ordered to appear before the court on Tuesday, the 17th of April, 1702, which was an impossible date, as the 17th of April on that year was Friday. Granting a motion to have the conviction quashed, the court held that, if a conviction state that the defendant was summoned and did by virtue thereof appear on Tuesday, the 17th of April, and it appears by the almanac, which is a part of the law of England, and of which the court is bound to take judicial notice, that the 17th day of April was on Friday, the conviction shall be quashed, for the time of the summons being impossible, it is the same as if there had been no summons.[15]

It was also held that a writ of inquiry, executed on a Sunday, was void, that the court was "bound to look into the Almanac and take notice of it, though not specially assigned as error," for now, it is said in the same

[14] Norton vs. Shelby County, 118 U. S. 425.

[15] Queen vs. Dyer, 6 Mod. 41.

case, "the calendar is looked upon as a part of the law of the land."[16]

The American courts also judicially notice the rising and the setting of the sun and moon and other events based upon mathematical calculations. Reference to the adjudicated cases is made in this connection for the single purpose of illustrating the fact that that great body of mathematical truth by means of which men forecast with exact certainty the future movements of the heavenly bodies and which at once enter into the every day calculations and measurements of time and prices and wages of the people in the petty details of their business life, is an object of judicial knowledge in the light of which courts must of necessity ascertain the amount of damages they award, compute the interest they allow, ascertain the costs to be charged and determine the amount of the fines they inflict, or civil judgments they render. One Munshower having been tried for murder, the Supreme Court of Maryland in a review of the case made the following comments upon the point under consideration: "It was conceded that it became material and competent for the State to prove at what hour the moon rose on the night of Saturday, the 9th of August, 1879, and for the purpose of proving this, the State offered in evidence Gruber's Almanac for the year 1879. The prisoner objected to its admissibility, but the court overruled the objection and allowed the almanac to be offered for the purpose stated. To this ruling the prisoner excepted.

"This is all the exception states in regard to the almanac offered, and we must assume that it contained tables giving the periods of the rising and the setting of the sun and moon on each day of the year, such as are usually found in such works. The prisoner did not propose to offer proof assailing or impeaching the accuracy of the astronomical calculations upon which the tables in the particular almanac in question were made, but his counsel contend that the almanac was not the best evi-

[16] Hoyle vs. Cornwallis, 1 Strange, 387.

dence, nor indeed any evidence as to when the moon rose on that night. The argument is, that it was a mere calculation made by some one long anterior to the happening of the event, that the event would occur at a certain hour and minute; it was not evidence that the moon had risen at a certain hour, but the statement of a conjecture that it would do so. On the 2nd of January, 1880, when this case was on trial, there were surely better and surer means of proving when the moon did actually rise on the 9th of August, 1879, than by relying on the computation of an almanac maker that it would or ought to rise at a given time that night: how is the fact that it did rise at a particular hour proved by tendering as evidence the conjecture or calculation of some one that it would do so? If Gruber's almanac is evidence for this purpose, so then are all the other various ones published, because there is nothing in this one to make it more authentic than the others, and thus a fact susceptible of exact proof like any other event that has happened, may be established by the unsworn conjecture of almanac compilers. We do not propose to elaborate the question, nor to rely upon the fact that the Statute of 24 Geo. 2, ch. 23, is in force in this state. As has been well argued by the Attorney-General in his brief, the precise periods at which the sun and moon will rise or set at any particular period of twenty-four hours in the future is as absolutely certain and just as capable of exact mathematical ascertainment, as the occurrence of the day in which such setting or rising will take place. Courts have received as evidence weather reports, reports of the state of the market, prices current, and life insurance tables tending to show the probable duration of human life, though these are records which are not capable of mathematical demonstration, which cannot be tested by any certain law, and which may or may not omit the record of changes which have actually taken place. But an almanac forecasts with exact certainty planetary movements. We govern our daily life by reference to the computations which they contain. No oral evidence or proof which we could gather as to the hours of the rising or setting of the sun or moon could be as certain or accurate as that which we may obtain from such a source. Why then should not these computations which are, after all, but parts of the ordinary computations of the calendar, be admitted as evidence?"[17]

While reference in the above case is made to the admission of the almanac in evidence, strictly speaking no evidence of facts which the court judicially notices is required. Courts consult the book to inform themselves. They likewise consult books upon the sciences generally to ascertain the laws of chemistry, psychology, astronomy and many other branches of scientific learning.

The course of time and the fact that certain days of the week fall upon certain days of the month are equally within the judicial knowledge of the court. It was said by the judge in a comparatively recent decision that "courts will judicially take notice of the coincidence of days of the week with days of the month, as what days of the month fall upon Sunday. * * * Matters of which judicial notice is taken need not be stated in the pleading."[18]

The course of time and the regular or varying coincidence of days of the week upon certain days of the month, the hours of the day when the sun and moon rise and set, are often important facts frequently before the courts and for the purpose of satisfying himself upon these points, as we have before observed, the judge may refer to the almanac or any other book of reference for that purpose.[19]

The courts require no proof of things which must have happened according to the ordinary course of nature. The phenomenal order of nature is judicially noticed. *Lex spectat naturae ordinem.* As we have already observed in the foregoing pages, by the laws of nature in the secondary sense of the term is meant the

[17] Munshower vs. The State, 55 Md. 11.

[18] Clough vs. Goggins, 40 Ia. 325.

[19] Sasscer vs. The Farmers Bank, 4 Md. 409; Wilson vs. Van Leer, 127 Pa. St. 378; Donaldson vs. Mississippi, etc., 18 Ia. 291.

established order of antecedent and consequent that prevails throughout the finite universe. Whether in the realm of matter or of finite spirit, in addition to the primary truths of reason that direct the forces of the finite universe, there are certain factual sequences, certain established and orderly methods of operation in both matter and spirit to which the term law has been applied. That the planets revolve around the sun in elliptical orbits, that the earth rotates upon its axis, that bodies of matter attract one another directly as the mass and inversely as the square of the distance between them, that day follows night and summer follows winter, that the tides regularly ebb and flow, that the rivers run to the sea, that water seeks its level, that grass grows from grass seed and corn from corn and rice from rice, that heat radiates in straight lines, that the velocity of sound varies inversely as the square root of the density of the substance, that electricity follows the line of least resistance, that animals have the instinct of self-preservation; and that personal beings, living under both an intellectual and moral order, are morally responsible for their voluntary conduct, and that the feelings of self-respect naturally follow right action and that self-reproach follows low and vicious choices and unlawful behaviour,—this whole phenomenal order is judicially noticed. Without legal proof the courts render their decisions in the light of these notorious facts. The court no more requires proof of these so-called laws of nature than it does of the constitution and the general statutes of the state under which the court is operating. These common operations or laws of nature are frequently recognized and given effect in the trial of actual causes. In a certain case where the defendant had been accused of burglary and the question arose as to when the sun set upon that particular day the court said, "the time of the rising and the setting of the sun on any given day belongs to a class of facts like the succession of the seasons, changes of the moon, days of the month and week, etc., of which courts will take judicial notice."[20]

[20] State vs. Morris, 47 Conn. 179.

The natural law of the tides, their ebb and flow, is one of the generalized facts, which the court judicially notices. Where a libel was filed against the steamboat Planter, the court in trying the case felt authorized to judicially notice the situation of New Orleans for the purpose of determining whether the tide ebbs and flows as high up the river as that place; and was satisfied that, although the current of the Mississippi at New Orleans may be so strong as not to be turned backward by the tide, yet the effect of the tide upon the current is so great as to occasion a regular rise and fall of the water.[21] The court takes notice that the bay of New York is within the ebb and flow of the tide, and it judicially notices the fact that the tide did not ebb and flow within the range of a voyage made by a certain ship upon the Missouri River.

The courts judicially notice the "course of the seasons," the law of maturing crops, or the "general course of agriculture,"[22] the "operation and effect of natural forces,"[23] scientific principles, as the magnetic variation from the true meridian,[24] concerning which the court says it must take judicial notice as truly as it would of the law of gravitation, the descent of waters, the diurnal revolution of the earth, or the change of seasons. And the phenomena of vegetable and animal life generally are judicially noticed, so far, at least, as such phenomena are commonly known, as for instance, the regular period of gestation, as illustrated in the case where the court will take judicial cognizance of the fact that a child, born fourteen days after the first meeting of the mother and reputed father, could not possibly be his child.[25]

Laws of the Human Mind.

The courts also judicially notice the constitution and laws of the human mind as well as the constitution and laws of the material world and of impersonal beings. That

[21] Peyroux vs. Howard, and Varion, 7 Pet. 324.

[22] Ross vs. Boswell, 60 Ind. 235; Floyd et al vs. Ricks, 14 Ark. 286.

[23] Ware vs. Chew, 43 N. J. Eq. 493.

[24] Bryan vs. Beckley, 16 Ky. 91.

[25] King vs. Luffe, 8 East. 202.

the human mind possesses the constitutional powers of thinking, feeling and willing, requires no proof; nor does the fact that the intellectual power of mind is regulated by certain laws of thought, that there are certain uniform sequences of mental phenomena, as that self-approval follows a right choice and self-condemnation a wrong one, that the feeling of anger is aroused by unprovoked insult and abuse, that the will is free to choose obedience or disobedience to law and that a feeling of moral responsibility attaches to such choices, and further that there is in man an instinctive impulse which prompts him to self-defense when either his life is threatened or his safety is jeopardized. That laughter follows joy, and mourning grief, that fear follows threatened destruction, and pain physical torture need not be proved in any court of law. All these phenomena are uniform and, with many others, constitute the phenomenal order of the mental and moral world, and, being obvious to the common apprehension of mankind, are a "part of the law of the land," in the sense that they are recognized by the courts, and given effect without proof, the same as the constitution and general laws of the state are judicially noticed without evidence of their existence. When it is said that the courts notice the "order of nature," (*lex spectat ordinem naturae*), the meaning is that they notice the material order, the intellectual order, the emotional order, the moral order, and the constitutional instincts of animal life. All these systems of order are pre-supposed, judicially noticed, and, when occasion demands, they are given effect in the administration of human law.

The intellectual and moral order of the human mind is recognized by the courts in all those cases where they indulge the presumption of sanity. It is a presumption of human law that all men are of sound mind,—that the phenomenal order of the intellect, feelings and voluntary power are normal or undisturbed. In order to overcome this presumption of law, and shield a defendant from legal responsibility, the burden is on him to prove, to the satisfaction of the jury, by a preponderance of the whole evidence in the case, that at the time of committing a homicide, for instance, he was not of sound mind. "The law infers from the fact that a prisoner is a human being, * * * the further fact that he is a reasonable being, that is, that he is of sane mind, * * * and proof of the former fact is sufficient evidence of the latter, until the latter is disproved by a preponderance of evidence."[26]

The further fact that human choices are ever attended by motives and that motives influence the will's determination, is a mental law requiring constant judicial recognition. As nearly as possible in the application of legal principles to the conflicting interests of mankind, the judge and jurors should be free from bias. The will should be uninfluenced by affections or antipathies. The will "should hang in equal poise," so far as that may be possible: consequently we find abundant rules of court or legislation intended to secure this unbiased condition of mind as respects courts and jurors. A juror will be deemed disqualified from serving as such when it appears that he is a near relative of one of the parties, or "is under the power of either party or in his employment," or if he is to receive "part of a fine upon conviction," or if there are "actions pending between the juryman and one of the parties," which imply hostility or if the "juror have a pecuniary interest in the result of the cause." Perfect mental equilibrium it may be impossible to find in fact, but to guard against bias upon the part of those who hold the property interests, the liberties, and the lives of their fellowmen in their keeping is the constant effort of the courts. The courts judicially notice the mental constitution of man, and a judge or juror biased against either party in a cause, is not properly allowed to sit upon the bench or in the jury box.

So the laws of the human mind, no less than the laws of physical nature, are judicially noticed by the court. That men act from motives, that there must be an intent

[26] Commonwealth vs. Eddy, 7 Gray, 583.

in the committal of crime, that men possess conscience and know the difference between right and wrong are facts judicially noticed; in short, the courts take judicial notice of the constitution and laws of the human mind, just as truly as they recognize the laws and constitution of the material universe. Having occasion to discuss this point, Judge Christiancy said: "The laws of nature and of the human mind, at least such of them as are obvious to the common apprehension of mankind, as well as the more obvious dictates of common sense and principles of human action—which are assumed as truths in any process of reasoning by the mass of sane minds—constitute a part of the laws of the land, and may and must be assumed by the court without being found by the jury; indeed the finding of a jury which should clearly disregard them, should itself be disregarded by the court. In other words the courts are bound judicially to know and apply such laws and principles as part of the law of the land." [27]

The courts judicially recognize the laws of memory. "Constant repetition," is said to be the "first law of memory," so that a person who cannot read or write, and must therefore carry the details of his business affairs in his mind, recalling them from time to time, instead of consulting a book where they may have been recorded, has a more retentive and ready memory than those persons who commit to paper the record of their business transactions. In considering this point, the court in a recent case has said: "We take judicial notice of the fact that persons who are engaged in business and cannot read and write have their faculty of memory more acutely educated for the reason that they are compelled to depend upon their memory, and cannot rely upon written memoranda. The fact that this woman could not read or write would, according to common experience, tend to create in her a more accurate and retentive memory because it would be upon that faculty that she must rely in the conduct of her affairs." [28]

[27] L. S. & M. S. vs. Miller, 25 Mich. 291.

[28] People vs. Martin, 32 N. Y. Sup. 941.

Such are a few of the judicial utterances which claim that the eternal principles of reason, the generalized facts and orderly sequences of mind and matter, are a part of the law to which courts give effect in their administration of justice.

SUBJECTIVE JUSTICE.

The distinction of subjective and objective justice is important for the reason that the science of jurisprudence deals primarily and most exclusively with objective justice. Human law deals with overt acts, with outward conduct, not with inward states of mind. A may choose to murder B, and have his will fully set to that purpose, but so long as he does no outward act whatever, human law takes no jurisdiction over his immoral mental state or purpose. Simply because A hates B, is no ground for equity to interfere and issue an injunction restraining him from hating his neighbor. We are commanded to love our neighbor, but a court of law would not issue a writ of mandamus to compel it. In other words human courts do not concern themselves with mental states unconnected with any outward conduct. As a general rule it may be said that courts concern themselves only with outward actions, not with inward thoughts and purposes —however immoral they may be. And yet, we must notice the fact, that, as moral principles are so inseparable from outward actions, sometimes the inward moral purpose or motive prompting an outward act, will determine the legality or illegality of that act.

For example, there is a certain group of cases wherein the courts regard an act legally right or legally wrong according as the motive prompting the act was morally right or morally wrong. The ethical character of the motive in such cases determines the legal character of the conduct. If the motive of the defendant was morally right, then no cause of action exists; but if morally wrong, then his conduct is held to be actionable. In this class of cases, if the defendant was actuated by the immoral and unworthy motive or purpose simply to injure and harm the plaintiff, his injurious and harmful conduct will be regarded and treated by the courts as unlawful, and such damages as plaintiff may have suffered from such conduct would be awarded him. If, for example, the defendant should place poison in his barn for the purpose of killing rats that were infesting his premises, and his neighbor's dog, while trespassing there, should eat the poison and die as a consequence, the defendant would have done no moral wrong, and his conduct would be legal and so treated by the courts; but, if, on the other hand, he had placed the poison there for the sole purpose and with the intent to kill his neighbor's dog, and thereby injure the plaintiff, and succeeded in so doing, then his conduct being immoral would also be unlawful, and he would be legally liable in damages.

Again it has been held that where an insurance company issued a policy upon the life of A in favor of B, and X killed A, so that the company was compelled to pay the amount of the policy to B, no action for damages by the insurance company would lie against X, but on the other hand, if X had killed A, for the purpose of inflicting this injury upon the company, then, and in that case, an action by the insurance company against X for damages would lie. Here the purpose, or motive of the wrong doer, being immoral, makes the action of the wrong doer unlawful.

So it was held in England[29] that the plaintiff, an innocent man, who had been subjected to a criminal prosecution for theft, had no action for damages against the defendant for publishing all the criminal proceedings in his newspaper because he acted from a sense of public duty to bring the supposed criminal to justice. But if, on the other hand, the defendant had published the proceedings for the purpose, and from the motive to inflict injury and disgrace upon the plaintiff, then an action for damages would lie against the wrong doer. The moral character of the plaintiff's motive would determine the legal character of his action.

[29] Stevens vs. Sampson 5 Ex. Div. 53.

Again in Illinois[30] an insurance company contracted with a manufacturer to indemnify him against liability for the claims of employees, for injury sustained while in his employment. The plaintiff, one of the employees, got injured and the insurance company recognizing its liability, disputed the amount of his claim, and threatened to have him discharged by the manufacturer unless he would take a lesser sum which the company offered in full satisfaction of his claim. The plaintiff refused to yield to this demand, and the insurance company induced the manufacturer to discharge the injured employee, and threatened to cancel the policy unless he was discharged. The plaintiff brought an action for damages against the insurance company for injury sustained on account of this discharge, and in concluding its opinion the court said:

"We therefore conclude, both upon reason and authority, that where a third party induces an employer to discharge his employee who is working under a contract terminable at will, but under which the employment would have continued indefinitely, in accordance with the desire of the employer, except for such interference, and where the only motive moving the third party is a desire to injure the employee and to benefit himself at the expense of the employee by compelling the latter to surrender an alleged cause of action, for the satisfaction of which, in whole or in part, such third party is liable, and where such right of action does not depend upon and is not connected with the continuance of such employment, a cause of action arises in favor of the employee against the third party."

Again, the plaintiff was a hotel keeper, and he was also the assessor of the town, and in the discharge of his duties, as such assessor, he incurred the ill-will of certain citizens who claimed that he had placed too high a valuation upon their property. To retaliate and get even with him, these persons induced certain commercial travelers not to patronize plaintiff's hotel, whereby his business

[30] London Co. vs. Horn, 206 Ill. 493.

was ruined. Plaintiff sued the offenders for damages and recovered, the court finding that the defendants acted from an immoral motive, their actions being wilful and malicious.[31]

We find another class of cases illustrating the same fact, that the ethical quality of a man's motive may determine the legal character of his conduct. In modern days strikes are sometimes declared. And it sometimes happens where certain employees do not like some particular one of their co-employees, they threaten to strike, unless the employer will discharge their unwelcome colaborer. Should the employees insist upon the discharge of one of their number because he has a loathsome disease or other such cause, making him dangerous to them, they would be justified in their action, but on the other hand, if they induce the employer to discharge him because of spite and ill-will toward him, and use their influence to compass his discharge in order to injure him, then their conduct is actionable. An illustrative case to this effect is found in the King's Bench, where in the language of the Lord Justice it is said:

"A combination of two or more persons, without justification, to injure any workman by inducing employers not to employ him or continue to employ him, is, if it results in damage to him, actionable. What is a justification must depend upon the circumstances of the particular case.

"Even if a single individual who, by virtue of his position or influence, has power to carry out his design, sets himself to the task of preventing, and succeeds in preventing, a man from obtaining or holding employment in his calling, to his injury, by reason of threats to or special influence upon the man's employers, and the design was to carry out some spite against the man, or had for its object the compelling him to pay a debt, or any similar object not justifying the acts against the man, then that individual is liable to the man for the damage consequently suffered."[32]

31 Webb vs. Drake, 52 La. An. 290.
32 Giblan vs. Nat. Union, 2 K. B. 600 (1903).

Now, in all these cases the outward act of the defendant was performed in order to injure the plaintiff, not to help him, in order to harm him, not to serve him; in order to lessen his neighbor's welfare, not to promote it. He was not loving his neighbor by helpful deeds, but he was hating his neighbor by harmful deeds, and such harmful deeds, say the courts, shall be legally unlawful, because they are morally unlawful. In other words, what the human law, in this case, is, depends upon what the moral law is. The moral law forbids such conduct prompted by such a motive, so the human law shall forbid it. The human law is therefore based upon the moral law by judicial declaration.

Again, there is another group of cases where the courts themselves feel called upon to read exceptions into a statute where its strict enforcement would shock the moral sense of mankind. There are two especially tragic cases, where the violation of the moral law led the court to declare exceptions to the clearest language of a human statute.

A certain testator made his will, leaving small legacies to two of his daughters, and the remainder of his estate to his grandson, a lad 16 years of age. The boy being aware of this provision in his grandfather's will, and in order to prevent his grandfather from revoking the provision, which he had manifested some intention to do, and to obtain the speedy enjoyment and immediate possession of his property, wilfully murdered his grandfather by poisoning him. After the death of the testator the daughters, who were legatees, prayed the court to cancel and annul the will so far as it bequeathed property to the murderer, upon the ground that he was estopped to take under the will by his own immoral conduct. That is, this residuary legatee had violated the moral law, "thou shalt not kill," in order that he might obtain legal rights to certain property, and in deciding the question as to whether he could do so under the will, according to the clear provisions of the law of the state, the court said:

"Where, therefore, a beneficiary under a will, in order

that he might prevent revocation of the provision in his favor, and to obtain the speedy enjoyment and possession of the property, wilfully murdered the testator, *held* that such beneficiary, by reason of the crime committed by him, was deprived of any interest in the estate left by his victim, and so was not entitled to the property either as donee under the will or as heir or next of kin; and that an action was maintainable to cancel said provisions.

"All laws, as well as all contracts, may be controlled in their operation and effect by these general fundamental maxims of the common law, viz: No one shall be permitted to profit by his own fraud, to take advantage of his own wrong, to found any claim upon his own iniquity or to acquire property by his own crime."[33]

This decision is reached upon the ground that a thing which is within the letter of a statute, is not within the spirit and scope of the statute, unless it is within the intention of the lawmakers; and the court says that it could not have been the intention of the legislators to allow a legatee to take property under the will of a testator whom he had murdered.

Again, one Hunter had procured an insurance policy upon the life of another person, payable by assignment to himself, upon the death of the insured, and then killed the insured in order to get the money under the policy. In deciding this case, in an action to recover the money from the insurance company, Justice Field for the Supreme Court of the United States, said:

"Independently of any proof of the motives of Hunter, in obtaining the policy, and even assuming that they were just and proper, he forfeited all rights under it when, to secure its immediate payment, he murdered the assured. It would be a reproach to the jurisprudence of the country if one could recover insurance money payable on the death of a party whose life he had feloniously taken. As well might he recover insurance money upon a building that he had wilfully fired."

Under the civil law of Rome, evolved from the natural

[33] Riggs vs. Palmer, 115 N. Y. 506.

law of justice, by the juris-consults, philosophers and statesmen of many generations, it was held, "That no man could take property by inheritance or will from an ancestor or benefactor whom he had murdered." (Domat, Part 2, Book 1, Title 1, §3.)

Many of the legal maxims suggested by these cases are but brief statements of the moral law. "No one shall profit by his own wrong, or found any claim upon his own iniquity, or acquire property by his own crime," are recognized principles of the common law. They are the announcement of the truth, that no man shall gain a legal right to himself by violating the moral right of another. In all cases where these maxims control the decision, it may be said that the moral law prevails when it comes in conflict with the conventional rules of jurisprudence. In other words, the courts give effect to the moral law in these murder cases just cited. For why in fact is it that the lad who killed his grandfather could not take property under his will? The moral laws says, "Thou shalt not kill." The human law says, when the testator dies the legacy shall go to the legatee. Now according to this rule, if the testator dies a natural death title passes to the boy, but if the boy kills the testator it shall not, because the court itself would read an exception into the statute, making it accord with the demands of justice, or, in other words, with the demands of the moral law.

In these cases, the real law is the moral law; and the courts, taking that as a real rule intended by the legislature, make the statute conform to it. They base the human law upon the moral by construction on the ground that the law-maker intended to do so.

Summary.

Beginning with the fixed and changeless realities that surround us on every side, such as the essential characteristics of matter, and proceeding to that other large body of fundamental realities, known as self-evident truths, we have found that they are unchangeable, imperative, and set immovable limits to the actions of all physical, intellectual, moral, spiritual and social forces. We are all compelled to admit and recognize their controlling influence, and to submit to their imperative demands. Being regulative of power, in that they determine what power can and what it cannot accomplish, and being strictly fundamental, they are not only law in its primary and deepest signification, but they are also authoritative and reign supreme within and throughout the realms of both mind and matter.

Proceeding further we observed, in both personal and impersonal nature, large numbers of generalized facts and orderly sequences to which the term law is usually applied. These facts and sequences compose the phenomenal order in the physical and mental realms. They express the orderly on-going of finite nature. They are contingent rather than necessary truths, and they are law in a secondary sense rather than in the primary sense of that term. Yet relative to man they are to be regarded and reckoned with in determining what is duty and in the pursuit of his purposes in life. In this they are regulative of his action, and being fixed and changeless, so far as the power of man is concerned, they are law in its primary sense in so far as they determine what he can and what he cannot accomplish.

We also found a phenomenal order prevailing in human society, finding its expression in the so-called laws of sociology; and especially those wrought out and formulated in the science of political economy.

The moral law of love or service was emphasized as the all-comprehensive basis of jurisprudence; and the true meaning of rights, liberty and justice was considered as essentially involved in the science of human law and civil government. But while jurisprudence rests primarily upon the moral law, it nevertheless recognizes, and as we have seen from abundant authorities, courts judicially notice and give effect to the universal laws of reason and the phenomenal laws of mind and matter as they become generally known and recognized. Some judges even declare these laws of nature to be "a part of the law of the land."

In the consderation of these fundamental realities and the laws of finite nature amid which we live, we find law in its essential nature to consist in any truth or reality regulative of power, and we have found jurisprudence to chiefly rest upon the all-comprehensive moral law.

CHAPTER IX.

Human Law.

Human law, in its broadest signification, embraces all the rules of action which human beings adopt or enact for the regulation of their conduct. As in the realm of nature the word "law" is applied to the truths of reason, to the general properties of matter, and to the generalized facts and orderly sequences of both mind and material things, so in the sphere of human activity the term "law" is applied indiscriminately to almost every rule of human action whether regulative of the conduct of nations, the conduct of the individual citizens of a state, the conduct of persons associated in other than legal relations,—such as the members of literary clubs, political leagues, college fraternities and other similar voluntary associations; and the term is applied even to those rules of etiquette and fashion which depend entirely for their enforcement upon the power of public opinion; and hence we speak of the laws of nations, the laws of the state, the laws of a religious or political convention, the laws of fashion, and even the laws of whist, of chess, of football, and of the other games of chance and skill.

It is out of this confusion, arising from such indiscriminate use of the term "law," that jurists have been endeavoring, especially since the days of Austin, to bring order and system by assigning to the various rules of action some distinguishing term, such as "positive law," to those rules of conduct which are enforced by judicial authority, "international morality" to those rules regulating the conduct of one state or nation toward another; "imperfect laws," or "laws of imperfect obligation," as those which are without a sanction, and hence not enforcible by the courts of the land, "customary laws," being such as had their origin in the customs of society and became binding by subsequent judicial enforcement, "Divine laws," being those commands given by God to his human creatures, and so on throughout the entire list of those rules or precepts which are observed by rational beings as regulative of their external behaviour. But no jurist has, as yet, been successful in classifying human laws so perfectly, and naming them so appropriately, that succeeding writers have felt disposed to adopt his classification and nomenclature as final, or even as reasonably satisfactory in all their particulars. The subject of human law, however, is not peculiar in this respect: the same is true of the physical and mental sciences; and so long as our knowledge of mental and physical phenomena continues to expand, no finality of classification or perfection of nomenclature can be expected.

As human law, in its broadest possible signification, embraces all the rules of action adopted or enacted by human beings for the regulation of their conduct, it, of course, includes those rules adopted for the discipline or improvement of their mental powers, as well as those adopted or enacted for the regulation of their external behaviour.

In the cultivation and discipline of his mind, the individual adopts and applies various rules calculated to strengthen and quicken its several moral, religious and intellectual powers. In his Meditations, Marcus Aurelius records his rule for the cultivation of virtue, "When thou wishest to delight thyself, think of the virtues of those who live with thee; for instance, the activity of one, and the modesty of another, and the liberality of another, and some other good quality of a fourth. For nothing delights so much as the examples of the virtues, when they are exhibited in the morals of those who live with us and present themselves in abundance as far as possible. Wherefore we must keep them before us." [34] In the writings of the Ephesians there was the precept, "Constantly think of some one of the men of former times who practiced virtue." [35] and even the

[34] Marcus Aurelius, 180, 279. [35] Epictetus, 426.

pagan Epictetus was so profoundly religious that he prescribed the rule, "Think of God more frequently than you breathe," and the further moral precept, "What we ought not to do, we should not even think of doing." In accord with these rules is the injunction of St. Paul, that, whatsoever things are true, honest, just, pure, lovely or of good report, if there be any virtue and if there be any praise, "think on these things." If you would cultivate virtue, concentrate attention upon the good, and not upon the vile, is the precept of both pagan and Christian philosophy. It is a simple rule, prescribing what should and what should not be an object of contemplation.

While the feelings and emotions are not directly under the control of the will, yet indirectly a person can modify and discipline them, as when he declines to give expression to a passion, its excitability and the frequency of its recurrence diminish. In the culture of the feelings, the rule, "Refuse to express a passion and it dies," has been found most effective. The rule simply prescribes a uniform refusal under provocation to express the inflamed feelings, and it finds a terse expression in the precept of Epictetus, "Check your passions that you may not be punished by them." And the rules for mental discipline are also illustrated by that of Cicero which required him at night to mentally recall in order all the more important personal experiences and events of the day, that his memory might thereby become more ready and retentive. This rule simply fixed a definite and appropriate time when Cicero should comply with the requirements of that natural law of mental reproduction, "Frequent repetition is the first law of memory." This is further illustrated by the rule imposed by Agassiz upon his pupils, which required them to fasten their attention exclusively and for a long period of time upon a single object, that they might thereby observe the greatest possible number of facts or details exhibited by it, and that they might at the same time, and by the same process cultivate the mind's power of perception, as upon that process, followed by comparison, abstraction, and generalization, depend those true and accurate concepts, which embody those qualities common to an entire class of objects. "Form accurate concepts," therefore, becomes a rule for the guidance of mental energy.

Rules for the cultivation of the will have also been laid down as "Choose along the line of greatest resistance," and "decide with promptness and act with energy in the less important affairs of life," which rules are calculated to habituate the mind to promptness and vigor in the exercise of its self-determining power.

While these and other similar rules for the regulation of mental conduct do not fall under the popular conception of "law," yet they contain the essential elements of a law in its most fundamental signification. While they are not changeless, like the laws of nature, yet, while they exist as actually regulating rules of action, they are realities regulative of mental power, and they properly fall under the head of "human law," as above defined. It is true that they are self-imposed, capable of violation, subject to exception, modification and repeal, but so are all the laws which humanity has ever adopted or enacted for the regulation of its conduct, whether that conduct be individual, tribal, municipal, or international.

In turning our attention from those rules regulative of mental conduct to those which are designed to control the outward behavior of mankind, we notice first those which are individual in their adoption and application.

There are countless rules designed to regulate the external conduct of human beings, ranging in the extent of their influence and importance from the comparatively insignificant rule of the individual as to his hour for retiring up to the far-reaching and important rules regulating the action of states in their international relations.

Individual Conduct.—It is unnecessary to more than call attention to the numerous rules adopted by individuals for the regulation of that portion of their conduct which is exclusively personal. The different occupations, enterprises, and varying conditions of mankind make it necessary for individuals to adopt rules as to the character and extent of the physical exercise they may take and the time and perhaps the place when and where they will take it; rules fixing the hours for retiring and arising, and also fixing the time when they will begin and discontinue the labors of the day. Under this head of external conduct may properly be placed those rules regulating the personal attire and even the manners of the individual. Like the rules pertaining to mental development and culture, those relating to personal conduct are changeable, subject to numerous exceptions, and often they are of brief duration. But while they continue they are regulative realities, and hence embody the elements of a true law. In neither of these two classes of rules is there any enforceable sanction for their violation, unless the rule has taken on a moral aspect. If, in any instance, the rule is not followed by the individual, the circumstance preventing its application practically establishes an exception; but if the rules adopted for either the mental or physical behavior of the individual are actually calculated to aid in the perfection of his manhood, then a moral tinge is given to them, and conscience applies its sanction in case of their violation.

From these, the least stable, endurable and authoritative rules of individual conduct, we proceed to consider those rules of social conduct which are clothed about with a sanction, either applied by the power of public opinion, or by the power of the persons establishing the rules themselves.

Social Customs.—There is a large body of rules operative in human society, which silently and imperceptibly come into existence but exactly whence no one can tell, yet when they once legislate themselves upon a community, no tyrant was ever more exacting and cruel in his demands.

Of this class of laws, Mr. Austin has given the following account: "A few species of the laws which are set by general opinion have gotten appropriate names. For example, there are laws or rules imposed upon gentlemen by opinions current amongst gentlemen. And these are generally styled the rules of honor, or the laws or law of honor. * * * There are laws or rules imposed upon people of fashion by opinions current in the fashionable world. And these are usually styled the laws set by fashion." * * * "Now a law set or imposed by general opinion is a law improperly so called. It is styled a law or rule by an analogical extension of the term. The fact denoted by the expression is the following: Some indeterminate body or uncertain aggregate of persons regards a kind of conduct with a favorable or unfavorable opinion. In consequence of that sentiment, or the sentiment associated with that opinion, it is likely that they or some of them will be displeased with a party who shall pursue or not pursue conduct of that kind. And, in consequence of that displeasure, it is likely that some party (that party being undetermined) will visit the party provoking it with some evil or another. The body by whose opinion the law is said to be set does not command, either expressly or tacitly. For, since it is not a body precisely determined or certain, it cannot as a body, express or intimate a wish." * * * "It follows from the foregoing reasons, that a so-called law set by general opinion is not a law:—is not armed with a sanction; and does not impose a duty, in the proper acceptation of the expression:—but is closely analogous to a law, in the proper signification of the term."

The chief characteristic of these rules of action is the indeterminate source whence they spring, and also the fact that they generally have no specific sanction attending their violation. These rules have performed an important part in the peace, development and progress of human society. Many of the legal rules now enforced by courts of justice were once rules of this class, and were then attended by no sanction, except the displeasure of those persons affected by their non-observance, but as they became more generally observed they finally assumed the aspect of authoritative commands, and to rudely disobey or ignore them became such an offense against public sentiment that the courts regarded them as equivalent to legal enactments and enforced them as Law. There is, however, a great body of these rules now operative in human society which has never assumed sufficient importance in the estimation of the courts to warrant judicial enforcement, and to this body belong the so-called rules of honor, etiquette, fashion and many others which owe their origin to no known and conscious action of any determinate person or body of persons, and for whose violation no legal redress is obtainable. In certain parts of our country, and it is equally true in some other countries, if a person under particular circumstances challenges another to fight a duel, to decline or ignore the challenge would be looked upon with public disfavor as an act of cowardice, or indicative of a lack of true manliness. The law of honor, or public opinion, commands an acceptance of the challenge and an actual encounter. The person who violates this law suffers in the loss of public esteem, which to a sensitive person is one of the severest penalties that could be inflicted upon him.

There are also the rules of etiquette, which are fixed by the opinion and practice of the public, such as those regulating the salutations exchanged between persons meeting upon the street, in public conveyances and at public gatherings generally; and the rules observed by persons exchanging social calls, and others regulating the hospitality extended to friends or to strangers, and the customs observed at public dinners, social parties, receptions and balls, besides those numerous rules of conduct adopted by civilized people calculated to promote the harmony, civility and pleasure of human intercourse. These rules, adopted in social life, calculated to promote decent behavior, politeness, and good manners, are among the most important and influential laws operative in human society. Though not enforced by judicial decrees, they are nevertheless enforced by public opinion and humanity is unconsciously elevated and refined by this system of unauthoritative legislation.

Uniformity of conduct seems to be the tendency of personal no less than of impersonal nature; while in the latter necessity makes uniformity perfect, in the former freedom makes non-conformity possible. The principle of imitation, so deeply grounded in human nature, tends toward and insures a large degree of uniformity of human action. This principle imbedded in man's nature not only results in uniform usages and rules of social and uniform behavior in the various classes or communities of human beings; but it manifests itself quite as perceptibly in the uniformity of dress which public opinion most imperatively commands. A general uniformity in the style of dress and of personal adornments is prevalent wherever humanity exists. "Fashion in the distant wilds of Africa tortures and harasses poor humanity as much as in the great prison of civilization."[36]

National costumes are as characteristic as national systems of jurisprudence. Fashion fixes the style of dress within her jurisdiction as rigidly as the legislature fixes the rules for levying and collecting taxes within the scope of its authority, and the changes in one of these systems of law is quite as frequent as those in the other. The style of hat, the cut of the dress or coat, and the form of the shoe are not matters generally left to the choice of the individual, but they are determined by the decree of fashion, and compliance with that decree is enforced by a relentless infliction upon the offender of that peculiar discomfort which one experiences when confronting the chilly displeasure of the public, or when conscious of his own noticeable singularity.

These rules regarding dress extend from the poorest classes of society in some obscure province up to the diplomatic circles and royal courts of sovereign states.

The rules of etiquette and of fashion prevalent in royal circles form an interesting chapter in the history of any

[36] Fowler, Fashion in Deformity, p. 26.

civilized nation; and the persistency with which compliance with these rules is demanded is forcefully illustrated by the unpleasant consequences attending the attempt of Mr. Marcy, the Secretary of State under President Pierce, to have the representatives of the Republic appear at foreign courts in the simple dress of an American citizen. When Jackson became president, the diplomatic costume "informally or officially recommended, was a blue coat, lined with white silk; straight standing cape embroidered with gold; buttons plain, or if they can be had, with the Artillerist's eagle stamped upon them, cuffs embroidered in the manner of the cape, white cassimer breeches, gold knee-buckles, white silk stockings, and gold or gilt shoe buckles. A three cornered *chapeau bras,* a black cockade to which an eagle has been attached, a sword, etc." President Jackson recommended certain changes whereby the dress became more conformable to the simplicity of American institutions, but Mr. Marcy undertook to introduce into royal courts abroad an exception to their antique costumes and rules by requesting that the United States be represented there in the unostentatious attire of an American citizen. This breach of the unwritten law of royal custom was visited with manifest displeasure by Foreign Royalty, and even in England the public press denounced the innovation as due to General Pierce's republican ill-manners and to American puppyism."

These rules of etiquette and fashion, so exacting in their demands, are regulative of human conduct, leading to uniformity of external action and similarity of personal attire. Indeed they have the essential elements of a law in its primary significance. They are realities, fixed for the time being, and regulative of human power, in that they determine what man may and what he may not safely do. He is at liberty to obey and meets no opposition in obeying, but he is not at liberty to disobey them without the opposing power of public sentiment.

Conventional Rules.—In addition to the foregoing rules regulative of personal and social conduct, there are certain others originating with some determinate person or body of persons, and which, in addition to the sanction of public displeasure, have other sanctions enforceable by other than judicial authority. Belonging to this class are the rules established for the government of the family, for the government of tribes and clans, for the government of schools, universities, churches, literary societies, political, religious and other similar clubs, leagues, or voluntary associations, and even the established rules by which are played the games of chance and skill.

In these and many other similar instances, the rules originate with some particular and determinate person or persons, as with the parents in case of family government, with the chief or council in case of tribal government, and with the teacher or some governing board in the case of schools and churches. In all the instances of this class the regulative principles or rules spring from a definite source, and besides that they usually have some definite sanction attending thir violation, as that which parents and teachers may inflict; expulsion from membership of him who violates the rules of any club, league or other association, and the forfeits incident to the one who violates rules of the various games of chance. A fine of a few pennies is often inflicted by its rules upon him who neglects to return a book to a public library.

This class of regulative principles, springing from non-legal sources, is one of vast importance in the progress and development of human society. Illustrations of this class of rules are so numerous and easily called to mind that a further enumeration of them is not necessary. In no instance is the sanction attending their violation enforced by the courts of justice. If it were, then the rule itself, by the very act of judicial enforcement, would be transformed into a municipal or positive law. By the act of judicial enforcement it would be elevated from the great class of conventional rules of personal conduct and placed among the positive rules of Jurisprudence.

In these rules also are discovered the prime essentials of law in its primary meaning. They are realities fixed and established, though subject to change, violation, and even repeal, but during their existence they regulate man's power in the sense that they determine what he ought or ought not to do.

Had all these rules of action hereinbefore enumerated and adopted by man for the regulation of his conduct been denominated "rules" instead of "laws," and had the distinction been always observed by writers upon jurisprudence, clearness of thought would have been greatly subserved. But as the words "rules," "principles," and "laws" have been used indiscriminately by writers and speakers upon the subject, it has best subserved my purpose to regard the word "law" as generic, with the following species, "rules regulative of mental conduct," "rules regulative of external individual conduct," "social customs," "conventional rules" and "legal rules." Having considered the others, we will now consider the remaining species, "legal rules," or law in its legal sense.

Legal Rules.

Jurisprudence is the science of positive law, and positive law embraces all the rules of external human conduct enforcible by state authority, whether through the agency of the courts of justice, the military force, or other agency directed by the state. Whatever rule the state rightfully enforces, be it a principle of the common law, a statutory requirement, a constitutional provision, or a rule agreed upon by the civilized nations of the earth as regulative of their conduct toward one another, that rule, principle, or provision may be properly accorded a place under the general head of Positive Law. All such rules and provisions are either enacted or adopted by man for the regulation of human conduct either individual or national, and the state in one way or another undertakes to maintain and enforce those rules, or inflict punishment for their violation.

In its legal sense, "law" has been variously defined. Blackstone says that law, in its most general and comprehensive sense, "is that rule of action which is prescribed by some superior and which the inferior is bound to obey."[37] And civil law he defines as "a rule of civil conduct prescribed by the supreme power in a state, commanding what is right and prohibiting what is wrong."[38] Not satisfied with this definition, Austin says that "Law, in the literal and proper sense of the word, may be defined as a rule laid down for the guidance of an intelligent being by an intelligent being having power over him."[39] And positive law, he continues, is one "set by a sovereign person or a sovereign body of persons, to a member or members of the independent political society wherein that person or body is sovereign or supreme. In other words, it is set by a monarch or sovereign member, to a person or persons in a state of subjection to its author."[40] Neither of these definitions has satisfied the critical demands of more recent jurists, and the result has been that the numerous writers upon jurisprudence have multiplied definitions of law in general and of civil, or positive law, in particular, to an almost interminable extent.[41]

It will be observed in the foregoing definitions, that the *source* of law has been emphasized. In order to be a law, the rule of action, according to Blackstone, must be prescribed by some superior, and according to Austin it must be set by some sovereign to operate upon a person in a state of subjection. Educated under a monarchical form of government, it was natural for these learned authors to regard the sovereign as the supreme source of civil or positive law, as God was regarded as the author of natural law. The analogy was striking and plausible; and as the civil law had, as a matter of fact, been "prescribed," or "set," as a general thing, by a recognized sovereign to persons of admitted inferiority, the theory that all rules of action, in order to be binding

[37] Blk. Vol. 1 §38.
[38] Blk. Vol. 1, §44.
[39] Austin, Vol. 1, §2.
[40] Austin, Vol. 1, §189. 138.
[41] For a recent answer to the question, "What is Law," see "Law, its Origin, Nature and Function," by Carter, p. 14. Andrews Am. Law, 50 and 60.

upon inferiors, must emanate from some superior source, was the one which most closely accorded with the facts then known or existing.

But Austin, at least, recognized the insufficiency or inaccuracy of his own definition, and he enumerated certain laws, properly included within the province of jurisprudence, but which could not be regarded as the "commands" of a superior addressed to an inferior person. Among them were "the laws explaining the import of existing positive laws, and the laws abrogating or repealing existing positive law."[42] Nor can those laws which have arisen out of the customs of the people be properly said to have been "prescribed" by some superior for the control of an inferior, who is bound to obey, as must be the case according to the definition of Blackstone. Consequently modern jurists have not accepted the teachings of either Blackstone, Austin, or others, who like them have found the distinguishing characteristic of civil law in the superiority of those who may have "prescribed" or enacted it.

Among those who have justly criticised those definitions is Judge John F. Dillon, who says, "I cannot, after much reflection, but regard this definition (Blackstone's) as both inadequate and incorrect. To make it cover the actual body of the whole civil law of a state, the word "prescribe" and the word "command," here used, must be given an elasticity of meaning or an artificial meaning, not consonant with the general or appropriate use of these words.

"Austin's definition of law is equally defective, and the same criticism applies. 'Law,' according to Austin, is the aggregate of rules set by men as 'politically superior or sovereign to men as politically subject.'

"The definitions of Blackstone and Austin are apt and accurate as applied to the great body of what we call ordained, or enacted law of a state. But there is a large body of law to which the term 'rules prescribed,' or 'commands,' or 'rules set,' by a sovereign do not apply,

[42] Austin, Vol. 1, §37.

except by subjecting these words to a strain which alters or greatly expands their proper meaning.''[43]

A further difficulty with these definitions is found in the fact that they both exclude from the strict province of jurisprudence ''International Law.'' The law of nations comprises those rules of conduct which sovereign states agree to observe in their intercourse and relations with one another.

Certainly it cannot be properly said that these rules are ''prescribed'' by a superior power which an inferior power is bound to obey, nor can it be said that such rules are set by a sovereign power to a person or persons in a state of subjection. These rules of international conduct are adopted by free, equal and independent sovereign states—not politically superior or inferior; nor are they ''prescribed'' by one state for the guidance and control of another.

Austin recognized and acknowledged the fact that ''International Law,'' under his definition, could not be regarded as law, in the strict sense of the term; hence he designates those rules ''International Morality.''

Of such narrow and evidently inaccurate definitions of civil law, Sir Frederick Pollock has said, ''If therefore, we find that our definition of law does not include the law of nations, the proper conclusion is, not that there is no such thing as a law of nations, and that we are to talk pedantically of positive international morality, but that our definition is inadequate.''[44]

It will also be observed that constitutional law, and especially that of the United States, and others adopted by the people of a country, cannot be regarded as law within the restricted definitions of Blackstone and Austin, because such constitutions are not ''prescribed'' or ''set'' by a superior power for the control of inferior subjects. Such constitutions are adopted by the sovereign people for their own control and guidance, quite as much as for the control and guidance of those persons

[43] Laws and Juris. of Eng. and Am. Dillon, page 10.

[44] Oxford Lectures, page 19.

who compose the government under such constitutions. The people, the executives, the legislators, the judges, are all equally amendable to constitutional provisions.

In this instance Austin was obliged, as in the case of international law, to deny the dignified name of law to constitutional provisions, and to designate that body of rules "constitutional morality."[45] By holding tenaciously to his primary definition Austin was obliged to exclude from the realm of positive law that vast body of constitutional provisions, which constitute so important a part of modern jurisprudence. Had he written his work in the last quarter of the nineteenth century, in all probability he would have based his system of general jurisprudence upon a less restricted definition. To exclude international and constitutional law from the realm of positive jurisprudence at the present time would give to any system of law a one-sided, defective and faulty appearance.

It shows, however, that our definitions in the realm of jurisprudence, as elsewhere in scientific investigation, must be revised as new facts make their appearance. Doubt has been expressed as to the possibility in our present state of knowledge of framing a perfect definition of "law."

In his introductory chapter to International Law, William Edward Hall refers to this matter in the following language: "the various ideas of law formed in different societies and times, and the various groups of customs which have been obeyed as law, have not yet been sufficiently compared and analyzed, and until an adequate comparison and analysis have been made no definition or description of law can be regarded as final."

Other and later writers than Blackstone and Austin, recognizing the difficulty, not to say the absurdity of excluding the rules of international conduct from the province of "law" in its legal sense, have so enlarged the scope of their definitions as to properly include them. Thus Prof. E. C. Clark of Cambridge University has de-

45 Austin, Vol. 1, §249.

fined law in its ordinary sense to be "a rule of human conduct sanctioned by human displeasure," and concerning the rules regulating the conduct of states he says, "I maintain that the rules of international conduct, as now actually administered by the general consent and action of civilized nations, constitute a practical law to which it is absurd to deny the name, because it is not enacted or administered by a political superior."[46]

It will be observed that Prof. Clark does not regard it essential that a rule of human conduct in order to be a law must be the "command" of a superior to an inferior, nor that it be enforced by a political superior; but rather that the really essential elements in a law are, First, "a rule of conduct observed among a class of human beings," and Second, that the violation of that rule awakens human disapproval, or as the author says, the rule is "sanctioned by human displeasure." Further elaborating this conception of law he says, "Where there is amongst any body of human beings, however associated with one another, a rule of conduct actually operating upon their wills by virtue of human displeasure, whether that of the association at large, or some part of the association, or of some other human being or beings, people in general would not feel that they were employing any metaphor in calling that rule a law. Formulation, if not imposition, by a political authority is more and more the case with law as it approaches modern times, but it has not been always the case, and it is not essential to the true (that is the commonly received) signification of law in general."[47]

To the same effect Hall, in his introductory chapter to International Law, without defining law in general says, "If the rules known under the name of International Law are linked to the higher examples of typical positive law by specimens of the laws of organized communities, imperfectly developed as regards their sanction, the weakness and indeterminateness of the sanction of international law cannot be an absolute bar to its admission as

[46] Practical Juris., page 187.

[47] Practical Juris., p. 134.

law; and if there is no such bar the facts that international rules are cast in a legal mould, and are invariably treated in practice as being legal in character necessarily become the considerations of most importance in determining their true place. That they lie on the extreme frontier of law is not to be denied, but on the whole it would seem to be more correct as it is certainly more convenient, to treat them as being a branch of law than to include them within the sphere of morals."[48]

While Prof. Clark's description of human law as "a rule of human conduct sanctioned by human displeasure" disregards both the determinateness of its origin and the authority by which it is enforced, it seems nevertheless to embrace the essential elements of law in a general sense; yet, when we come to regard that species of human law known as legal rules, we find that they are characterized by the fact that they are enforcible in some manner by the state, or that their violation awakens the resentment of the state whose law is broken, or in case of international law the resentment of the state at least which is offended against. So the same learned writer says that "the law of a state is the aggregate of rules administered mediately or immediately by the state's supreme authority." And of those rules regulative of national conduct he says, "I maintain that the rules of international conduct, as now actually administered by the general consent and action of civilized nations, constitute a practical law, to which it is absurd to deny the name because it is not enacted by a political superior."[49]

This author would therefore give the name "law" to those rules of conduct, which obtain between the members of the same state, and which are "administered by the state's supreme authority;" and also to those rules which obtain between the states themselves, and are "administered by the action of civilized nations." And there is no sufficient reason why the name law should be applied to the rules regulative of individual action, but denied to those rules regulative of state action. In the

48 International Law, p. 17.

49 Practical Jurisprudence 172, 186.

former instance the rules regulate the conduct of individual persons, and in the latter instance, they regulate sovereign aggregations of persons.

It is true, to be sure, that in ancient days customs had the force and effect of law before the courts actually declared them to be law. It is contended by some that these customs must have been law, otherwise the courts could not have enforced them without performing the odious act of judicial legislation. However this may be, it is true that until a rule of action is recognized by a court, as binding upon individuals, or recognized by civilized nations as binding upon them, and its violations punishable by state authority in the usual methods adopted by injured states, that rule is not properly regarded as a part of the positive law. It may have the effect of law upon the action of persons, it may supply a sufficient motive to induce men to act in accordance with its demands; but obedience is secured to its demands by moral or prudential reasons alone, for until the state actually undertakes to enforce it, or actually asserts its right or purpose so to do, no one can be certain that any state enforcement will ever be undertaken. Such rules of action or customs may be law in the making; but the actual enforcement of such rules, the assertion of the right and purpose by the state in some form to enforce them is necessary to complete the process and convert the customs into a part of the positive law of the land.

Positive law then may be defined as "a rule of external human action, enforcible by state authority." This definition embraces municipal law, including the written and unwritten constitutions of states; and it also embraces the provisions of International Law for they are often enforced by authority of the state which has been offended by its violation; and not infrequently enforced or given effect by the established courts of the land. While in case of municipal or civil law, there is an arbiter or court that enforces the rights of the respective parties; in controversies between states themselves there is no such arbiter or Court, but the injured state asserts its rights and inflicts such penalty as the conditions and circumstances of the case may require or permit. In any event the sanction, whatever it may be in any given instance, is administered by state authority.

The true test of a "law" in the legal sense of the term, is not found in the source whence it originates; but rather in the character of the power which enforces it. The power that enforces rather than the power that originates, determines what rules of human conduct shall be elevated to the dignity of positive law. Some of those rules may have their origin in the moral constitution of man, such as those forbidding murder or theft. Some of them may arise from the customs of the people such as the laws regarding primogeniture and conveyance of land by deed. Some of them may have been enacted by the sovereign power of a state, and still others may have been adopted by sovereign states as rules regulative of their conduct toward one another; but whatever the origin of the rule, unless the state in one form or another undertakes to enforce it, or claims the right to do so, the rule cannot be regarded as a law in the legal sense of the term. But when the state does rightfully administer it, then such rule is a part of the great body of positive law, and must be considered in discussing the subject of jurisprudence.

When legal rules are violated, when law in its legal sense is broken, some state, in its capacity as a state, has occasion to act. It may exert its power through the executive, as in case of removal of an official for malfeasance in office, or through the legislature as when a corporate charter is repealed for an abuse of the franchise granted thereunder, or through the courts in the ordinary methods of inflicting fines, or awarding damages in cases where the criminal or civil law has been violated, or still further by a sovereign state in declaring war, or enacting retaliatory measures against another state that has improperly or wrongfully violated some established provision of international law. In every case, where a legal rule, a law in its legal sense, is broken, the State in one method or another may be called upon to set in operation its sovereign power. Such infraction of law furnishes a legal occasion for the state to act. In accordance with these facts, a law in its legal sense may be defined as "a rule of external human action, enforcible by state authority."

As to whether the rules of International Law should be regarded as belonging to Jurisprudence or to the realm of morals, there has been much discussion. The following quotations are instructive:

"Is it well at this stage of our English legal history to refuse the name Law to the rules which regulate the mutual dealings of States?

"To confine the term Law to the commands of determinate human authority, to commands enforced by determinate sanctions, would doubtless facilitate the framing of a formally faultless Science of Jurisprudence. But, on the other hand, to deny to any rule the name of Law, on whatever ground, would be in the popular mind to deprive it of all that peculiar halo of respectful reverence which has undoubtedly attached to the term in the passing of the ages. Either a rule governing human conduct is law or it is not; if it is not law, it is not binding. So argues the average man, 'the man in the street,' and it is useless to talk to him of the obligation of morality, more particularly if he be taught that the test of morality is utility. The popular mind, as Austin's master, Jeremy Benthem, saw, does not draw fine distinctions. Were it not for its deleterious practical consequences we might be content to leave the great logical precisian in the undisturbed enjoyment of his logic and his verbal purism, but, if the choice must indeed be made, rather let us seek out some other unoccupied route to a legal scientific perfection than, by claiming as private a hitherto public high road, block the way of a progressive International Law. Rather let us have peace and peacefulness without the blessings of neat terminology than precise language and therewith the spirit of lawlessness. It is well to have a formally faultless Science of Jurisprudence; it is better to have English-speaking peoples displaying ready obedience to the dictates of Honour, Justice and proved Utility enshrined in the rules as the Law of Nations or International Law." [50]

To the same effect are the following words of Mr. Hall:

"In what has been said up to this point the rules governing the conduct of states have been spoken of as legal rules; it has, therefore, been implied either that they constitute a body of true law, identical in its essential characteristics with law regulating an organized political community, or at least that, if not identical with such law, they are so closely analogous to it as to be more properly described as law than by any other name. It is, however, not uncommonly thought—in England at any rate—that neither of these views is correct. The only fundamental distinction, it is said, which separates legal from moral rules, is that the former are, and the latter are not, commands given and enforced by a determinate authority; both are general precepts relating to overt acts, but in the one case a machinery exists for securing obedience, in the other no more definite sanction can be appealed to than disapprobation on the part of the community or of a section of it. Judged by this test, it is urged the rules of International Law are nothing more than counsels of morality, sanctioned by the public opinion of states.

"That there is an element of truth in this criticism must be frankly admitted. International Law does not conform to the most perfect type of law. It is not wholly identical in character with the greater part of the laws of fully developed societies, and it is even destitute of the mark which strike the eye most readily in them. But it is now fully recognized that the proper scope of the term law transcends the limits of the more perfect examples of law. To what extent it transcends them is not equally certain. The various ideas of law formed in different societies and times, and the various groups of customs which have been obeyed as law, have probably

[50] A history of the Law of Nations, T. A. Walker, Vol. 1, p. 18.

not yet been sufficiently compared and analyzed, and until an adequate comparison and analysis have been made, no definition or description of law can be regarded as final. During the continuance of this state of uncertainty as to the proper limits of law, it is impossible, in dealing with International Law to ignore the two broad facts, that it is habitually treated as law, and that a certain part of what is at present acknowledged to be law is indistinguishable in character from it." [51] To the same effect are the words of Mr. Pollock: [52]

"There is another branch of legal science of which I have as yet said nothing, and which stands by itself; I mean that which deals with existing or possible relations not between citizens of the same State but between independent States. International Law is a true branch of jurisprudence, notwithstanding all that may be said about its want of sovereign power and a tribunal. You may define it as 'positive international morality' not having the nature of true law, but if you do, the facts are against you. For what are the facts?

"1. The doctrines of International Law are founded on legal not simply on ethical ideas. They are not merely prevalent opinions as to what is morally right and proper, but something as closely analogous to civil laws as the nature of the case will admit. They purport to be rules of strict justice, not counsels of perfection.

"2. Since they assumed a coherent shape they have been the special study of men of law, and have been discussed by the methods appropriate to jurisprudence, and not those of moral philosophy.

"3. There is also a practical test, and a conclusive one. If international law were only a kind of morality, the framers of State papers concerning foreign policy would throw all their strength on moral argument. But as a matter of fact this is not what they do. They appeal not to the general feeling of moral rightness, but to precedents, to treaties, and to opinions of specialists. They assume the existence among statesmen and publicists of

[51] W. E. Hall, International Law, page 14.
[52] Pollock Sir F., Oxford Lect., 18.

a sense of legal as distinguished from moral obligation in the affairs of nations.

"4. Further, there is actually an international morality distinct from and compatible with international law in the usual sense. As a citizen among citizens, so a nation among nations may do things which are discourteous, high-handed, savouring of sharp practice, or otherwise invidious and disliked, and yet within its admitted right and giving no formal ground of complaint. There is a margin of discretionary behaviour which is the province not of claims and despatches but of friendly representatives and 'good offices.' "[53]

It is safe to say that in the opinion of most modern jurists those rules of conduct which regulate the intercourse of civilized nations should be regarded as law in the legal sense of that term. Though there is no separate and distinct court to enforce those rules in their application to an offending individual nation, yet, when violated the offended state through its established government seeks such redress as is generally recognized and sanctioned by civilized nations. These rules of conduct are recognized, maintained and enforced by state authority. If war is declared, or retaliatory legislation enacted, or diplomatic relations discontinued, or any other customary redress sought, it is through the authority of the state that all such sanctions are applied. And any rule of conduct intended to regulate the intercourse of individuals, states, or civilized nations, whose violation is recognized and dealt with by state authority, is a law in its true and legal sense.

[53] Oxford Lectures, etc., Pollock, p. 18.

CHAPTER X.

Divine Law.

As to what constitutes "Divine Law" there has been a great variety of opinions. In the works of James Wilson the author says: "The law of Nature, and the law of Revelation are both Divine; they flow, though in different channels, from the same source. It is indeed preposterous to separate them from each other."[53]

From our foregoing analysis we have observed that "law" in its primary sense consists in the fundamental truths of reason, and that these truths and principles are eternal in the Divine Mind. Being thus constituent elements of the Eternal and Divine Reason, they may, with the strictest propriety be designated "Divine Law." But, as a matter of fact, we find them operative throughout the entire realm of finite nature constituting both laws of things, and laws of thought, and therefore, if we name them from their original source they may be pronounced Divine; while if we name them from the realms wherein we find them operative, they may properly be called "Natural"; and we have considered them in the foregoing pages as "Natural Law." And it may also be said that the generalized facts and orderly sequences which we have observed both in the realms of matter and of finite mind are established through the Divine Intelligence and Power; and hence might be regarded for that reason as Divine. But here, too, if we consider principally the realms wherein these generalized facts and orderly sequences appear, we should regard them as Natural Law, being found operative in the realm of finite nature. Hence we may consider, with reference to their sources, all these laws both primary and secondary, as Divine; and with equal propriety we may say, with reference to the spheres wherein we find them operative that

[53] Wilson's Works, Vol. 1, p. 106.

they are Natural. Thus it becomes largely a matter of choice as to whether we shall declare them to be Divine or Natural. In either event they are of God.

Finally, the laws, "to be found only in the holy scriptures," or the "laws of revelation," to employ Blackstone's words again, are generally called divine. So far as they are the re-announcement of natural law they may be called either divine or natural, for reasons already mentioned; but if the laws of the Hebrews generally, recorded in the Bible, are to be called divine laws because they are conceived as specifically formulated, written out and given to Moses or other Hebrew leaders by the Divine Creator, in a manner altogether peculiar, it is more than questionable whether the word divine should be applied to them. As an example of some of the laws in the scriptures, we have the following: "Ye shall not eat anything that diest of itself; thou mayest give it unto the sojourner that is within thy gates, that he may eat it, or thou mayest sell it to a foreigner." This law sounds very human. In fact it sounds inhuman. The most candid view possible for us to take of it is that it is of human origin, like the code of Hammurabi; the codes of Lycurgus, of Solon, and the ancient Romans. To call such a law divine in the sense that God originated it and imposed it upon the people would be to shock our faith in God's impartial love.

The view is coming to prevail that the laws of the ancient Hebrews as found recorded in the Holy Scriptures, came into existence very much in the same manner as the laws of the Assyrians, the Babylonians, the Egyptians, and all the other peoples of the earth, ancient and modern, and came to their end also just as other human laws have become extinct or inoperative.

But it is asked whether the law of love to God and to our neighbor is not peculiarly a divine law, and hence cannot be regarded as natural. We have seen that man's duty to choose God as the Supreme Object of service, and to serve Him with all his mind, and heart, and strength is involved in his moral constitution, or, as we say, the sense of obligation to serve and obey God is a part of man's moral nature. So the obligation man is under, to love his fellow men, in the sense that he should choose them as objects of service is grounded also in his moral constitution, consequently they may both, with strict propriety, be designated natural laws, the same as the laws of thought, of imagination, and of memory are regarded as natural.

The law of love to God and man are involved in the moral order. They are a constituent part of man's moral nature. They are not external commands imposed by arbitrary authority; but they are internal commands written upon the heart of man by his Creator; hence, they, too, like the laws of the physical universe, may be called divine laws as given by the Divine Ruler, or they may be regarded as natural laws, operating as they do, in the sphere of man's moral nature.

In the foregoing chapters we have classified them as "Natural Laws," but with the conviction that they, like all other laws considered, except the rules of human origin, may be as properly regarded as Divine.

CHAPTER XI.

General Summary and Conclusion.

That we live in a Universe subject to unchanging law has been assumed by the most thoughtful minds from the earliest times. There seems to be an instinctive belief in the human mind, that, behind the ever changing phenomena of the finite universe, there exists some changeless and regulative principle. To the changeless and controlling principles, and to the ever changing phenomena, general facts, forces, hypotheses and uniformities of nature the name *law* has been given indiscriminately. This name has also been given to the rules of human conduct, and there have been accorded to it attributes of power, intelligence, royalty, and even it has often been spoken of as an actual entity possessed of creative energy. The ancients referred to law as the King of Kings: they also spoke of it as an eternal principle that governed the Universe, and even in modern days it has been apparently regarded as a controlling entity exercising dominion over mind and matter. We are bewildered by the conflicting senses in which the word is employed, and embarrassed and confused by its conspicuous and careless use in science, philosophy, ethics, theology and in general literature. This led to our inquiry into the essential nature of law.

The human mind desires to hold all its knowledge in the unity of one grand system, and so we ever find ourselves endeavoring to construct a perfect system or classification of the laws of the universe, both natural and human. The inquiring mind desires also to discover the essence of things, and hence in the realms of law, especially where the word is applied to such numerous and varying conceptions, it becomes a matter of interest and importance to discover, if possible, its real and essential meaning. The idea of fixedness dominates in the general conception of law, so to find the changeless and established truths and facts of the universe seemed to be the first step in discovering the true conception of the term.

In order that we might discover the nature of law in its primary signification, we enumerated among others the following fundamental truths which are regulative of all power. It is self-evident that every beginning or change of being must have a cause; the same complex of causes always produces the same effects; something cannot come from nothing; with finite agents reception must precede production; nothing can both be and not be at the same time; the shortest distance between two points is a straight line; a straight line cannot enclose a portion of space; a thing cannot be in two different places at the same instant; two bodies cannot occupy the same space at the same time; things that are equal to the same thing are equal to each other; there can be no knowledge unless there is some reality to be known; all events must occur in past, present, or future time; no body can exist without occupying space; whatever is predicated of a class of objects may be predicated of all that is contained in that class; there can be no attribute without a substance to which that attribute belongs; there can be no motion without a body to move; and the moral intuitions, that a rational being ought to act rationally; obedience to moral law is right and disobedience is wrong, the product resulting from exact compliance with law must be a perfect product; the product resulting from non-compliance with law must be imperfect; as an engine constructed in exact conformity to every law of mechanics involved in its construction must be a perfect engine, and a moral character constructed in exact compliance with the all-comprehensive law of love must be a perfect character.

These few fundamental truths and inferences are examples of that vast body of primary and regulative realities which are law in the primary and deepest sense of the word. They are primary realities. They are ultimate. We cannot go back of them. The mind rests upon them without uneasiness but in perfect tranquillity. The truth that the shortest distance between two points is a straight line is a final *reality*. We can give no other reason for it than the assertion that *it is*. We cannot go behind the fact. In it we find the ultimate, and so it is with the whole body of primary principles. In the moral realm the truth that man *ought* to choose the right, and *ought not* to choose the wrong expresses a fundamental *reality*. We cannot go back of the fact. It too is ultimate. Conscience apprehends the fact by original insight, and accepts it without question as final. We cannot overemphasize the fact that in the quest for primary law we are looking for ultimate realities. They set the limits to all action. They determine what power can and what it cannot do. They are *law*, and these ultimate principles comprise the first great code of supreme and final authority which we have found operative within and throughout the realms of both matter and mind. This Supreme Constitution of the Universe, as it has been called, fixes the limits for all power. It commands society no less than the individual. It speaks with authority to the legislator, the judge and the executive. It prescribes what physical power may and what it may not do; it announces to the intellect what it can and what it cannot conceive, and it tells the will what it *ought* and what it *ought not* to choose. Its provisions are universal, imperative and changeless. It constitutes that *eternal* law to which Demosthenes and Cicero referred, and to which impassioned orators have ever since referred in their heated efforts to ground their arguments upon an immovable and eternal foundation. Being realities regulative of all power, these truths of reason are law in its primary and truest sense. The power-regulating element is the essential element in *law*.

Besides these regulative and fundamental principles, science has given the name *law* to many general facts and orderly sequences of the finite universe. They are law, however, only in a secondary sense. They are not, like primary truths, regulative of all power, but they are rather the orderly manifestations of power. Force manifests itself uniformly under the same conditions, and to this uniformity of expression the name law has been given. The whole phenomenal order of impersonal nature, embracing the general facts and uniformities of the inorganic, the vegetable and the animal kingdoms, excluding man as a rational being, constitute that great body of natural law so-called with which Science largely concerns itself. In order that we might observe the factual and phenomenal character of these laws so-called, an enumeration of a few of them was made and considered, among which the following were mentioned:

Every planet moves in an elliptical orbit: the radius vector of a planet sweeps over equal areas in equal times: every body continues in its state of rest, or of uniform motion in a straight line, except in so far as it is compelled by force to change that state: to every action there is always an equal and contrary reaction: every particle of matter in the universe attracts every other particle with a force directly proportioned to the mass of the attracting particles, and inversely to the square of the distance between them: in a medium of uniform density light goes in straight lines with a uniform velocity: in passing into a denser medium light is bent toward a perpendicular to the surface at the point of incident: and in passing into a rarer medium light is bent from the perpendicular; the angle of incident is equal to the angle of reflection in case of both light and sound; electricity follows the lines of least resistance: everywhere under the law of the conditioning and the conditioned, the earth precedes and conditions the existence of the roots and trunk of the tree; the trunk in turn conditions the existence of the branches; the branches condition the existence of the buds, the buds precede and condition the flower and the fruitage: in the struggle for existence the fittest survives: in the language of Goethe "in order to spend on one side Nature must economize on the other," to which fact is given the name of the law of Compensation: the use of one's powers enlarges them: the offspring tends to resemble its parent or parents: "man as an individual is capable of indefinite improvement. Society and nations, which are but aggregations of men, and finally the human family or collective humanity are capable of indefinite improvement" is a statement of fact merely, but is given by Charles Sumner as the Law of Human Progress. And to these so-called laws may be added the general facts of evolution, the continuousness of Nature, and all the orderly sequences observed in the realms of matter and mind, such as the fact that light and darkness alternately follow the rotation of the earth upon its axis, the varying seasons follow the revolutions of the earth around the sun; and in the realm of animal life instinct secures uniform migrations from cold regions to warm in winter, and from warm to cooler regions in summer, while in human society abundant illustrations of uniform sequences are recognized: If the price of an article falls (other things remaining the same) the quantity demanded increases, and if the price rises the quantity demanded decreases; and if cheap money is put in circulation the better money will disappear: if land is made to bear a heavy burden of taxation, then, as a general thing, the price of land will decrease: if there is a rise in the rates of interest then there will be a decline in the price of stocks: and if the population of a state greatly increases, then we may reasonably expect the price of land there will increase. All these so-called laws, as will be observed, are simply statement of general facts. They are not self-evident truths but contingent. It is conceivable that a planet should revolve around the sun in a circle instead of an ellipse; it is conceivable that a falling body should descend forty feet the first second instead of sixteen, but it is not conceivable that the shortest distance between two points should be a broken line instead of a straight one. It is perfectly obvious that these generalized facts and orderly sequences to which the term *law* has been applied, are law only in a secondary sense.

They had a beginning and may have an end, hence they are not eternal. They are generally manifestations of force, rather than regulative of force. They have received the dignified name of law, though they lack the essential element of law. We have observed, however, that relative to man's power they are regulative, in that they often determine what he can and cannot do.

Then again we observed a similar phenomenal order in the realm of finite rational beings. Man as a person, possessed of reason, free will, and conscience presents another realm of law in this secondary sense. There are certain general facts, observed in the realm of the human mind, unlike any that are found in the impersonal sphere. They constitute a body of secondary law different from any observed in the other two spheres. Among those which were considered may be mentioned the following: Under the so-called law of association of ideas, we find the following general tendencies: the sight of a person, who resembles in appearance a distant friend, will generally suggest the thought of that friend: the sight of a mountain peak in a foreign land resembling one in our own land, will as a rule suggest the thought of the latter: the thought of the very rich suggests by way of contrast the thought of the very poor: the coldest days of winter suggest the hottest days of summer: on the battle-field of Waterloo one acquainted with its history will think of Napoleon and Wellington: the thought of Wilkes Booth will suggest the thought of Abraham Lincoln to one familiar with the history of their day, as the name Guiteau will suggest that of Garfield. This tendency of one thought to suggest another is called a law. It is a general fact and is so universally true that it is recognized as a part of the established order of thought. Again under the law of memory we find that matters which occupy the mind for the longest period of time are, other things being equal, more likely to be recalled: and also those objects which are apprehended most vividly, and brought before the mind most frequently, are most readily reproduced in memory: and here too we find many uniform sequences among the thoughts and emotions, as the thoughts of success inspire hope, and apprehension of defeat awakens fear: a choice of right is followed by an emotion of self-approval, and a choice of the wrong is followed by self-condemnation: cheerful obedience to the laws of God is followed by spiritual peace, and willful disobedience is followed by spiritual discord and unrest. Many other illustrations might be given of that large body of so-called law that operates within and throughout the finite rational realm. These suffice to show their character. They are facts and nothing more. They are called laws as that whole group of uniform tendencies and sequences in the physical world are called laws. We may properly look upon them as a body of so-called laws unlike those in the other two spheres, and to a certain extent separate from them, and possessing essential characteristics of their own. They belong to that great class of somewhat similar laws which had a beginning and hence are not eternal. They are secondary, not primary law.

From the foregoing enumeration of observed laws we find three systems more or less distinct and separate, yet constituting one all-comprehensive body of natural law.

The immutable and eternal principles of reason constitute the first system and by reason of their universality and supremacy, they have been called the Supreme Constitution of the Universe. To their authority all cosmic, psychic, and social forces must submit. In harmony with them all created things have been fashioned. They are laws of thought in the world of mind, as they are laws of things in the world of matter. They determine what physical power can and cannot effect, what intellectual power can and cannot conceive, and what voluntary power ought and ought not to choose.

The second system embraces all those generalized facts and orderly sequences found within and throughout the impersonal realm, including the phenomenal order of physical nature as well as the instincts and impersonal intelligence of the animal kingdom. Relative to man all these so-called laws are established facts and are regulative of his power, in that they set limits to his action. He cannot annul the law of gravitation, but he can accomplish many things in harmony with it.

Within the third system are embraced all those established facts and uniform occurrences peculiar to the rational constitution of man, such as the law of moral obligation, of scientific imagination, of rational reproduction or memory, the laws of association of ideas, and all the factual sequences prevailing within the realms of ethics, esthetics, and religion.

Thus man lives under and is implicated in a three-fold system of Natural law, in a way somewhat analogous to that in which an American citizen lives under a three-fold system of human law. He lives under the Constitution and Statutes of the United States, under the Constitution and Laws of his State, and under the Charter and Ordinances of his City or other municipality.

We then considered in what sense *human* law or jurisprudence rests upon *natural* law.

This triple system of nature antedates all human law. Man is born into it. No person or race can escape its jurisdiction. Every system of positive law is based upon it, or in some way related to each one of the three bodies of natural law composing the triple system. But Jurisprudence is related to the finite *rational* system in a peculiar and special manner. The principles of Ethics belong to the body of rational law, and the one all-comprehensive law of love or service to man furnishes the basis of Jurisprudence. We observed that the moral law, "Thou shalt love thy neighbor as thyself" was the genus, under which all the principles of justice, of benevolence, of veracity, of gratitude, of mercy and others are found to be but species.

This all-comprehensive principle of the moral law is rooted in the rational constitution of man, and has been recognized by all races of men with greater or less distinctness. The literatures of the ancients in both the Orient and the Occident disclose the idea that man was not made to live for self alone. Terence voiced this thought in his saying, "I am a man and nothing which is human can be alien to me."

The system of moral rights and duties is developed fundamentally from this universal law. The statement itself, that man shall love his neighbor as himself, necessarily implies that man is to love or serve himself. Love to *self* is the standard of duty; love to our neighbor ought to come up to that standard. A moment's consideration shows that this is necessarily true. If man would serve his neighbor in any capacity he must have served himself first. If one would give money to the poor, he must first get the money, if he would impart knowledge to the ignorant he must first acquire the knowledge; if he would bless the world in any manner he must first acquire the instrumentalities of power by means of which he can bestow that blessing. In short, if a person would give he must get; he must be egoistic before he can be altruistic. We have seen that in all finite action reception must precede production, and the moral law of love is but an aspect of that universal principle. Man must serve himself before he can serve others; he must perfect his own powers before he can assist others most efficiently to perfect theirs.

But what does love to self involve? It means that man must make the very most of himself. He must cultivate, refine, enlarge, and perfect all the susceptibilities and powers of his being. Doing this is to love self, and to do this requires the discharge of all duty. If he owes a debt, it is his duty to pay it, and it is a right of the creditor to receive it. It is man's duty to respect his neighbor's rights to life, liberty and property. Only by performing those duties can man serve himself best; only by performing those duties can man make the most of himself; only by performing them can he ever hope to perfect himself; only by performing them can he comply with the law "love thyself." But the discharge of one's duties, and the corresponding satisfaction of another's rights, the adjustment of rights and duties, is what we call the *principle of justice.* So it transpires that the principle of justice and the law of service or love are identical. When we apply the law of love to the reciprocal rights and duties in the business or other transactions of human life, we call it the principle of justice, and when we apply it in those cases where man finds it his duty to give to his neighbor hoping for nothing in return—in all gratuitous transactions—we call it benevolence, and when we apply it in transactions involving the impartation of truth, we call it veracity: so these principles of justice, benevolence and veracity, are only different names given to the law of love, according to the nature of the transactions wherein the law is applied, as is the case with the general *legal principle* of fixtures, which, when applied to articles of personal property annexed to premises for domestic purposes is called the principle of domestic fixtures; and when applied to such articles annexed to the premises for purposes of trade is called the principle of trade fixtures, and when applied to such articles annexed to premises for agricultural purposes is called the principle of agricultural fixtures, one principle receiving three different names according to the peculiar facts involved in its special application.

It may be said that the administration of justice is the essential work of courts of law. Positive law has primarily and chiefly to do with the enforcement of duties and the protection of rights. To see that the outward adjustment of men's rights and duties is secured is the prime object of human law; and as the principle of justice is, in essence, the moral law, it may be said, as we have contended, that jurisprudence or positive law is founded upon and draws all its vitality and force from the one fundamental and all-comprehensive moral law of service or love.

But much legislation has to do with the establishment of almshouses, institutions for the insane, for the feeble-minded, and other defective fellow beings. Such legislation is in a sense an application of the principle of benevolence. The people, by taxation, bestow their money upon the unfortunate and feeble, hoping for no equivalent in return. It is essentially a gratuity, and yet such legislation becomes a part of the law of the land and is included in the subject matter of Jurisprudence.

The principle of veracity also finds a most prominent place in the realm of Jurisprudence. The violation of this principle is the occasion of much legislation, and judicial ruling. It enters into every business transaction. Fraud, deceit, and misrepresentation of every kind play a conspicuous part in the transactions of human life. The law has many legal provisions calculated to establish truth and to eliminate falsehood in human affairs. Even a good or bad motive often determines the legal or illegal character of the outward action inspired by such motive. The morality of his motive may determine the legality of one's conduct. The principle of veracity, the moral principle of love applied in human affairs respecting truthful statements and honest conduct, is ever before the court for application. Witnesses must tell the truth and the whole truth. No one can gain a legal right by his own fraud, lying, or deceitful behavior. If a person does not speak the truth when he ought to, the court will not permit him to speak it when he wants to in order to gain an advantage over his adversary.

In the ever present demands of justice, benevolence, veracity, and perhaps other moral principles, we find the foundation of human law; and as these separate principles, are, in reality, but aspects or component parts of the one all-comprehensive law of love, the conclusion is fairly established, I think, that at the bottom of all jurisprudence we find as the basal law that one all-controlling command of reason, "Love thy neighbor as thyself."

If this is true, the advantages gained by recognizing the fact are many. It makes jurisprudence a branch of applied ethics; it gives to jurisprudence itself the highest possible dignity; it raises the administration of justice from a selfish scramble by litigants and counsel for unrighteous ends, to a dignified effort on the part of judge, counsel and advocate, to discover where the golden thread of moral principle runs in the complicated affairs of human life, and to settle the rights of the parties interested according to the demands of that principle; it dignifies the office of the judge, by making him a priest at the altar of moral law, and it raises the office of counsel to the exalted life work of one devoted to the advocacy of unselfish love in the complicated details of human life. Judge and counsel together become the unselfish arbiters of the conflicting interests of their fellow-men, ever seeking to discover and satisfy the demands of the all-controlling law of love. From such a conception of jurisprudence, and from such a conception of its administration, what judge or advocate or even what minor officer of the court can fail to gain an uplifting and ennobling inspiration?

But we have seen too that jurisprudence bears a distinct relation to the other two systems of natural law, that of primary truth, and that of impersonal nature. The courts everywhere necessarily recognize the fundamental principles of reason, and give force and effect to the generalized facts and established sequences in the worlds of finite mind and matter.

If a person is indicted for the committal of a murder in the city of Boston, and, on the trial, he completely establishes the fact that on the day the crime was committed he was in London, no further proof of his innocence is necessary. The court, the jury and the counsel as well, all apply the primary and universal law that no body or person can be in two different places at the same instant. This law is decisive of the case. All parties concerned submit without question or argument to the imperative demands of this self-evident principle of intuition. While this law is not counted by the jurist as one of the positive laws of the land, and while that whole body of rational, self-evident principles is not regarded or treated as a part of jurisprudence, yet, as a matter of fact, we have found from numerous judicial authorities that the courts take judicial notice of this vast system of fundamental truth, and give to the individual principles the force and effect of positive law, wherever they are found applicable in the trial and final decision of actual cases before them. There is, therefore, a real and close relationship existing between jurisprudence and this vast system of universal and imperative principles.

Then, too, we find a similar relationship existing between jurisprudence and the phenomenal order of the physical universe and all impersonal nature as well. The courts take judicial notice of the laws of the material world, the instincts of animal life, and all the established uniformities in that vast realm of generalized facts and orderly sequences, whenever they become the subject of general observation and knowledge. When one who is alleged to be the father of a child, born out of lawful wedlock, fully establishes the fact before the court that for two or more years immediately before the child's birth, he was constantly in a land foreign to that where the child's mother resided during all that time, he must be pronounced innocent of the offence, as, under the natural law of gestation, he could not have been the child's father. The law of gestation need not be proved. The court takes judicial notice of that general fact, and applies it as he might apply a statute or a principle of common law where such application would be appropriate. The courts give force and effect to all such laws whereever they are involved in the subject matter of the litigation before them, and their application often becomes the decisive factor in the controversy. Such laws, when necessarily applicable in any given case, perform the same office that positive law performs. They are the decisive factor in the controversy. This fact illustrates the close and vital relationship existing between jurisprudence and this great system of natural law.

While the expounder of positive law would confine his inquiry to the principles enforceable by state authority, yet, if we would notice and consider every decisive principle operative in the decision of human controversies before our courts, we should be surprised to see how many of the laws or controlling principles involved in those decisions, are but universally admitted principles of so-called natural law. They are given effect through judicial notice and application. They are in fact a part of the "law of the land." They exert a decisive influence in the litigated cases before our courts; and respecting them Judge Christiancy says, "The laws of nature and of the human mind, at least such of them as are obvious to the common apprehension of mankind, as well as the more obvious dictates of common sense and principles of human action—which are assumed as truths in any process of reasoning by the mass of sane minds—constitute *a part of the law of the land,* and may and must be assumed by the court, without being found by the jury; indeed the finding of a jury which should clearly disregard them, should itself be disregarded by the court. In other words the courts are bound judicially to know and apply such laws and principles as part of the law of the land."

So, while we observe the peculiar and essential relation of jurisprudence to the moral law, whence it draws its essential life and nature, we see also how the whole system of natural law, embracing the primary intuitive principles, the impersonal phenomena and the personal order constitute the real foundation or basis of the world's systems of human law. Hence it is not enough that the student, the lawyer, the judge, and the jurist should become familiar with the common law of the land, with the constitutions and statutes of states and nations, and even with the broad principles of international conduct, but they should look above, beyond, and back of all these human enactments, rules and compacts to the superior principles of that great triple system of natural law, whose regulative influences are felt in all the details of human life. While we find the basis of jurisprudence to be essentially ethical, we also observe that it sustains a close relationship to the system of universal principles, and to the phenomenal order of the impersonal realm.

Having considered the essential nature of law in its most general sense, and having considered the foundation of human law as enforceable by the state, we proceeded to consider the particular nature of human law itself. We observed that human law in its broadest signification embraces all the rules of human conduct which human beings have adopted or enacted for the regulation of their conduct. We observed that the word law is applied indiscriminately to all the rules of human action, whether regulative of national conduct, the conduct of the individual citizens of a state, to the conduct of persons associated in the various relations of social life as members of literary clubs, political leagues, college fraternities, ball teams, improvement societies, and other similar voluntary associations; and it is applied also to rules of etiquette and fashion, and even to those which regulate the games of chess, whist, checkers, and all the other games of chance or skill, as well as to the rules adopted by industrial, political, and religious conventions to facilitate the transaction of business. So we find ourselves speaking of the laws of golf, the laws of football, the laws of polite society, the laws of good manners, the laws of etiquette, the laws of library associations, the laws of labor organizations, the laws of the women's federation, the laws of political conventions, at the same time we are speaking of the laws of nations, the laws of the state, and "the law of the land." We observed too that had the word law been reserved for and applied exclusively to those rules of human conduct which are enforced by state authority, and the word *rule* applied to all others, then the classification would have been made easy. Little, however, is to be gained by mere classification. The only distinction, important to be made among these rules, is that afforded by the fact that some of them are enforcible by the state and others are not. Those which are so enforcible are strictly *law* in the sense that they impose upon persons civil obligations cognizable by the courts of justice, and all other rules are law only in the sense that they tend to subserve some good end and secure regularity of conduct, but persons are in no way answerable to the courts for violating them, being subject only to such disadvantages of personal loss or public disapproval as their violation may involve.

Among the rules adopted by persons for individual improvement may be named the following: What we ought not to do, we should not think of doing: refuse to express a passion and it dies: check your passions that you may not be punished by them: frequent repetition is the first law of memory: choose along the line of greatest resistance: decide with promptness and act with energy in the less important affairs of life has been given as a helpful rule in the cultivation of the will: and here too we might mention rules adopted by individuals for the preservation and improvement of physical health, such as the rules fixing the hours for arising and retiring, for exercise, for recreation, and for labor.

These rules for individual improvement, mental and physical, though self-imposed and self-repealable, are the least stable and authoritative of all the rules adopted by mankind. They are the lowest order or type of regulative realities. They are adopted for a worthy end, and so long as they are unrepealed they *tend* to regulate the conduct, hence they have in them the essential element of law.

Proceeding from these rules of *individual* conduct we next considered those rules of social conduct which are attended by a sanction either applied by the power of public opinion, or by the persons themselves prescribing the rules. Among others we mentioned the law of honor, whereby in some places a person challenged to fight a duel must accept it or suffer disgrace in the public mind: the laws of etiquette, the laws of fashion, rules regulating the salutations of persons upon the street or at public gatherings: rules observed by those exchanging calls, rules observed by hosts and guests on occasions of hospitality, the customs observed at public dinners determining, among other things, the position of guests at the table, or in the receiving line at a public reception: and here too may be mentioned those rules of court etiquette in our own and other countries, which, when sovereigns, presidents, ministers, ambassadors, and other dignitaries assemble, regulate their conduct in a manner as tyrannical as the decree of a despot regulates the conduct of his subjects. Among the laws of fashion we observed those most common ones which dictate the form of the hat, the cut of the shoe, and the style of the dress or coat which are so exacting in their demands that a fair degree of uniformity is secured throughout the land in the case of all men, women, and children alike, and they affect all classes of people as a rule from the poorest of society up to the royal courts of sovereign states.

These rules too are regulative of human conduct, and possess therefore the essential element of law. The chief characteristic of these rules or laws aside from their regulative element, is their indeterminate source, and they are not as a general thing attended by any specific sanction. Their violation arouses public disapproval which is one of the most severe forms of punishment.

In addition to these rules of a non-legal character we considered one other class of important rules or laws established for the government of the family, for the government of schools, churches, literary societies, political, religious and other similar clubs, leagues and voluntary associations, to which rules there are, in addition to the sanction of public displeasure, other sanctions specifically provided and enforced by the person or persons prescribing them. In these and similar instances the rules originate with some particular and determinate person or persons, as with the parents, the chief of a tribe, the teacher, the governing board of the voluntary association or other organization. These sanctions vary in form and character to suit the demands of each particular rule, as expulsion or suspension from school in case of disobedience, forfeits incident to the violated rules of games of chance, fines in money for the non-return of books to a library at the proper time, and many other similar sanctions prescribed by such bodies or associations, but in no instance is the sanction attending the violation of any of this class of rules enforced by the courts of justice. Should the courts undertake to enforce the performance of these rules, that very act would raise the rule from a mere conventional regulation to the dignity of law in its legal signification.

This class of regulative principles, springing from non-legal sources is one of vast importance in the progress and development of human society. These rules are peculiarly regulative in their nature, being specifically prescribed for the regulation of human conduct. They are fixed and established, and, while remaining in force, possess that regulative element that characterizes law in its essential nature.

Having examined this class of non-legal human laws, positive law only remained for our consideration; and after reviewing various definitions of law we decided that the following statement correctly expresses all the elements essential to law in its legal sense. *Positive law is a rule of external human action enforcible by state authority.* Our examination satisfied us, that both constitutional and international law are fairly embraced within both the spirit and the letter of this definition: and that all positive law is characterized by that regulative element essential to law in its most general sense.

As to whether the vast body of laws, which we classify as natural, might be also called divine, with as much propriety and exactness as they might be called natural, we concluded in Chapter X that they might be so named. Regarding this matter James Wilson said: "The law of nature, and the law of revelation are both divine; they flow, though in different channels, from the same source. It is indeed preposterous to separate them from each other."

There would be an advantage, indeed, in calling the whole body of law, excepting that of purely human origin, Divine. It would bring into our study of the laws of Nature the thought of a divine presence which the use of the term *natural* has largely excluded. In scientific thought with many, God and Nature have been divorced, or, more accurately, perhaps, Nature is looked upon as all-sufficient, and the presence of God unnecessary. But in more recent days the immanence of God is gaining favor, especially in religious thinking, and the laws and uniformities of Nature are now regarded as immediate manifestations of God actually present and actively energizing in the movements and ongoing of the finite universe. In harmony with this view of Nature and of God's immediate presence within it, the laws of Nature, which are but God's uniform activities, might with strict accuracy be called Divine; and we should then say: All laws are either Divine or human.

APPENDIX.

For the benefit of those students who wish to pursue philosophical inquiries, and to consider *natural law* in both its primary and secondary sense, the following outline of questions and authorities is appended. The *laws of thought* and the *laws of things* are necessarily involved in the subjects considered. The three objects of all human thought, it has been said, are "the Ego or person, the World, and God," or as others express it, "The World-ground, Physical Nature, and Soul." If these are the three continents of all possible human knowledge, then all the *laws* of which we can have any knowledge must be found within these realms. By perusing the works referred to, we learn something of the nature of *law* as viewed by these authors. As our objective point, however, (in addition to learning the nature of law in general) has been to see clearly the relation of jurisprudence to the *moral law,* we are especially concerned with the *ethical* nature of man. As the finite reason knows intuitively that a thing cannot both be and not be at the same time, so intuitional ethics teaches that the finite reason knows intuitively that "a rational being *ought* to act rationally." In the abiding and illuminating presence of its rational intuitions the soul both sees and feels its *obligation* to choose and to act in harmony with them. The soul both recognizes and knows them as law to its action. This knowledge of *oughtness* is itself an essential element in man's rational nature. It is this original and fundamental intuition that constitutes man a moral being. When an occasion in experience arises, man knows by original insight that "a body cannot be in two different places at the same time," and that " a straight line cannot enclose space," and so by the same immediate insight he knows, when an occasion in experience arises, that he *ought* to act rationally, that he *ought* to use his powers for rational ends, that he *ought* to seek his own welfare, rather than his own destruction, that he *ought* to seek his neighbor's welfare, rather than his injury and ruin, that he *ought* to conform his choices to the demands of truth, and thereby secure the perfection of his being, and that he *ought* to "love (or serve) his neighbor as himself."

Throughout the following authorities *natural law* is incidentally referred to and employed in a variety of senses: and the *moral law* in particular is fully considered in those works devoted to the subject of ethics. The nature or essence of human law is discussed in the works referred to under that topic. In general, the problems in philosophy are considered under the theories of Knowledge and the theories of Being.

THEORIES OF KNOWLEDGE.

Are there intuitive truths? If not, there can be no intuitive ethics.

ISSUE.

Intuitionalism or *Rationalism* alleges that a knowledge of intuitive truths is acquired through Rational Intuition.

The Opposing Theories deny that knowledge of intuitive truth or of any other truth is acquired through Rational Intuition.

AUTHORITIES

Intuitionalism

Harris, Phil. Basis of Theism, 109 ch. 3, 7.
McCosh, Intuitions of the Mind, 20, 101, 309-310.
Hopkins, Outline Study of Man, ch. 3, 4.
Haven, Mental Phil., 238.
Browne, Theory of Thought and Knowledge, ch. 3, 4.
Hickok, Rational Psychology, Introduction, and ch. 1, Book 2.
Wayland, Intellectual Phil., ch. 3.
Fiske, Outline of Cosmic Phil., Vol. I, p. 46, Vol. II, p. 161.
Lotze, System of Phil., ch. 3, pp. 450, 513.
Mivart, On Truth, ch. 4.
Mivart, Groundwork of Science, ch. 8.
Leibnitz, Phil. Works, by Duncan, 307.
Des Cartes, Phil. of, by Torry, 2, Med. 113.
Kant, Critique of Pure Reason, Muller, Vol. I, p. 398.
Paulsen, Introduction to Phil., 373.
Farrier, Institutes of Metaphysics, 79.
Porter, Human Intellect, 61, 497.
Mansel, Prælegomena Logica, ch. 4, p. 92.
Mansel, Metaphysics, 221, 242.

Empiricism	Spencer, First Principles, 70. Bain, Mental Science, 181. Fiske, Outline of Cosmic Phil., Vol. I, p. 56, 287, Vol. II, p. 161. Mill, System of Logic, Book 2, ch. 5, p. 152. Hegel, Logic, ch. 4, p. 76, and ch. 5. Carpenter, Mental Physiology, 237. Lewis, The Study of Psychology, ch. 10. Lewis, Problems of Life and Mind, Vol. I, 191, 338. Reply: McCosh, Intuitions of the Mind, 294, 361. Bowne, Theory of Thought and Knowledge, ch. 4.
Sensationalism	Locke, Sources of our Knowledge, Bk. 2, ch. 1, § 3, 4, 5, ch. 12, § 8, ch. 22, § 1, 2, 3. Condillac, Origin of Human Knowledge, ch. 1. Hume, Treatise on Human Nature, part 4, § 6, Bk. 1, part 1, part 3, § 5.
Relativity of Knowledge	Mill, Examination of Sir Wm. Hamilton's Phil., Vol. 1, p. 13. Fiske, Outline of Cosmic Phil., Vol. I, p. 3. Reply: McCosh, Intuitions of the Mind, 340. Harris, Phil. Basis of Theism, 109.
Positivism	Auguste Comte, Postitve Phil., Vol. I, ch. 1.
Phenomenalism	Kant, Critique of Pure Reason, Muller, 2d Vol. Reply: Harris, Phil. Basis of Theism, 99.

General Reply: Harris, Phil. Basis of Theism, ch. 5.

Theories of Being.

I.

ABSOLUTE BEING.

Accepting the intuitional theory of knowledge, there must be an uncaused, unconditioned, or absolute Being, from which all things emanate. What is its *essence?* Is it spirit or matter, or something unlike either?

Philosophy supplies the following answers.

ISSUE.

Spiritualistic Philosophy or *Spiritualism* alleges that matter is the product of mind.

Materialistic Philosophy or *Materialism* denies this, and alleges that mind is the product of matter.

- **Ontology**
  - Pluralism
    - Atoms of Democritus
    - Monads of Leibnitz
  - Dualism — Des Cartes
    - Extended Being
    - Thinking Being
  - Monism
    - Materialism
    - Spiritualism
    - Parallelism or Identity theory — Spinoza, Spencer, Fechner — Matter and mind phases of a third substance.

AUTHORITIES

Spiritualism

Anaxagoras, Ueberwig His. of Phil. Vol. I, p. 60-3-5.
Plato, Ueberwig His. of Phil. Vol. I, p. 127.
Aristotle, Bk. XI, ch. 6, 7 and 8.
Descartes, Third Meditation.
Liebnitz, Phil. Works, by Duncan, 100, 218.
Crooker, The Theistic Conception of the World, 95-7.
Maxwell, Nature, Vol. 8, p. 441.
LeConte, Princeton Review, March, 1881, p. 149.
McCosh, Princeton Review, May, 1881, p. 369.
Bowne, Princeton Review, Nov., 1881, p. 344.
Flint, Theism, ch. 4.
Mivart, On Truth, ch. 26.
Bowne, Studies in Theism, 375.
Bowne, The Phil. of H. Spencer, 218.
Harris, Phil. Basis of Theism, 428.

Materialism

Lucretius, Watson's Edition.
Buchner, Force and Matter, ch. 1.
Hæckel, History of Creation, Vol. I, p. 20, 75, 316.
International Encyc., Vol. 9, p. 593.
Lange, History of Materialism.

II.

The Cosmos.

Accepting the spiritualistic theory, the Absolute Being is *spirit*. What then, is its relation to the cosmos? Does it constitute an underlying unity ever manifesting itself in the manifold phenomena of the universe?

Philosophy furnishes the following suggestions.

FIRST CAUSE

- Cosmology
  - Polytheism
  - Monotheism
    - Theism
    - **Deism**
      - Lord Herbert
      - Locke
      - Voltaire
    - Pantheism
      - Spinoza
      - Feuerbach —Thoughts on Death and Immortality.

Issues.

Theistic Philosophy alleges that Spiritual Being is the First Cause of the universe and thus transcends it, is immanent in it, ever sustaining it and revealing thought and purpose in its evolution.

Deistic Philosophy admits the transcedence of the First Cause, but denies its immanence.

Pantheistic Philosophy admits the immanence of Spirit in the universe, but denies its transcendence.

AUTHORITIES

Theism	Harris, Self-revelation of God, 251, 341. Flint, Theism, ch. 4. Bowne, Studies in Theism, 287. Fisher, Princeton Review, July, 1881, p. 16. Bowne, Phil. of Spencer, 219. Harris, God, Creator and Lord, Vol. I, p. 78.	
Deism	Lord Herbert.	
Pantheism	Spinoza.	Ueberwig, His of Phil., 55, 60-78. Fullerton, Phil. of Spinoza.

As to its Manifestations.

Theistic Philosophy suggests that the First Cause may reveal itself in the phenomena of the universe, according to the law of scientific evolution.

ISSUE.

Scientific Evolution alleges "that the existing arrangement of the physical Universe, is the result of a continuous and progressive evolution from simple and lower to more complicated and higher conditions and forms," according to certain laws, and by means of resident forces. (P. b. 455).

Materialistic Evolution admits this, but alleges further that the existing Universe, including life and mind, is the result of matter and force which are alone eternal.

AUTHORITIES

Scientific Evolution
- Harris, Phil. Basis of Theism, 455.
- Drummond, Ascent of Man, 1.
- LeConte, Princeton Review, March, 1881, p. 149.
- McCosh, Princeton Review, May, 1881, p. 367.
- Bowne, Princeton Review, Nov. 1881, p. 344.
- Abbott, Outlook, Jan. 2 and 9, 1897.
- Fiske, Destiny of Man, ch. 1 and 2, and p. 110.
- Harris, God, Creator and Lord, Vol. 1, p. 72.
- Bowne, Metaphysics, 271.
- Harris, Self-revelation of God, 278-280.

Materialistic Evolution
- Hæckel, Princeton Review, May, 1880, p. 144.
- Buchner, Force and Matter.
- Reply:
- Bowne, Phil. of H. Spencer, p. 146, 240.

III.

The Soul.

PSYCHOLOGY.

As there cannot be motion without a body to move, nor an action without something to act, can there be thought and feeling and choice without some being (Self) to think, to feel, and to choose?

ISSUE.

Realistic Philosophy or *Substantialism* alleges that there is a separate *self*, distinct from the phenomena of consciousness.

Nihilistic Philosophy or *Non-Substantialism* denies that there is any separate self, distinct from the phenomena of consciousness, and alleges that *mind* consists in a series of states of consciousness.

AUTHORITIES

Substantialism
- Mivart, On Truth, 19.
- Haven, Mental Science, 252.
- Muller, Science of Thought, 64.
- Hopkins, Princeton Review, Jan., 1881, p. 1.
- Fisher, Princeton Review, July, 1881, p. 1.
- Ladd, Elements of Psychology, 607.
- Harris, Phil. Basis of Theism, 155, 94-99.
- Mivart, Groundwork of Science, ch. 8.
- Bowne, Metaphysics, 314.
- McCosh, Intuitions of the Mind, 127.
- Hickok, Rational Psychology, 714.

Non-Substantialism

- James, Psychology, ch. 10, p. 90.
- Spencer, Psychology, Vol. 1, p. 193, Vol. 2, p. 501.
- Mill, Examination of Hamilton, Vol. 1, p. 253.
- Fiske, Cosmic Phil., Vol. 2, p. 119.
- Hume, Treatise of Human Nature, Bk. 1, part 4, § 6.
- Clifford's Lectures and Essays, Vol. 1, p. 288, Vol. 2, p. 57.
- General Reply:
- Harris, Phil. Basis of Theism, ch. 7.
- Harris, Self-revelation of God, 80-1, 342.

In General.

Realism alleges that there is a real existence of the external world, independent of all human thought about it.

Idealism alleges that all *reality* is in its nature psychical; that the souls of men, and God, and the ideas in them are the only existences.

Realism

- Harris, Self-revelation of God, 75-82, 193.
- Mivart, On Truth, 77, 3.83.
- McCosh, Intuitions of the Mind, 108.

Idealism

- Berkeley, Principles of Human Knowledge, Philosophical Works, Vol. 1, p. 155.
- Royce, Spirit of Modern Phil., 341.
- Bowne, Theories of Knowledge, Idealism.
- International Encyc. Vol. 7, p. 789.
- Discussion, Hamilton Metaphysics, 198.

Ethics.

The supreme question in ethics, both for the individual and the state is: What is the greatest good man can possess?

The correct answer to this question gives the supreme law of human action. Some have said it is happiness, others have said it is the perfection of one's being, and others claim that it is the perfection of one's being, *plus* the happiness necessarily involved in the process of attaining and in the possession of that perfection.

I.

Any correct answer to this question must recognize the controlling fact that persons are *ends* in themselves, and are beings to be served. This is the supreme fact in ethics.

AUTHORITIES

Kant, Fundamental Principles of the Metaphysic of Morals. Abbott's Trans.
Harris, Self-revelation of God, pp. 285,501.
Harris, Philosophical Basis of Theism, 266-285.
Seth, Ethical Principles, 214.
Kant, Theory of Ethics, pp. 52, 56, 302, 306.

II.

If persons are to be served, what is the greatest service that can be rendered them, or what is the greatest good that they may attain for themselves, or help others to attain?

Issue.

Hedonism says that happiness is the greatest good, and the supreme end of human conduct.

Intuitive ethics says that the perfection of one's being and the happiness necessarily connected with it is the greatest good and the supreme end of human conduct.

AUTHORITIES

Hedonism

Zeller, Socrates and the Socratic Schools, ch. 7, and ch. 13.
Zeller, Stoics, Epicureans, and Sceptics, Part 2.
W. Wallace, Epicureanism.
H. Sidgwick, History of Ethics, ch. 2, § 3, 4, 16 and 17.
Bentham, Introduction to the Principles of Morals and Legislation.
J. S. Mill, Utilitarianism.
L. Stephens, Science of Ethics.
H. Spencer, Data of Ethics, Part 1.
H. Sidgwick, Method of Ethics, Bk. 3, chs. 13 and 14; Bk. 4.
T. H. Green, Prolegomena to Ethics, Bk. 3, ch. 4, § 219-239; Bk. 4, ch. 4.
J. Martineau, Types of Ethical Theory, Vol. 2, Part 2, Bk. 2, chs. 1 and 2.
Hume, Enquiry Concerning the Principles of Morals: Treatise on Human Nature, Bk. 3.
E. Albee, History of English Utilitarianism.
J. Dewey, A Study of Ethics, pp. 41-68, 115-123.

Intuitive Ethics

- Kant, Fundamental Principles of the Metaphysic of Morals. Abbott's Trans.
- Seth, Ethical Principles, 79-235.
- Harris, Philosophic Basis of Theism, Chap. 9.
- Harris, Lord and Creator of All, Vol. 2, p. 147, 178-192.
- W. W. Capes, Stoicism.
- Windelband, History of Philosophy, § 72-85.
- Butler's Sermon's, 1-3, 11 and 12.
- J. Dewey, Outline of Ethics, pp. 78-95, 147-152.
- J. S. Mackenzie, Manual of Ethics, Bk. 2, ch. 3.
- F. H. Bradley, Ethical Studies, Essay 4.

THE STATE.

Persons are ends to be served, and the state and civil government are means by which their highest good and general welfare are to be secured.

In order to do this the state and the individual must both observe the universal moral law, seeking to realize their perfection and well-being through the exercise of justice, benevolence and veracity.

AUTHORITIES

- Harris, God, Lord and Creator of All.
- Woolsey, Political Science, Part 2, chs. 4 and 5.
- Burgess, Political Science, Vol. 1, p. 83.
- Bluntschli, Theory of the State, 305-326.
- Wood, Government and State, chaps. 2 and 3.
- Humboldt, Sphere and Duties of Government.
- Mill, J. S., Liberty, Political Ec., Book 5.
- Locke, Treatise on Government, Bk. 2, ch. 9.
- Seth, Ethical Principles, p. 287.
- Lieber, Political Ethics, Vol. I. 159.
- Harris, God, Creator and Lord of All, Vol. 2, p. 388-525 and 538.
- Spencer, Principles of Ethics, 212, 222.
- Willoughby, Nature of the State, Ch. 12.
- Ency. Britannica Government.

INDEX.